STREETS BROAD
and NARROW

THE HISTORY AND HERITAGE OF BRITAIN'S TOWNS

STREETS BROAD and NARROW

THE HISTORY AND HERITAGE OF BRITAIN'S TOWNS

Compiled and edited by Terence and Eliza Sackett

STREETS BROAD and NARROW

MARKET DRAYTON, MARKET DAY 1911   63338T

CONTENTS

FRANCIS FRITH, founder of the world-famous photographic archive, was a complex and multi-talented man. A devout Quaker and a highly successful Victorian businessman, he was philosophical by nature and pioneering in outlook.

By 1855 he had already established a wholesale grocery business in Liverpool, and sold it for the astonishing sum of £200,000, which is the equivalent today of over £15,000,000. Now a very rich man, he was able to indulge his passion for travel. As a child he had pored over travel books written by early explorers, and his fancy and imagination had been stirred by family holidays to the sublime mountain regions of Wales and Scotland. 'What lands of spirit-stirring and enriching scenes and places!' he had written. He was to return to these scenes of grandeur in later years to 'recapture the thousands of vivid and tender memories', but with a different purpose. Now in his thirties, and captivated by the new science of photography, Frith set out on a series of pioneering journeys up the Nile and to the Near East that occupied him from 1856 until 1860.

INTRIGUE AND EXPLORATION

These far-flung journeys were packed with intrigue and adventure. In his life story, written when he was sixty-three, Frith tells of being held captive by bandits, and of fighting 'an awful midnight battle to the very point of surrender with a deadly pack of hungry, wild dogs'. Wearing flowing Arab costume, Frith arrived at Akaba by camel sixty years before Lawrence of Arabia, where he encountered 'desert princes and rival sheikhs, blazing with jewel-hilted swords'.

He was the first photographer to venture beyond the sixth cataract of the Nile. Africa was still the mysterious 'Dark Continent', and Stanley and Livingstone's historic meeting was a decade into the future. The conditions for picture taking confound belief. He laboured for hours in his wicker dark-room in the sweltering heat of the desert, while the volatile chemicals fizzed dangerously in their trays. Back in London he exhibited his photographs and was 'rapturously cheered' by members of the Royal Society. His reputation as a photographer was made overnight.

THE RISE OF FRITH & CO

Characteristically, Frith quickly spotted the opportunity to create a new business as a specialist publisher of photographs. He lived in an era of immense and sometimes violent change. For the poor in the early part of Victoria's reign work was exhausting and the hours long, and people had precious little free time to enjoy themselves. Most had no transport other than a cart or gig at their disposal, and rarely travelled far beyond the boundaries of their own town or village. However, by the 1870s the railways had threaded their way across the country, and Bank Holidays and half-day Saturdays had been made obligatory by Act of Parliament. All of a sudden the working man and his family were able to enjoy days out and see a little more of the world.

With typical business acumen, Francis Frith foresaw that these new tourists would enjoy having souvenirs to commemorate their days out. Frith's studio was soon supplying retail shops all over the country. To meet the demand he gathered together a team of photographers, and published the work of independent artist-photographers of the calibre of Roger Fenton and Francis Bedford. In order to gain some understanding of the scale of Frith's business one only has to look at the catalogue issued by Frith & Co in 1886: it runs to some 670 pages, listing not only many thousands of views of the British Isles but also many photographs of most European countries, and China, Japan, the USA and Canada. By 1890 Frith had created the greatest specialist photographic publishing company in the world, with over 2,000 sales outlets.

POSTCARD BONANZA

The ever-popular holiday postcard we know today took many years to develop. The Post Office issued the first plain cards in 1870, with a pre-printed stamp on one face. In 1894 they allowed other publishers' cards to be sent through the mail with an attached adhesive halfpenny stamp. Demand grew rapidly, and in 1895 a new size of postcard was permitted called the court card, but there was little room for illustration. In 1899, a year after Frith's death, a new card measuring 5.5 x 3.5 inches became the standard format, but it was not until 1902 that the divided back came into being, so that the address and message could be on one face and a full-size illustration on the other. Frith & Co were in the vanguard of postcard development: Frith's sons Eustace and Cyril continued their father's monumental task, expanding the number of views offered to the public and recording more and more places in Britain.

Francis Frith had died in 1898 at his villa in Cannes, his great project still growing. The archive he created continued in business for another seventy years. By 1970 it contained over a third of a million pictures showing 7,000 British towns and villages.

FRANCIS FRITH'S LEGACY

Frith's legacy to us today is of immense significance and value, for the magnificent archive of evocative photographs he created provides a unique record of change in the cities, towns and villages throughout Britain over a century and more. Frith and his fellow studio photographers revisited locations many times down the years to update their views, compiling for us an enthralling and colourful pageant of British life and character.

We are fortunate that Frith was dedicated to recording the minutiae of everyday life, for it is this sheer wealth of visual data, the painstaking chronicle of changes in dress, transport, street layouts, buildings, housing and landscape that captivates us so much today. His images offer us a powerful link with the past and with the lives of our ancestors.

THE VALUE OF THE ARCHIVE TODAY

Historians consider The Francis Frith Collection to be of prime national importance. It is the only archive of its kind remaining in private ownership. The archive's future is both bright and exciting.

Francis Frith, with his unshakeable belief in making photographs available to the greatest number of people, would undoubtedly approve of the computer technology that allows his work to be rapidly transmitted to people all over the world by way of the internet. His photographs depicting our shared past are now bringing pleasure and enlightenment to millions around the world a century and more after his death.

Introduction

STREETS BROAD AND NARROW, busy and tranquil, grand and humble – the variety and individuality of Britain's streets typify the unique character of our towns. In this book, we attempt to show some of this variety through the vivid photographs taken by the Francis Frith company over the years. Frith's fascinating archive contains thousands of scenes of urban life from 1870 to 1970, an eventful century that changed our towns for ever. Here in this book we can trace the history of our towns, and enjoy their rich variety, through the character of their streets.

Most towns have their origins as market centres. From the dawn of history, small farmers and growers gathered in open-air markets, driving their livestock in through the lanes. As the reputation of these produce markets grew, they were held on regular days of the week. Soon it became necessary to build a market hall to accommodate them all. Then other tradesmen such as cobblers and blacksmiths took advantage of the regular gathering of potential customers, and the growth of the town was set in motion. By medieval times traders and craftsmen had grown wealthy, and this is reflected in the fine guildhalls and covered arcades. Coaching inns sprang up to cater for the needs of travellers.

Life was not all trade. Prosperity encouraged schools, and fine churches and chapels in which to worship. From the medieval period onwards, market towns expanded outwards, with radiating residential areas for both rich and poor. The Victorian period was one of civic splendour, although around the great buildings the poor continued to live in humble houses. The streets of most British market towns are thus a rich jumble of architectural styles and building types, and reflect the long history of the settlement of which they are a part.

Other towns took advantage of distinctive local resources. Thanks to their mineral springs, Leamington, Buxton and Great Malvern grew into spa towns where the rich went to have their ills cured. Villages on the coast with attractive cliff scenery or a beautiful bay or beach were patronized by the rich and later by the working man and his family – the railways and bank holidays created a boom for the seaside. From such modest beginnings sprang up popular resorts like Scarborough, Bournemouth and Torquay. Other towns traded on some local strength – Newmarket on its horse racing, Bakewell on its puddings, Cheltenham on its schools.

Many towns eventually grew to the point where they became cities. Oxford and Cambridge gained a worldwide reputation for their universities. Towns on the coast like Liverpool and Newcastle were the conduits for the transportation of heavy goods such as iron and timber, and so developed into international ports. Other towns, such as Lichfield and Durham, had fine cathedrals, and though relatively small in size, developed the unique charm of the British cathedral city.

During the 20th century Britain's rapidly growing population and World War II bomb damage made the building of new towns a vital necessity. These settlements, often built on open fields, grew into towns almost overnight, telescoping the building process of centuries. It is fascinating to see how their architects tried to give the streets of these new towns both civic dignity and neighbourliness.

Today, with the predominance of chain stores, shopping precincts and ring roads, our towns are all beginning to look the same. As we walk down any typical town street, it is often hard to tell whether we are in Market Drayton or Melton Mowbray. Yet if we look above the chain store fascias in most main streets, or along the terraces of side streets, another world is revealed: we see the streets of our towns as they once were – individual and characterful. This book peels away the layers of unsympathetic modern changes; Frith's fascinating period photographs show the streets of our towns before the planners altered them for ever.

REDHILL, SURREY, HIGH STREET 1906 55035T

A glorious jumble

BROAD OR narrow. Steep or flat. Crowded or empty. Medieval or Victorian. The streets of our towns are so varied and so full of character that it is almost impossible to define a typical street.

We will see bustling market places and broad cobbled shopping streets. We will see the architecture of many periods in sharp juxtaposition, with timber-framed shops next to dignified Georgian hotels. We will see narrow lanes, steep steps, and congested closes and yards. Some streets are prosperous, lined with large shops and busy with smartly-dressed people; others are humbler, or even shabby. Here is the bustling town centre – and here also the quiet suburb with its corner shop. Here is the grand terrace – and here too is the artisan's cottage. Our first chapter is a glorious jumble of every kind of street.

Luton

LUTON, BEDFORDSHIRE,
THE CORN EXCHANGE 1897
39700T

THIS PHOTOGRAPH illustrates the Victorian zeal in tidying up traditional market clutter – in Luton's case the clutter of the straw plait markets – by the building of a market house or corn exchange. Luton's corn exchange, an ornate building in the Gothic style, was sited on Market Hill at the south eastern end of George Street, near the junction with Chapel Street. The first Corn Exchange had been built by the lord of the manor. He leased the tolls to the Board of Health, who wanted the new building off the streets as part of the 19th-century improvements. In the photograph we can see an urchin displaying a billboard advertising Starke's clearance sale – for this task he will have earned a few pennies. We can also see from the photograph that at this date market stalls still spilled over onto the road and pavement. Chapel Street was previously known as Hog Lane, a narrow rough road, lined with some very poor dwellings. Bad housing was a consequence of the town's growth from 2,986 in 1821 to 36,404 in 1901.

Guisborough

GUISBOROUGH, YORKSHIRE, WESTGATE 1899 44758T

GUISBOROUGH is one of the many towns of Britain that retain their medieval street pattern. The street plan of the present-day town centre is heavily influenced by the medieval land holdings. The curved medieval strips running between Westgate and the north and south back lanes (present-day Bolckow Street/Park Lane and Rectory Lane) were passed from one generation to another, and during the late 19th and 20th century, speculative builders developed the area literally strip by strip. Whilst today Westgate forms the heart of the town, it is not actually mentioned by name until 1549; before this it was simply a track running on an east/west orientation through the strips, which ran north to south. Guisborough has never had a High Street, and Westgate has simply come to be known as 'the Street' or 'the main street'.

In this delightful and evocative view with its wide sweep of cobbles, we see the north or 'top' side of Westgate. On the extreme left is the watchmaker's and jeweller's shop of George Page, a keen amateur photographer; many of his photographs of events in the town were taken from his first floor drawing room window, shown here, with the distinctive clock below.

By the 1950s, cars were parking on both sides of Westgate, and it lost the broad, spacious feeling shown in this photograph.

SHIFNAL, SHROPSHIRE, MARKET PLACE 1898 41818

BECAUSE OF Shifnal's terrible fire of 1591, all the picturesque timber-framed buildings in the town's streets were built after that date. This range of shops in the market place displays ornate timber framing. Generally, when old buildings like these are restored the plaster is often removed to reveal the old timber beneath; however, on some in Shifnal the timber has since been plastered over.

The road here has since been widened by the demolition of Mason's, the butcher's shop. On the left is the Georgian bow-window of Meyrick's the chemist's and druggist's. It is clearly a swelteringly hot day – the awnings and blinds are down on many of the shops – yet the joints of meat are still hung outside Mason's window for the flies to feast on.

Shifnal is thought to have been the model for P G Wodehouse's 'Market Blandings'. Despite the growth of the town as it developed to provide accommodation for both Birmingham and Wolverhampton to the east and the new town of Telford to the west, it has managed to retain much of its charm and individuality.

Shifnal

HERE WE HAVE a nostalgic scene at the very heart of old Northwich, at a time when tradesmen used horses and carts to transport their wares and tools around the streets. The Bull Ring was once the central meeting place and the hub of activity for the town. It was originally the location of a weekly market in the 17th century. Technically, Northwich is the name given to the six-acre township surrounding the Bull Ring.

As a result of the immense damage and destruction caused by subsidence, many of the old buildings in the town had to be pulled down. For a time, between the late 1800s and early 1900s, Northwich resembled a shanty town with shops and single-storey timber sheds filling in the gaps where buildings had disappeared. However, owing to new building regulations which insisted that any new developments be based on a light timber framework, the town slowly recovered, and fine black and white timber-framed, multi-storey buildings began to emerge, decorated with ornate carvings and plasterwork. This has given the town a very attractive 'olde-worlde' feel, particularly along the High Street; the Old Post Office, built in 1911, and the Brunner Public Library, rebuilt after subsidence damage in 1909, are particularly fine examples from this period.

Not only were many buildings demolished and replaced but several were jacked up, particularly during the 'big-lift' of 1920-24 when the Bull Ring was also raised by 6ft in the battle against subsidence. How sad that the splendid Georgian Angel Hotel had to be pulled down.

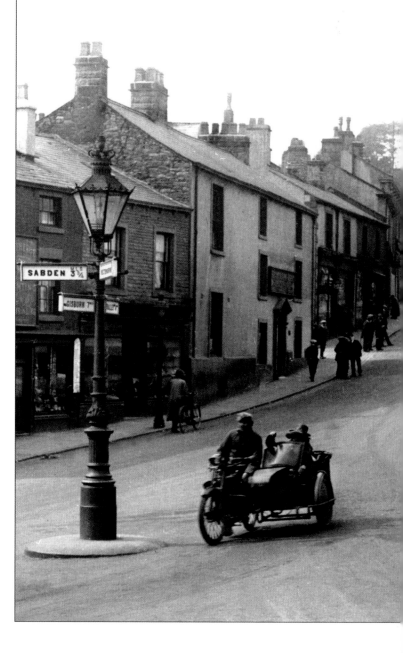

Clitheroe

CLITHEROE, LANCASHIRE,
MARKET PLACE 1921 71131

Northwich

Above: NORTHWICH, CHESHIRE, THE BULL RING 1903 49678

Cheshire is famed for its salt-workings. Henry VI brought Dutchmen over to instruct the English in its extraction. At Northwich salt was found at deep levels. In 1781 miners penetrated to a new stratum, 40 yards thick. The American traveller Louis Simond describes his descent into the mine in 1810.

'We descended into the mine. My companions, dressed in the costume of the place, a flannel over-all, were seated in a large tub, suspended by a rope; one of the miners stood on the edge, to keep the tub steady in its descent. At the depth of 330 feet, we found ourselves in a sort of palace of salt. The ceiling, about 20 feet high, was supported by pillars 15 feet thick, at very bold, and, I should think, alarming distances, considering the prodigious weight above. I measured 53 steps (159 feet) between some of them!'

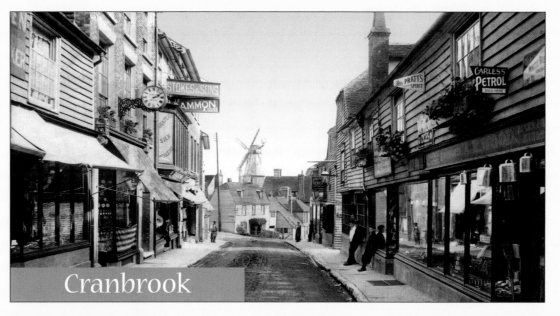

Cranbrook

CRANBROOK, KENT, STONE STREET 1906 56971T

SOME VILLAGES expanded into small towns by having a local industry. A good example is Cranbrook in Kent: Flemish weavers came here in the 14th century, and made the village a centre of medieval cloth making, using wool from the local flocks. The long main street, the Hill, bordered by tile-hung or weather-boarded cottages, turns in the middle, with St Dunstan's Church set back above the bend. Cranbrook Mill in the background was built in 1814. Restored in 1958, it is regarded as the finest remaining smock mill in the county.

Brick, painted brick, vertical hung tiling, weatherboarding with natural slate, and tiles for roofing are all visible in this photograph. These building materials are commonly used in the streets locally;

they are characteristic of the Kentish Weald, with its rich source of timber for building. Glass shop fronts line this Edwardian street, which boasts a jeweller's, a draper's and silk mercer's named Stokes & Sons, and a trader by the name of J F Gammon. The licensee J Fread at the Prince Albert pub (right) offered 'good stabling' for drinkers' horses.

CLITHEROE, an ancient market town, dates back to the 11th century. Its name comes from the Anglo-Saxon for 'rocky hill', and indeed the town grew around a prominent limestone outcrop upon which stands a Norman castle. The parish church, although not as high as the castle, has an equally prominent position. The street we see in this photograph runs like a spine between the castle (centre background) and the church, and it is along this ancient route that the town has developed.

Our photographer stood in Church Street with the church behind him; the part we see is the Market Place, where markets have been held since early times. The White Lion Hotel on the right is still there today. Notice the horse-drawn vegetable cart on the right – at this date, despite some motorised traffic (two fine examples are visible in the foreground), horse-drawn vehicles were still popular. The café's proprietors in 1921 were Messrs Taylor & Hughes: their slogan was 'we are noted for our pork pies'.

Minehead

THIS PART of Minehead is Higher Town (or Church Town), and is set on the side of a steep hill. A network of charming, narrow streets culminates in this even narrower lane with its flight of steps leading up to the church. It was the Lower Town which generally prospered, while the poorer houses were in the Higher Town.

Leland, writing in the 1540s, stated: 'The fairest part of the Toun standith in the bottom of an Hille. The residew rennith stepe up a longe hille, yn the toppe where of is a fair paroche chirche.' The Rev Richard Warner, visiting in 1800, was disappointed by Higher Town, feeling that it had 'nothing to recommend its shabby, irregular lanes, but the extensive prospect necessarily given to it by its elevation.' It was the poorness of Higher Town that saved its character. Prebendary Hancock wrote in 1903: 'We can find a sentimental sigh for the low, old houses, myrtle-clad to their overhanging roofs, which until recently were to be seen even in the heart of the town'. Higher Town is certainly no longer shabby, and has become a desirable residential district. In essence, however, Church Steps has changed little since those days.

The oldest cottages we see in this photograph are built in what is known as a 'cross passage' design: a passage runs straight from front to back door, dividing the house. There were usually two rooms on the up-slope side of the passage and a shippon (cow shed) on the down-slope side. In medieval times the living quarters would have been heated by a fire in the middle of the floor of the main room with the smoke simply drifting out through a hole in the roof.

Right: MINEHEAD, SOMERSET, CHURCH TOWN 1888   20893

Frome

THE OLDEST trading street in Frome is traffic-free, and still retains its medieval character with a stream running down its centre (photograph 58850, right). There is a Domesday reference to a market here in 1086 – Cheap Street's name comes from 'chepe', meaning market. Note the open-fronted, stall-like frontage of Vincent's the fishmonger's (left of photograph). Opposite, with a jettied timber-framed upper storey supported by brackets, is one of the oldest buildings in Frome. The town can now boast more listed buildings than any other in Somerset, despite the fact that the early 1960s saw the beginning of the Trinity clearances. These caused such a local outcry that a halt was put on the demolition. The result is that the buildings and streets that did remain have been restored and renovated, leaving us with a most important collection of 17th- and 18th-century industrial housing.

The industry in question was the textile industry. With an abundance of sheep nearby on the Mendip hills, and Frome's proximity to water, cloth mills began to be established, and from the 17th century onwards they prospered and grew – at one time there were about two hundred mills, and it is said that seven wagons weekly were taken to London laden with cloth. The increasing work force needed for spinning and weaving raised the demand for accommodation (one weaver needed between seven and eight spinners).

Other industries in Frome included bell casting and foundry work, stained glass, and printing, which all helped it to survive through many changes, although its population has remained about the same. William Cobbett once referred to Frome as being 'a sort of little Manchester'. If he could ride again to this Somerset town, he would see that Frome has done well in preserving the streets and houses of its industrial past.

Frome was noted for its 'blue cloth', which was used for army uniforms during the Napoleonic Wars. The Russian Imperial Bodyguard were also dressed in this cloth up until the time of the Crimean War. The dye was obtained from woad, which was grown locally. Teasels were used for raising the nap of the cloth, and they grew abundantly hereabouts.

Right: TEASELS 2004 ZZZ00881

Above:
FROME,
SOMERSET,
CHEAP STREET
1907 58850
Above left:
FROME,
SOMERSET,
MARKET PLACE
1907 58843

THE ROWS made up a pattern of narrow streets unique to Great Yarmouth. They often began in a tunnel under a building. The Rows had many nicknames before they were formally numbered in 1804. Row 60 was sometimes called Ostend Market Row, the word Ostend being a corruption of Austin: in the Middle Ages a cell of the Augustinian or Austin friary in Gorleston stood at the end of this Row.

The Rows may have been quaint to visit in the daytime, but they had their unpleasant side too. In the days before street lighting it was a bold man who ventured into a strange row at night. Hygienic conditions before the days of sewers and water supply are best left to the imagination. Each Row had an open drain running down it. In 1898 it was estimated that 12,000 people lived in the Rows: about a third of the living-rooms received an hour's sunlight, the others no sunlight at all. By 1911 the Borough Engineer, J W Cockrill, had paved or concreted the surface of every Row: as a consequence he acquired the nickname of 'Concrete Cockrill'!

A sort of tunnel or tubular passage

The writer Charles Dickens was fascinated by Great Yarmouth and describes the Rows very well:

'A row is a long narrow lane or alley, quite straight, or as nearly so as may be, with houses on each side, both of which you can sometimes touch at once with the finger-tips of each hand, by stretching out your arms to their full extent. Now and then the houses overhang and even touch above your head, converting the row, so far, into a sort of tunnel, or tubular passage. Many and many a picturesque old bit of domestic architecture is to be hunted up amongst the rows. In some rows there is little more than a blank wall for the boundary. In others, the houses retreat into tiny courts, where washing and clear-starching were done, and wonderful nasturtiums and scarlet-runners are reared from green boxes'.

Great Yarmouth

Left: GREAT YARMOUTH, NORFOLK, ROW NO 60 1908
60654

Rochdale

ROCHDALE'S 122 steps lead down from the parish church to the town centre 80ft below. The churchwardens' accounts for 1660 record that 24 shillings was paid for 8 loads of 'great stone' from Blackstone Edge for the steps. Taylors House on the right was occupied by Worth & Worth, solicitors, for many years. When it was demolished in 1934 it was found to have contained a huge stone water tank, the town's first reservoir, constructed by the Taylors in 1760. The water was drawn from Packer Spout.

Rochdale's famous daughter

Rochdale is famous as the home of Gracie Fields. It was at the Hippodrome that she began her singing career, coming joint first in a talent show at the age of 10. She won 10s 6d.

Left: ROCHDALE, GREATER MANCHESTER, CHURCH STEPS 1913 65603T

Below: KENDAL, CUMBRIA, STEELE'S YARD, 123 HIGHGATE 1914 67393

Kendal

THE YARDS that are so characteristic of Kendal developed from medieval burgage plots, long narrow strips of land running back from the main streets. They were usually named from a feature in them – in Two-Seater Yard off Highgate, for instance, a seat for the weary was placed on each side of the entrance – or from a business, like Post Office Yard, or Cumstey's Yard (Cumstey's were a firm of fat refiners), or from the owner or a prominent resident. Dr Manning's Yard off Highgate was named after the doctor who lived and practised in the house at the head of the yard in the late 19th century.

In the old yards, the ground floors were often used as workshops. Typical businesses might be rope works, dye works, tanneries and woollen warehouses. Cottages were crammed in too, and conditions in the yards were cramped and not very hygienic. Each yard might have a midden, a single earth closet, and one communal tap, all combining to produce health hazards despite the efforts of housewives to keep their homes and families clean and healthy. Disease, especially cholera, took its toll. Eventually many of the yards succumbed to the efforts of town planners; many were severely truncated and others completely lost in a flurry of removing old and unhygienic housing where changes in trades and occupations had made many of the buildings redundant.

Left: KENDAL, CUMBRIA, YARD 59, STRAMONGATE 1914 67387

Tiverton

MANY MEDIEVAL streets had drains running down the centre of them. However, what we see in this photograph is certainly not a drain: the Leat was installed back in 1250 as the town's water supply. The present day Castle Street was once, rather aptly, named Frog Street because the Leat contained many of those amphibious creatures. This charming view is instantly recognisable today. Notice the boy with the scooter to the left; scooters are coming back into fashion now, and perhaps some day children will once again sail yachts in the Leat. Sad to say, it normally carries no water today.

Above: TIVERTON, DEVON, CASTLE STREET 1920 69888P

THIS PHOTOGRAPH of Whitby (right) shows one of the many narrow yards running down to the river near the harbour, which at the time of this photograph were occupied by fishermen and poorer families. Here children could play safely, and the fishermen could prepare their nets. Argument's Yard is named not as a result of a quarrel but after a family that once owned property there. The house on the right is derelict, the stone stairs have seen better days and the outside toilet looks ready to collapse. A fisherman's oilskin is slung over the stair rail, and the boy on the right is showing a large fish to his friends – it is part of his father's catch, and they will be having it for supper.

   Situated in a deep ravine on the estuary of the River Esk, Whitby earned its living from the sea, either by whaling, fishing, coastal trading or shipbuilding. For centuries it was often easier for people coming to or going from Whitby to make their journey by sea rather than attempt to travel overland.

'The houses of the old town – the side away from us, are all red-roofed, and seem piled up one over the other anyhow, like the pictures we see of Nuremberg.' BRAM STOKER, 'DRACULA' 1897 (DESCRIBING WHITBY)

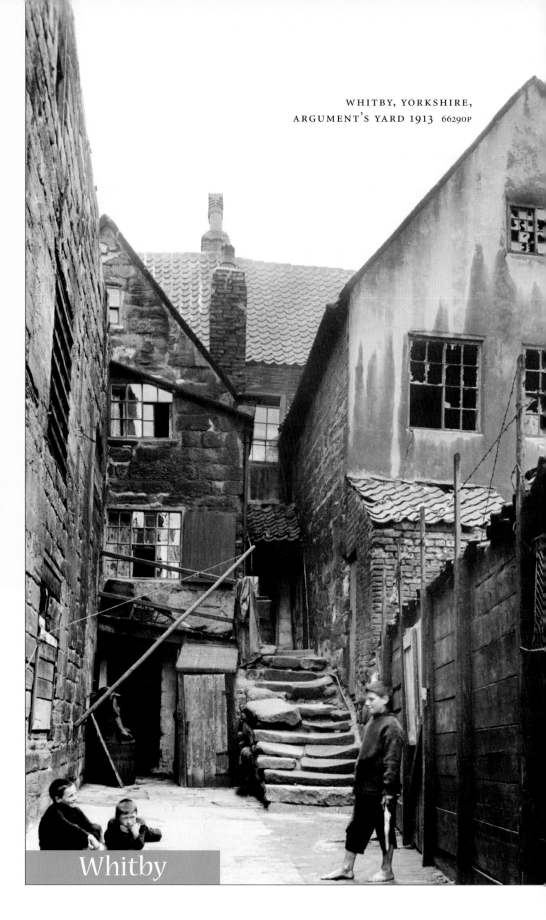

WHITBY, YORKSHIRE,
ARGUMENT'S YARD 1913 66290P

Whitby

SOUTHPORT, MERSEYSIDE, LORD STREET 1913 66507T

THIS STREET is a contrast to the humble yards of Kendal or Whitby. Laid out as an extravagant boulevard in the 1820s, Lord Street contains many elegant buildings that reflect the town's ambitions as a high-class residence and resort. Perhaps the street's most distinctive feature is its elaborate arcade or veranda of decorative cast iron and glass which extends along its length (left of photograph).

The buildings display a wonderful medley of architectural styles, and apart from the loss of the stone setts and tramlines, the street's general appearance has changed little with the passing years. Southport's residential make-up was reflected along Lord Street where quality shops abounded. By the beginning of the 20th century the national retail chains were opening branches along what was considered one of the finest streets for shopping in England. Note the large gilt signs on the left of the picture. These had been a popular form of advertising for many years. Thompson & Capper's sign has been modified at some time so that it can be lit up with electric lights.

Farnham

FARNHAM, SURREY, THE BOROUGH 1913   65926P

THIS PHOTOGRAPH was taken at a time when long exposure was needed. The cyclists, a man in a horse-drawn cart, pedestrians and even the window cleaner were all told to freeze and look like statues. Signs stretch far down the street and include those for the Bush Hotel, Frisby's and for G & A Hewitt, china, glass and earthenware dealers, whose premises would later be taken over by W H Smith. Real ceramic urns stood above the window of Miss Paget's Spinning Wheel (right). The most noticeable architectural difference in the last 100 years is the loss of the Victorian Town Hall and Corn Exchange, with its highly decorative 88ft-high clock tower. It was replaced in the 1930s by the present building, which was designed by Falkner, Aylwin and Benslyn. Note the painter on his long ladder (left) – today, health and safety rules would no doubt compel him to work from scaffolding.

The Borough, a typical small town shopping street, and Farnham's main east-west route, is the successor to ancient trackways. The Saxons and the Romans built settlements here; as cross-roads have always been a favourite stopping place, the market area, at the foot of the street which leads to the castle (left), became the nucleus for the town. In his book 'The Old Road', Hilaire Belloc writes: 'Farnham was always a place of capital importance. The fact that it was a meeting place of the roads that came from London and the Straits of Dover, necessarily made it a key to Southern England'.

Literary inspiration

Over the centuries many writers have been born, lived and found inspiration in Farnham, including Izaak Walton (near right), author of 'The Compleat Angler'; William Cobbett, politician, writer and founder of Hansard; J M Barrie (far right), who wrote 'Peter Pan' two miles out of town; Jonathan Swift, author of 'Gulliver's Travels'; and, in more recent times, the novelist Joanna Trollope, who was a teacher at Farnham Girls' Grammar School.

Great Yarmouth

KING STREET is the busiest shopping street in Great Yarmouth: this photograph looks north past the junction with Regent Street towards the Market Place. The 'King' in the street name is Charles II, who visited Yarmouth in 1671. Note the many forms of transport in this photograph, including a delivery handcart.

There are no fewer than four ladders in this picture! The three tall ones are almost certainly window cleaners, while the man on the short ladder next to the street lamp appears to be making some minor adjustments to the blind in front of his shop.

GREAT YARMOUTH, NORFOLK, KING STREET 1896   37958

'Its sands are magnificent; its seafront five miles long … [Yarmouth is a] great national playground, a quick-change sanatorium for multitudes of jaded mortals … David Copperfield thought it the finest place in the universe.'

ARTHUR MEE, THE KING'S ENGLAND 'NORFOLK' 1959

Poole

Echo! Echo! Street-wise children in Poole in the early 1900s

Ron Alderman, speaking in 1992, said most working class Poole families had nine or ten children. 'We were hungry because our parents had so many children to feed. As kids just after the First World War, we used to go and sell Echo newspapers in the High Street. We would shout 'Echo! Echo!' and if we sold a dozen the shop would give us another dozen so we could make a few coppers. Then we would go and buy faggots and peas and have a good feed. For a sweet we would go scrumping for apples'. Mr Alderman and his mates employed other tricks to aid their survival. When a coal-grabbing crane unloaded ships at the Quay, they collected any lumps that fell on the ground. Sometimes at dinner time they would pop out of school to persuade wealthy trippers visiting the Viewpoint on Constitution Hill to part with their pennies. For entertainment, they sent one boy into the cinema at the Amity Music Hall in the High Street. 'He would pay to go in, then go and open the fire door and the rest of us would get in for nothing', he said. 'We were never caught. We were too fly for that'.

HERE WE SEE an extraordinary selection of architectural styles, showing how our High Streets developed piecemeal. On the extreme left is an old thatched cottage, on the corner of Carter Lane, which survived until 1919. It was the home of the Town Crier and Bill Poster. A notice in the window reads 'Poole Bill Posting Company'. The cottage was replaced by Poole's first Woolworth's. The rest of the street is a wonderful mixture of more restrained Georgian and Regency with riotous Victorian, and the many passers-by attest to the commercial importance of this busy port town. The clock on the right belonged to watchmaker James Cole.

Above: POOLE, DORSET, HIGH STREET 1908 61164

Reigate

CORNFIELD ROAD, part of a 19th-century housing estate, is an archetypal street of terraced houses with handy shops on the corner. The houses are small, and not exactly beautiful, but intensely respectable, each with its tiny front garden and low boundary wall. Solidly built houses like these, with proper plumbing and mains drainage, must have seemed the height of modernity to their first occupants. Photograph 62762, taken four short years after photograph 56205, shows that the pavements have been demarcated from the road, but no metalled surface has yet been applied.

The steps and shop (left of 62762) survive, but the shop is now selling soft furnishings. Many of the products emblazoned in the windows are still available today. It is quite remarkable that an area such as this could support two almost identical shops. The house on the left now carries a blue plaque informing us that Oscar Wilde lived here at one time.

Top: REIGATE, SURREY, CORNFIELD ROAD 1906 56205
Above: REIGATE, SURREY, CORNFIELD ROAD 1910 62762

Braintree

BRAINTREE, ESSEX, SOUTH STREET 1909 62116

AFTER the Industrial Revolution, many towns increased in size, and housing was needed for the workers. Braintree was no exception. With the introduction of the silk industry in 1810, followed by the arrival of the railway in 1848, the town grew. The census returns for the 100 years from 1831 show not only the growth in population, but also the growth in the working population. Housing and industrial development spread out away from the town centre.

In South Street, the houses were typical of those that were built in Braintree from the 1890s to house the increasing number of people coming into the town to work. In this view, looking away from the town, the houses near the telegraph post have decorative brick tiles in panels between the windows. Both these and the bricks would have been made in local brickfields – at one time there was a brick works behind the houses on the right.

Note the wall post box, once quite a common feature in our towns. According to Kelly's Directory, post was collected from this particular box at 7.50am, 10.30am, 3.40pm and 7.35pm on weekdays. Quite prominent in the distance is the gable end of a large building. This is the Braintree Brewery in Railway Street, founded in about 1868 and owned in 1909 by Ernest Ingold. The brewery closed in 1939, and the site was re-developed for housing in 2001.

HIGH WYCOMBE, BUCKINGHAMSHIRE, AMERSHAM HILL 1906   53668

High Wycombe

THIS STREET of semis is a step or two up from the more workaday terraces of Reigate and Braintree (see opposite page). Amersham Hill is High Wycombe's grandest Victorian and Edwardian suburb. The first phase in its development was alongside Amersham Hill, the old turnpike road to Amersham, immediately north of the station. This evocative view shows the 1880s and 1890s houses, many of them large semi-detached ones to the west; at this time vast detached houses behind substantial boundary walls were built too, these ones to the east.

Prosperous housing spread up Amersham Hill, much of it in detached villas in large and well-wooded grounds; this middle-class housing continued along roads like Rectory Avenue and Lucas Road in the 1920s. This was where factory owners, chair manufacturers, lawyers, successful builders, bank managers, doctors and the professional classes gravitated. Also, more and more commuters to London settled here, their journey made easier by the 1906 opening of the line to Marylebone. East of this middle-class enclave you were back into working-class and lower middle-class housing in the Totteridge Road area.

High Wycombe also saw streets of artisan terraced housing built between 1880 and 1914. Their occupants were mostly employed in the factories and workshops scattered in amongst the houses. Schools were built by the Borough Education Authority set up after the 1870 Education Act, and some of these survive (such as Green Street School of 1895), as well as pubs and shops. To the north of the railway, smaller semi-detached and terrace houses spread up the Hughenden Valley and north of Priory Road's substantial middle-class late Victorian semi-detached villas.

Exmouth

Above: EXMOUTH, DEVON, ALEXANDRA TERRACE 1906   56768

Below: EXMOUTH, DEVON, THE ESPLANADE 1906   53941T

THIS STREET is a typical example of a seaside terrace. With the advent of bank holidays and more prosperity in Victorian times, seaside resorts flourished, and many streets like this were built where seaside landladies crammed in as many holidaymakers as they could.

Exmouth is proud of the fact that it is the oldest seaside resort in Devon, a town that attracted fashionable Georgian society in great numbers. The resort owes much to its setting, located as it is on a spit of land between the waters of Lyme Bay and the mighty estuary of the River Exe. Exmouth's history as a watering place began around 1720 when the wealthier members of early Georgian society found their way to the town, and the Napoleonic Wars, which closed the Continent to the wealthier traveller, brought new visitors and prosperity. Exmouth's sea front at this time was very different to how we see it today. The long sea wall and esplanade did not exist; between the growing town and the sands was a landscape of marshland and dunes. Exmouth came into its own as a seaside resort during Queen Victoria's reign, particularly after the opening of the railway in 1861.

The way the town developed was probably most influenced by the building of the sea wall in 1842; this was a massive feat of engineering, given the sheer length of Exmouth's sea front. Its creation, topped by the Esplanade – a glorious place for a promenade – presented the opportunity to develop the frontage of the town, along with gardens and leisure facilities. Alexandra Terrace overlooks the line of Exmouth's sea front, its view as uninterrupted today as when this photograph was taken a century ago. The terrace is relatively unchanged, though there has been the intrusion of modern windows in some of the top storeys. Many of the original houses are now blocks of flats.

Worthing's beauty, fashion and unalloyed purity

According to the Wallis Guide Book of 1826, 'Nothing can excel the spectacle that the Esplanade presents when thronged, as it is every fine summer's evening, with all the beauty and fashion of the place; while the opportunity it presents for inhaling the ocean breeze in unalloyed purity, and the defence it affords against the sea, stamp it with an importance commensurate with its attractive appearance'.

HERE WE SEE a somewhat grander seaside street than the one at Exmouth, and the buildings are earlier in date, for Worthing had been a popular watering place since the 18th century. However, before 1820 the expansion of Worthing had been haphazard. There had been no grandiose schemes comparable, in either size or style, with the squares and crescents that had been created at Hove or Brighton. York Terrace, the imposing building shown in the centre of the picture, was built circa 1822 by Edward Evershed. This terrace of five separate lodging houses, with their stucco facades, ionic pilasters, porches and balconies, was without doubt one of Worthing's most impressive Regency buildings.

In all the emerging resorts, the provision of accommodation for visitors had been a high priority, and at Worthing terraces of lodging houses were constructed on the former agricultural land that adjoined the foreshore. Once complete, they were immediately let at exorbitant rents. During the first two decades of the 19th century, the more affluent of Worthing's Georgian visitors often took over entire houses on a long lease, so that they could cater for themselves and also entertain. In many cases, they brought their own servants with them.

Below: WORTHING, SUSSEX, THE ESPLANADE 1890 22706

Worthing

Stafford

Left: STAFFORD,
STAFFORDSHIRE,
MARKET SQUARE c1960
S411087

HERE WE SEE how post-war architects often showed scant respect for existing building lines and styles. It is hard to believe that the architect of the new Boots building ever visited Stafford or even saw a photograph of the town centre with its ancient timber-framed buildings, dignified Georgian and classical-style shops and businesses, and the medieval St Mary's Church rising in the background. Boots stands queasily on its thin legs cocking a snook at the town's history and heritage. There is also a colossal Burton's menswear building here in the art deco style, built in the 1930s. Lining the square nearby are other chain stores such as F W Woolworth, but this occupies a building dating back to the 15th century.

A market was held in Stafford's Market Square from at least the 12th century until 1853, when a new covered hall was built behind the Guildhall. Through the centuries, the square was the setting for many fairs, parades and celebrations. In 1800 the local newspaper reported that a chimney sweep had auctioned his wife here for 5s 6d!

Right: WARRINGTON, CHESHIRE, BRIDGE STREET c1950 W29006

Warrington

WARRINGTON, CHESHIRE, BRIDGE STREET c1955
W29060T

THESE EVOCATIVE VIEWS of Warrington (above and opposite page) show an archetypal town centre not so very long ago – yet the cars and vans, and the fashions, make it seem a world away! Bridge Street was one of four main streets intersecting at Market Gate. All of these streets were not only shopping streets, but a key part of the regional road network, as we can see from the signpost in the foreground of W29006 (opposite page). From 1938 to 1966 Market Gate roundabout attempted to speed the flow of traffic on the A49 and A57 routes through the town centre.

The original concept of 1908 was to create four matching corners, 'a spacious circus, perfectly symmetrical in shape with a ring of singularly graceful buildings'. Piecemeal redevelopment of Market Gate prevented the realisation of this ambitious scheme.

The corner of Bridge Street and Buttermarket Street (left) was rebuilt just before the First World War. At the time the photograph W29060T (above) was taken, Boots the chemists were still firmly entrenched on the corner of Sankey Street. The banner on Boots' Corner advertising Warrington's annual Walton Horse Show suggests the photograph was taken near Whitsuntide. Meanwhile, shoppers could pop into Longs for unrationed sweets or stand and admire the dexterity of the assistants in the Maypole Dairy next door as they patted a pound of golden butter into shape.

From ancient origins

THE STREETS of Britain's towns lead us back into the remote past. Some streets even have their origins as ancient prehistoric trackways or as Roman roads, and many towns retain their medieval street patterns. The buildings on the streets tell us their ancient history too. In this chapter we will see how the centuries jostle together in our ancient towns. Medieval buildings stand on Roman streets, or Tudor and Georgian ones are set in a Norman stronghold. Monks, merchants, ship owners, benefactors – all these people from the distant past have made their mark on the streets of their towns.

Right: COLCHESTER, ESSEX, THE OLD SIEGE HOUSE 1921   70362T

Opposite page: COLCHESTER, ESSEX, ST JOHN STREET 1921   70363P

Opposite page: COLCHESTER CASTLE (DRAWING)

Colchester

COLCHESTER'S HISTORY is a long one – it was founded as a Roman town by the Emperor Claudius in the 1st century. Its conquest was vital to the establishment of Roman power, and Emperor Claudius himself, in a brief visit to the conquered lands, came to Colchester where he received the surrender of numerous native tribes personally. The town became a legionary fortress, its port at Fingringhoe playing a crucial role in supplying the troops and ferrying them and their supplies along the coast in support of the conquest. Parts of the Roman walls can still be seen. Every era since, from the Saxon, the Norman, the medieval, the Tudor, the Stuart, the Georgian, and the Victorian to the modern age has left its mark on the streets of the town and added to the richness of its heritage. In this photograph (left) we see East Street with its charming jumble of 15th- and 16th-century timber-framed, jettied and gabled buildings.

The Old Siege House (in the foreground), a 15th-century timber-framed terrace of three houses (now joined into one), played an important part in the siege of Colchester during the second phase of the English Civil War in the summer of 1648. The Parliamentarian town was taken by the Royalists and was promptly besieged for eleven weeks by Cromwell's New Model Army. The house was peppered by Royalist shot: red rings now surround the bullet holes in the old beams.

ALTHOUGH MANY BUILDINGS in St John Street and Vineyard Street in Colchester have been lost, this wonderful group of jettied buildings survives, clustering up to Schere Gate, possibly a medieval gate through the town wall. There are steps under the gateway, and the Roman town wall is incorporated in the house. The rendered façades and Georgian sash windows conceal the medieval timber-framed structures of houses built immediately outside the wall and its gateway. The house on the right was altered to make a shop front; note the striped barber's pole and the signs in the window - 'Shavallo Shaving Soap' and 'Kolene for the Hair'. Much has changed hereabouts, and the dual-carriageway southern bypass, Southway, is a mere 50 yards away.

During the Middle Ages and later, Colchester was a noted cloth-making town. This prosperity was marked by an increase in the number of parish churches to eight within the walls and eight outside, together with the monastic houses of Greyfriars and Crutched Friars.

Colchester's ghostly cavalier

The ghost of a cavalier is said to walk down East Street, and he disappears when he reaches Siege House. One of the rooms in the building (now a restaurant) is so haunted that staff will only work there in pairs. A phantom Puritan has also been seen nearby.

Ludlow

THIS PHOTOGRAPH shows clearly why Ludlow has been an important town for so long: sited on a hill surrounded on almost three sides by the River Teme, it was comparatively easy to defend. It was some twenty years after the Conquest that the castle was built (top centre), probably by Roger Lacy whose family had come from Normandy with William I. The Lacy family held several castles in the region, but Ludlow was to become the most important. It was built right beside the cliff overlooking the river, and within a very short time a settlement was established beside it with a market that brought traders from far and near.

We can also clearly see the route that the traders took when they came to market. Dinham Bridge was built in 1823, but it replaced a much older medieval bridge. Sometimes in dry weather when the river is low the old medieval stone piers can still be seen. There is a weir just beyond the bridge to the left. In fact there were several weirs all along this stretch of the River Teme; they were built to hold up the river so that there would always be water available to power the mills.

Ludford Bridge (drawing, opposite), in its present form dates from the 15th century. The first bridge on the site, however, was probably built in Norman times to give easy access to the castle and the town.

BROAD STREET in Ludlow was described by Nikolaus Pevsner as 'one of the most memorable streets in England'. It is a wonderful mix of architectural styles, with 15th-century buildings at the top and elegant Georgian buildings further downhill, all overlooked by the tower of St Lawrence's Church, the largest parish church in Shropshire.

The timber-framed Angel Hotel has in recent years been sold and refurbished as shops and apartments. It was built as an inn in 1555, and it is therefore older than the famous and even more ornate Feathers. Later it became a coaching inn, and among its most renowned visitors were Admiral Nelson and Lord and Lady Hamilton (Lady Hamilton was Nelson's mistress).

The Butter Cross (the dignified classical-style building at the end of the street) was built in 1744 at a cost of £1,000 as the Town Hall, and ever since it has dominated the view along Broad Street. It served at one time as a butter market, hence its name. The upper floor was used for a school, the Blue Coat Charity.

Left: LUDLOW, SHROPSHIRE, DINHAM BRIDGE AND THE CASTLE c1955 L111018

Above: LUDLOW, SHROPSHIRE, BROAD STREET AND THE ANGEL HOTEL 1936 87393T

Right: LUDLOW, SHROPSHIRE, LUDFORD BRIDGE (DRAWING)

Abingdon

THIS VIEW demonstrates how many of our towns and their streets were shaped by the great medieval abbeys. Of the Benedictine Abbey of St Mary in Abingdon little survives above ground. Once the sixth wealthiest of England's medieval monasteries, it was dissolved by Henry VIII in 1538, and much of its stonework was carried by river to London.

This view looks east from Bridge Street past the bridge across the mill stream (the river itself is out of shot a hundred yards away to the right) which was dug for the abbey in the 10th century and drove the two abbey corn mills. The Abbey Brewery which occupied many of the buildings closed in 1895, and the watermill became Langford's Coal and Corn Merchants. In this view the mill had only a couple of  years left as a corn mill. The buildings on the right were cleared away in the 1960s, along with a carpet factory (originally a Victorian hemp and twine works), and were replaced by the Upper Reaches Hotel. The site of the houses on the right is now part of the hotel car park.

ABINGDON, OXFORDSHIRE, ABBEY MILL AND THE BRIDGE 1890 26993

IT IS THOUGHT that Shrewsbury was founded in the 7th century by the Saxons. Its name is certainly Saxon in origin – 'Scrobbesbyrig' means 'fortified settlement in scrubland'. But the town we see today was shaped by the Normans. After the Norman conquest Roger de Montgomery built the castle (1074) and the abbey (1083). The castle stood on a defensive site occupying the only land entry into Shrewsbury, and the settlement that grew up around castle and abbey was enclosed by a loop in the River Severn. Later the settlement was walled for added protection; the remains of the wall can be found throughout the town, most notably along the street known as Town Walls. They also survive in the foundations of many buildings along Pride Hill. By the 1260s merchants in the town felt so secure that they began to build their town houses abutting the walls.

The merchants who built these houses were extremely wealthy and powerful. They were wool merchants, and it was their trade that made medieval Shrewsbury one of the wealthiest towns in England. As time went by the wool trade was replaced by the cloth trade. To this day evidence of the wealth of these merchants can be seen in the many glorious timber-framed buildings throughout the region. It is hard to believe that Lloyd's Mansion was demolished in the 1930s – the demolition of a building of this quality would never be allowed today. Notice the superb carving detail all over the building and particularly at the gable end.

Above: SHREWSBURY, SHROPSHIRE, LLOYD'S MANSION, PRINCESS STREET 1904   51360

Right: SHREWSBURY, SHROPSHIRE, IRELAND'S MANSION 1891   28915

Opposite: SHREWSBURY, SHROPSHIRE, WYLE COP c1891   38099

Shrewsbury

THIS ENORMOUS TOWNHOUSE below was nicknamed 'Ireland's Folly' by local people when it was first built in the 1500s. It is an early example of speculative building: it was one building divided into three so that Ireland, the merchant who built it, could rent out the two end sections in order to help him with financing the building – very astute.

Nikolaus Pevsner describes it as 'the only timber-framed house in Shrewsbury to which one might grant grandeur'. Many people find it hard to believe that it is genuine Tudor rather than a more recent fake, if only because of its size and position in the town centre.

THIS PHOTOGRAPH, although so rich in Victorian detail, gives us a fascinating impression of what a 15th-century street might have looked like. The timber-framed shops with dwelling space above are large and ornate, the working places and homes of wealthy merchants. The fish shop, Mudd's, behind the pump, dates to the 1430s. It is now known as Henry Tudor House – Henry VII stayed here on his way to fight Richard III at Bosworth Field.

But we also see here a vivid picture of the bustle of Victorian street life. Notice particularly the boy filling a bucket from the street pump (right), the handcart, and the variety of shops and shop signs. Also we have evidence of improved rail communications with fresh fish being brought all the way from Grimsby by Mudd & Sons.

The name of this street is a fascinating blend of old Welsh and old English. 'Wyle' means 'the road up the hill' and 'cop' means 'the top', so here we have simply 'the road up the hill to the top'.

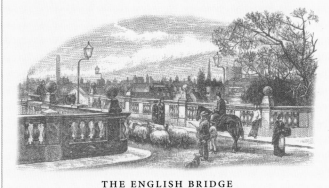

John Byng's melancholy Sunday

THE ENGLISH BRIDGE

The traveller John Byng visited Shrewsbury in 1793. Witty and mordant, he manages so often to see the dark, gloomy face of wherever he is staying. But he is always perceptive and rarely dull.

'I return'd to my inn and order'd dinner; and till it was ready, walk'd over the new bridge, an ugly structure, which would look lighter, were the balls with their pediments removed.

What a melancholy place is the best country town; and especially on Sundays, when no business is carrying forward! And their streets too, their grandest streets, are like the outlets of Spitalfields, or of Ratcliffe Highway.'

JOHN BYNG, 'RIDES ROUND BRITAIN', 1790
ED D ADAMSON, FOLIO SOCIETY

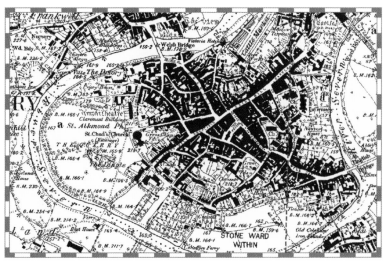

Dartmouth

THE ANCIENT BOROUGH of Dartmouth has a history going back to prehistoric times, when a settlement stood at the top of the hill above the River Dart, well away from coastal marauders. By the 11th century, trade had grown and danger lessened, and the town spread down the hillside to become a wealthy fishing and trading port – in medieval and Tudor times it was one of the foremost ports in Britain, rivalling the Cinque Ports in importance and fame. Many of the streets in the lower part of the town have been reclaimed from the river in various stages since medieval times, as we might guess from some of the street names – for instance King's Quay and Vavasour's Slip.

The photographs show two wonderful examples of Tudor buildings in the narrow medieval streets near the river. The house on Foss Street stood near its junction with Duke Street. The supports for the oriel windows and jettied upper floors were finely carved wooden animals. But alas, they are no more to be seen, as the building was destroyed on 1943 by the same bomb that damaged Parade House (D7110).

The lovely Tudor building on Butterwalk seen in D7110 survived unchanged for 300 years before being badly damaged in the bombing of 1943. The exterior carvings and plasterwork were removed for safekeeping, and the building was restored in 1954.

Left: DARTMOUTH, DEVON, FOSS STREET 1889 21602

Royal visitors to medieval Dartmouth

Since William Rufus sailed from Dartmouth to Normandy in the 11th century there have been many royal visitors here. King John (right) stayed in the town for three days in June 1205, and was here again in October 1214, when he reputedly 'gave privilege of Mairalte to Dertmouth'. Other royal visitors include Charles II, Queen Victoria, Edward VII, George V, Edward VIII, George VI, and Elizabeth II. Many members of the royal family have attended Britannia Royal Naval College.

DARTMOUTH, DEVON, BUTTERWALK c1960 D7110

Ipswich

IPSWICH, SUFFOLK, THE ANCIENT HOUSE 1921 70398P

THE BUTTERMARKET contains the town's most famous building, the Ancient House. Also known as Sparrowe's House, this remarkable building is over five hundred years old; it was around 1670 that Robert Sparrowe remodelled this jettied structure – the walls of its upper floors, with their bay windows, overhang the lower part. Its interest lies in the elaborate moulded plasterwork designs on its outer walls - it is probably the best surviving example of pargetting in Britain. The panels below the first floor windows represent the continents of the known world at that time – Europe, Asia, Africa and America - along with the arms of Charles II (who, it is said, hid here after the Battle of Worcester) over the main doorway.

Life in Ipswich was not always peaceful. Charles Dickens tells of a great storm endured by David Copperfield when he travelled through Ipswich by stage-coach to Great Yarmouth.

'When the day broke, it blew harder and harder … We came to Ipswich – very late … and found a cluster of people in the market-place, who had risen from their beds in the night, fearful of falling chimneys. Some of these, congregating about the inn-yard while we changed horses, told us of great sheets of lead having been ripped off a high church-tower, and flung into a by-street, which they then blocked up.'

THIS STREET is the principal route into Saffron Walden from the north. Its narrowness, and the fine old houses and shops to be found here, betray its medieval origin. The wonderful building on the right was described as 'the finest unspoilt mediaeval building in the town' by Mary Whitehead in her book 'A Portrait of a Market Town'; it dates from the 15th century. It was one of a group of shops strung out along the street, and not one of those clustered round the Market Square; Myddylton Place is some 200 yards into the town as we enter from the north. It was the house of a wealthy merchant connected with the wool trade. In the 14th and 15th centuries, the cloth fullers used the springs behind it in Freshwell Street. By the end of the 16th century the back part was used as a malting. At this time the timber loft was added with an oak wheel-hoist to raise the barley, which was laid out to ferment on the vast upper floor.

At the time of this photograph, the beams were partially exposed, but about half the house was plastered. The dragon post at the corner is beautifully carved. Inside there is fine panelling and carved beams. Upstairs, the huge room with timbers rising unhindered to the roof is now used as a dormitory for youth hostellers. The Society for the Preservation of Ancient Buildings took the building on in the 1930s; it was used by evacuees in the Second World War, and it was leased by the Youth Hostel Association in 1947.

Beyond and covered with Virginia creeper is Myddylton House. At this time there was a shop on the left corner, Thomas Barsham's grocer's shop, which stood on this spot from 1873 to 1914.

King's Lynn

CENTURIES AGO the Wash was much larger than it is today. Located on its south-east corner, King's Lynn was built on the edge of the sea, probably with help from the Romans, and later from the Dutch, who were experts in cutting dykes. All the navigable rivers in the area met at King's Lynn harbour. From ancient times, therefore, it was always a populous and flourishing seaport, borough and market town. Trade in all kinds of commodities developed, including furs, cloth, farm produce, fish, wine, and wood, bringing in merchants and buyers from home and abroad.

This street, like so many in Britain, bears traces of a long history. Napoleonic prisoners laid the granite cobbles. John Hampton, a master baker, lived in the first house on the right; one of his famous products were ship's biscuits that travelled the world – often accompanied by weevils. If we enter the courtyard on the right, immediately under the balcony containing Read & Wildburn's building paraphernalia, we will find a wonderful quadrangle called Hampton Court. This was an addition built by the Ampfles family in the late 15th century, and their mark is carved into the courtyard entrance. Tall people must mind their heads when they enter because there is a cannonball suspended from its ceiling, which is said to have smashed through St Margaret's Church west window during the siege of Lynn.

Saffron Walden

Above: SAFFRON WALDEN, ESSEX, MYDDYLTON PLACE 1907   58811
Above right: KING'S LYNN, NORFOLK, NELSON STREET 1908   60025
Right: KING'S LYNN, NORFOLK, THE QUAY 1898   40893P

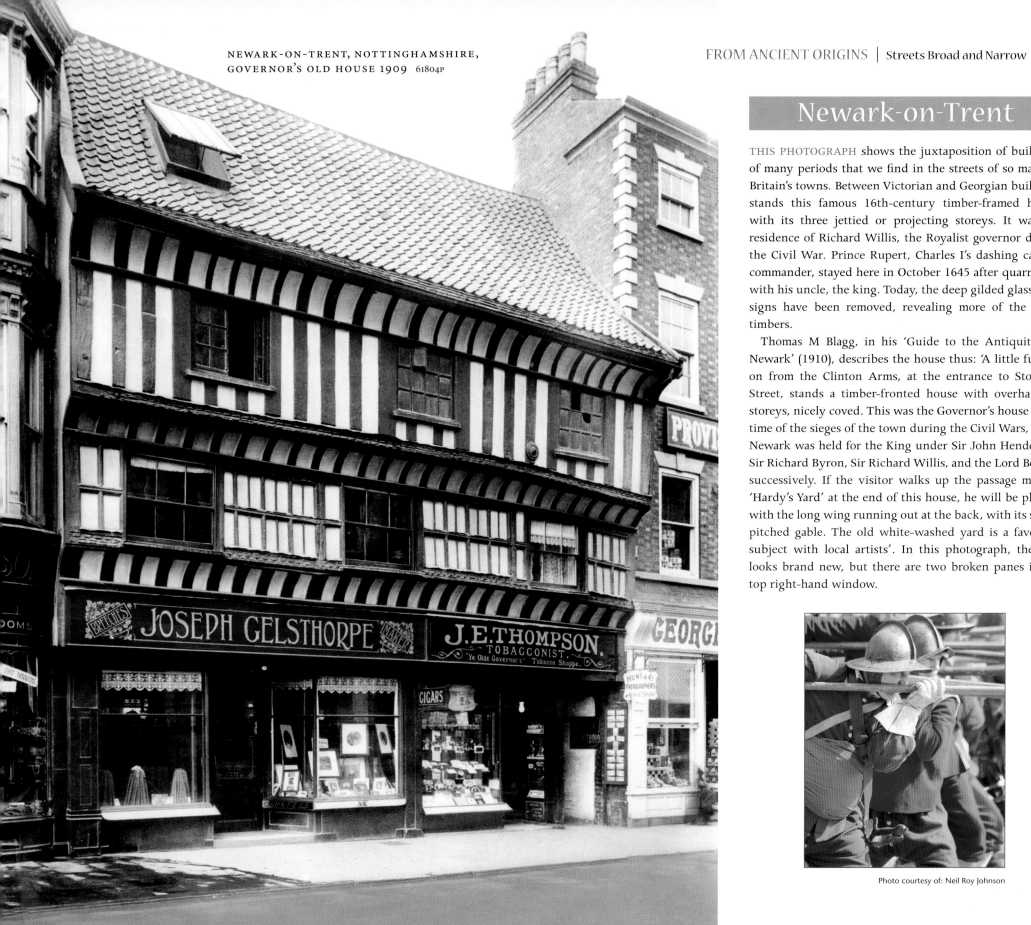

Newark-on-Trent

THIS PHOTOGRAPH shows the juxtaposition of buildings of many periods that we find in the streets of so many of Britain's towns. Between Victorian and Georgian buildings stands this famous 16th-century timber-framed house, with its three jettied or projecting storeys. It was the residence of Richard Willis, the Royalist governor during the Civil War. Prince Rupert, Charles I's dashing cavalry commander, stayed here in October 1645 after quarrelling with his uncle, the king. Today, the deep gilded glass shop signs have been removed, revealing more of the black timbers.

Thomas M Blagg, in his 'Guide to the Antiquities of Newark' (1910), describes the house thus: 'A little further on from the Clinton Arms, at the entrance to Stodman Street, stands a timber-fronted house with overhanging storeys, nicely coved. This was the Governor's house at the time of the sieges of the town during the Civil Wars, when Newark was held for the King under Sir John Henderson, Sir Richard Byron, Sir Richard Willis, and the Lord Bellasis successively. If the visitor walks up the passage marked 'Hardy's Yard' at the end of this house, he will be pleased with the long wing running out at the back, with its steep-pitched gable. The old white-washed yard is a favourite subject with local artists'. In this photograph, the roof looks brand new, but there are two broken panes in the top right-hand window.

Photo courtesy of: Neil Roy Johnson

Chipping Campden

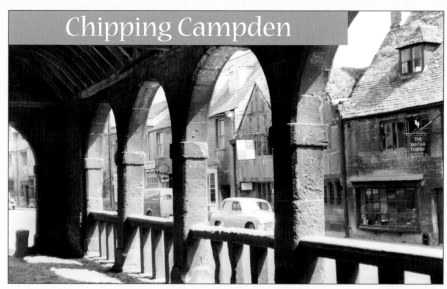

CHIPPING CAMPDEN, GLOUCESTERSHIRE, HIGH STREET c1960 C335047

THIS TYPICAL Cotswold town, with its buildings of honey-hued limestone, was one of the great wool towns of the Middle Ages before becoming a thriving market centre. The name 'Chipping' means market.

Here we glimpse the High Street through the arches of the Market Hall, which was built in 1627 at the expense of Sir Baptist Hicks. This rich London merchant won favour with James I by lending the monarch money, and in return he was granted 'our rectory and church at Cheltenham, our chapel at Charlton Kings and our church at Campden'.

Thanks to restoration work by the Campden Trust, this exquisite stone town has some of the finest buildings in the county. Just beyond the Market Hall behind the war memorial is the Town Hall, which dates back to the 14th century. Other fine examples in the High Street include the 18th-century Bedfont House, the 14th-century Woolstaplers Hall and the early 19th-century Lygon Arms.

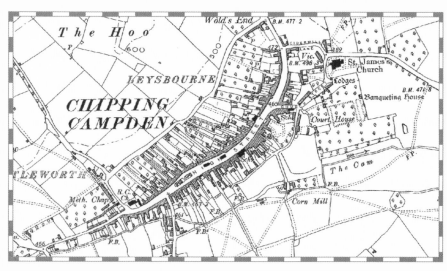

Boston

THIS STRIKING and imposing building is an outstanding example of the way in which many of the buildings in our streets are altered and restored over the years. The original building may have been the Hall of the Corpus Christi Guild, founded in 1335. What we see today is basically a 15th-century timber-framed building. Then the ground floor, first floor and part of the second floor were restored by J Oldrid Scott, the son of the distinguished architect Sir George Gilbert Scott, in 1874; at the same time he added the upper part of the building and the gables in the same ornate 15th-century style. This Frith photograph shows the building with its timbers in their natural state and the infill panels decorated with painted plaster and rosettes. Today the building has had its timbers blackened and the panels whitewashed.

Above: BOSTON, LINCOLNSHIRE, SHODFRIARS HALL 1889 22274

Right: BOSTON, LINCOLNSHIRE, PACKHOUSE QUAY AND SHODFRIARS HALL, SOUTH STREET 2005 B155706K

Market Harborough

At nine o'clock, I enter'd Market Harborough, where, to my sorrow, was a feast – and revelry, tipsy dance, and Jollity, with wonderful drunkeness, owing to the extreme heat; and I found myself consign'd to an alehouse inn, the George, an hot, stinking, narrow house without a breath of air ... I supp'd upon nasty sweating ham and beef, and soon retired to an old chamber hung with painted arras.

JOHN BYNG, 'RIDES ROUND BRITAIN', 1790
ED D ADAMSON, FOLIO SOCIETY

THIS is the kind of ancient public building that adds character to our streets. The Old Grammar School in Market Harborough was founded in 1614 by Robert Smyth, Harborough's very own answer to Dick Whittington. He was a poor boy who left Harborough for London 'with his cup empty' to seek his fortune and found work as an archivist for the Lord Mayor's Court. There he gained an understanding of Latin, the language used in most legal documents at the time, and became very successful. But he always remembered the place where he was 'bred and fed' and wanted to do something good with his life.

In order to establish the word of God in the hearts of the people of Harborough, Smyth would often send money up from London to provide bread for the 'godly honest poor' of the town and which would be handed out on the Sabbath day. But he is remembered today for founding the schoolhouse in the Market Place. The Old Grammar School was fully restored in 1977 and now hosts public events. It has pride of place in Harborough's heritage, reminding us all of an historical age we can only imagine.

The group of young children posing for this photograph underneath the Old Grammar School have for a backdrop the 1889 extension of the Symington's factory (now the Harborough District Council offices, the library and the museum); what a startling architectural contrast!

Market hustle and bustle

THE STREETS of our market towns find their focus in the market place. From the earliest times, this has been a place of hustle and bustle – and in the days when animals still thronged in the centre of town on market day, a place of dirt and smells too. This hub of the town's radiating streets, the place where much of its wealth was generated, is often still marked by a market cross; it may be a simple column, or a wonderful example of the medieval mason's skill, or even an elegant Georgian construction. Whatever it looks like, it still reminds us of market days long gone.

Right: MARKET DRAYTON, SHROPSHIRE, MARKET DAY 1911 63338P

Market Drayton

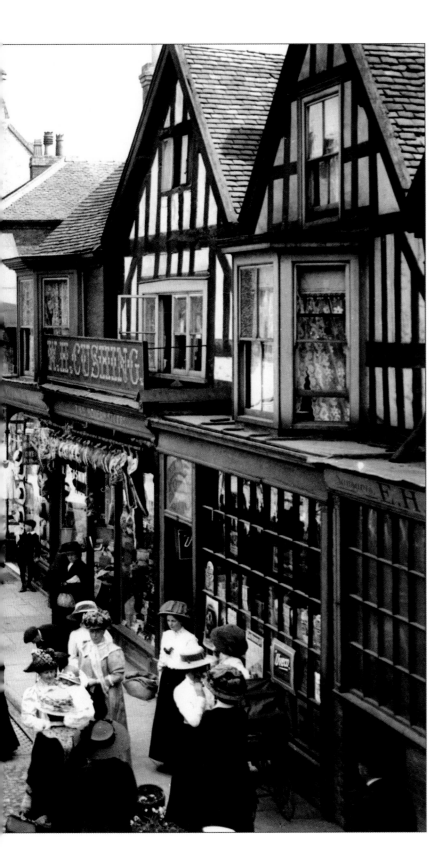

THIS WONDERFULLY lively photograph gives us a vivid picture of what a market town's streets look like on market day. Well-dressed ladies jostle and gossip, while the stalls erected on the cobbles are doing a roaring trade.

The first charter for a market was granted by Henry III in 1245, and the town is still famous for its Wednesday markets which have now been held on this day each week for over 750 years. This first charter did not just give the town the right to have a regular weekly market; it also gave permission for an annual three-day fair each September. A clause in the charter states that the new markets and fair must not in any way harm any that are already trading – a reminder that all markets of the time had to be more than $6\frac{1}{2}$ miles from each other. That distance was considered a reasonable distance for traders to walk to market in the morning, trade in the market, and then walk home afterwards.

Fountain to celebrate Victoria's glorious reign

The wonderfully ornate fountain sitting at the top of Market Drayton's High Street (extreme left of 63338) was erected in 1898 to commemorate Queen Victoria's Diamond Jubilee the previous year. It was removed when the road was widened. Today this section of road has become a one-way route, and so there is once again plenty of room for the fountain. Unfortunately, however, when it was removed in the 1930s it was broken up, and various bits ended up in different gardens all over town. Another Jubilee is now commemorated here - that of Queen Elizabeth II - with a clock on the wall of the buildings behind.

Settle

SETTLE, YORKSHIRE, MARKET DAY 1921 71339

SETTLE LIES between Skipton and Ingleton, and here we find a fascinating mixture of alleyways, courtyards, and shambles. Many of the houses date from the 17th century, after the Civil War. Trade in the town increased dramatically once the Keighley to Kendal turnpike road opened, making Settle a premier coaching route. Two railways touched the town; the North West line was followed by the famous Settle-Carlisle line in 1876. Here we see the market on a busy Tuesday. On the right is the Elizabethan-style Town Hall built in 1832, and in the background, somewhat smothered by washing, is the Shambles. Dating from the 17th century, the Shambles comprised several shops in an arched arcade with living accommodation over the top.

THE 12TH-CENTURY Market Place is central to Banbury's development. Alexander the Magnificent, Bishop of Lincoln, planned a new town around the market protected by his new castle. By the time the market charter was renewed in the reign of Henry II, Banbury had become more recognisably urban in character with a market every Thursday and a fair at Whitsun.

In the 1920s, Banbury's produce market was a huddle of stalls on a triangle of land towards Butchers Row, a medieval way which entered the Market Place by the side of Robins Bros shop (centre background of 70569 – Robins's has twin white gables). Bicycles and cars were then free to occupy the road which ran diagonally along one side of the stalls. Many permanent shopkeepers in this part of Banbury resented the loss of some of their trade to those regulars and casuals who did business under the awnings. In an attempt to tackle this problem they paid rent on the land in front of their premises and sometimes laid out goods there, as we can see.

Nathan's Domestic Stores (left) and Robins Bros were typical examples of stores whose owners made good use of the pavements. At Nathan's, a common sight was a pile of galvanised buckets and baths, some wicker hampers and, this being summer, a few deck chairs. The ash pan trade sign was typical of many examples of trade signs still to be found around the town.

Next door to Nathan's shop is a 17th-century building with fine dormers, one of the very few of its period to have three full storeys, which according to tradition was the Bishop's Palace. It is often called this today. By 1921 the house had turned into Spencer's Hotel and Restaurant, and must have been thronged with those who came to Banbury on market days.

Below: BANBURY, OXFORDSHIRE, THE MARKET 1921 70569

Banbury

Great Yarmouth

Great Yarmouth's market place was not always as salubrious as it has become in the 20th century. The local diarist William Youell saw bear-baiting taking place in the Market Place in the late 18th century. In the same period Beatniffe wrote that 'it is shocking to see butchers daily slaughtering calves, sheep etc in the centre of such an opulent town, resorted to by crowds of genteel company from almost every part of England'.

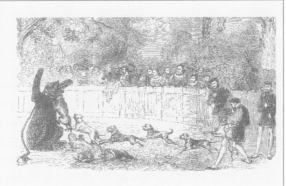

THE MARKET has been the heart of Great Yarmouth for at least 800 years, and this photograph shows it bustling with activity. In the 20th century it has become famous for the high quality of chips sold on its stalls; the stalls in this photograph include Brewer's Chip Potato Saloon. The dramatic – but short-lived – effect of the electric tram upon the urban landscape is captured in this image. The tramlines were installed c1901, and in 1913 the track was to be doubled to cope with increasing demand. In the distance is St Nicholas's Church, claimed to be one of the largest parish churches in England. Just off the far end of the Market Place is the old Fishermen's Hospital, founded in 1702 for retired fishermen and their wives. The character of the southern end of the market has now been altered by the introduction of permanent covered stalls.

GREAT YARMOUTH, NORFOLK, THE FISH MARKET c1900 G56503

THE SUCCESS of Great Yarmouth depended on two factors: fish and trade. The fish involved was the herring. Yarmouth began when herring fishermen put up temporary shelters while they spread their nets out on the sands to dry. The first inhabitants were men from the Cinque Ports, and eventually they were holding a herring fair at Yarmouth every year: thousands of people and hundreds of boats gathered from all over Europe for the occasion. The size of the herring catch was staggering: the average catch in the early years of the 20th century was 40,000 lasts, or about 528 million fish! The greatest daily catch was probably that of 23 October 1907, when nearly 80 million herrings were brought into the town. In some years there were so many fishing boats in the harbour that it was possible to cross from one side of the river to the other on their decks. This evocative photograph shows hundreds of swills, the specially made wicker baskets for herrings which were unique to Yarmouth and Lowestoft. When this picture was taken, Great Yarmouth was the herring capital of the world.

Great Yarmouth's fish train

The railway came to Yarmouth relatively late, but it had a dramatic impact on the town. Communications with the Midlands and London were soon opened up when the line between Norwich and Cambridge opened in 1845. The line was extended from the main station to South Quay as early as 1847, and ran all the way down the Quay to the Fish Wharf by 1882. This line was for freight traffic only: it was used to carry fish, and also to supply coal to steam drifters moored against the Quay. The line closed down in 1976.

Crawley

A CENTURY ago Crawley was a thriving village mid-way on the road from London to Brighton. In 1585 it had been described as 'the village or streate of Crawley' – in those days still basically a correct description. There had been some expansion because of the coaching trade, but much more followed in the 19th century after the opening, in 1848, of a branch line to Horsham from Three Bridges station on the main London to Brighton railway line. It crossed Brighton Road at the southern end of the High Street, which is where Crawley station was sited. Houses were then built near the station and extending along Brighton Road and behind the old High Street in West Green. More shops were built, and the first commuters moved in.

Crawley had a street fair twice a year, in May and September. When this happened the High Street was closed. Photograph 53326T gives a flavour of what the fair was like at a time when agriculture was still very important. It also shows the inconvenience the fair caused. Some shops had to erect barriers in an attempt to protect their windows. The area from the level crossing to the Upper Square was reserved for cattle. Beyond, in the Middle Square, there were more cattle, but horses were also traded. The Lower Square held a fairground with rides, swings and stalls.

The photograph shows the Upper Square itself. Since the square is wide, it was unnecessary to barricade shop fronts here. At Warren's store (left) much of its merchandise is hanging outside. One lone car is trying to thread its way through the cattle. A policeman stands outside Ockenden's shop, keeping his eye on things. Note the mixture of flat caps and bowler hats worn by men. Some farmers wear riding boots and leggings, a wise precaution for a muddy area. There is a wide mixture of cattle breeds to be seen, and a farm machinery firm has brought along a hay elevator, surrounded by other pieces of equipment, in an attempt to interest local farmers.

The 1922 Crawley Parish Guide reported: 'Many now feel that [the Fair] has outlived its usefulness. Various attempts have been made to get rid of it or to have it removed from the streets, but the Home Secretary appears to have no power to remove a Chartered Fair, and can only abolish it by the unanimous desire of the inhabitants. The Fair lingers on, a relic of bygone days'. Shortly afterwards it was removed to fields behind the east side of the High Street, and eventually closed.

Left: CRAWLEY, SUSSEX, THE FAIR, UPPER SQUARE 1905 53326T

Blackburn

BLACKBURN, LANCASHIRE, THE MARKET AND THE TOWN
HALL 1894   34307

HERE we have a busy and bustling view of Northgate. The Town Hall did not need or get a clock, because the Market House had the town's clock on a freestanding tower in front of it. The Market House and its tower are on the right of our picture, and the square, solid Town Hall is beside the market. The Market House opened on 28 January 1848. It opened every day except Sunday, and was famous for stalls selling black puddings and sarsaparilla. Unfortunately, the old Market House and Clock Tower were cleared away in the 1960s when the new Market Hall opened.

Romford

Market Day Noise and Bustle

Into some of the shops you stepped from the pavement down, as it were, into a cave, the level of the shop being eight or ten inches below the street, while the first floor projected over the pavement quite to the edge of the kerb. To enter these shops it was necessary to stoop, and when you were inside there was barely room to turn round ...

But mean as a metropolitan shopman might have thought the spot, the business done there was large, and, more than that, it was genuine. The trade of a country market-town, especially when that market-town dates from the earliest days of English history, is hereditary. It flows to the same store and to the same shop year after year, generation after generation, century after century. The farmer who walks into the saddler's here goes in because his father went there before him. His father went in because his father dealt there, and so on farther back than memory can trace ...

On a market-day like this there is, of course, the incessant entry and exit of carts, waggons, traps, gigs, four-wheels, and a large number of private carriages. The number of private carriages is, indeed, very remarkable, as also the succession of gentlemen on thoroughbred horses – a proof of the number of resident gentry in the neighbourhood, and of its general prosperity. Cart-horses furbished up for sale, with strawbound tails and glistening skins; 'baaing' flocks of sheep; squeaking pigs; bullocks with their heads held ominously low, some going, some returning, from the auction yard; shouting drovers; lads rushing hither and thither; dogs barking; everything and everybody crushing, jostling, pushing through the narrow street. An old shepherd, who had done his master's business, comes along the pavement, trudging thoughtful and slow, with ashen staff. One hand is in his pocket, the elbow of the arm projecting; he is feeling a fourpenny-piece, and deliberating at which 'tap' he shall spend it. He fills up the entire pavement, and stolidly plods on, turning ladies and all into the roadway; not from intentional rudeness, but from sheer inability to perceive that he is causing inconvenience.

Photo courtesy of Julian Hight   RICHARD JEFFERIES (1848–1887), 'FROM HODGE AND HIS MASTERS'

ROMFORD has changed dramatically over the last 30 years. The construction of ring roads and the pedestrianisation of South Street and other areas of the town centre, together with the building of huge shopping precincts and superstores, has all but erased the atmosphere of what was essentially a country market town.

In 1247 King Henry III granted Romford a charter permitting a livestock market to be held in the town every Wednesday. It provided a centre on the Essex Great Road where sheep and cattle farmers in the area could sell their stock. The Wednesday cattle market continued for over 700 years, the final one being held in 1958.

Romford Market concentrated on livestock on Wednesdays, although there were always some general traders to serve the stockmen and farmers. Saturday offered a general market and Friday also became a day for miscellaneous traders. Farmers, nurserymen, smallholders, manufacturers, craftsmen and traders of all household goods came from a wide area to ply their trades at Romford.

The many cattle trucks surrounding the pens in this photograph indicate that cattle were brought in from distant farms to be sold here. However, even in the 1950s some cattle were herded through the streets. Boys could earn a few pennies from the herdsmen by going ahead of the herd and closing garden gates to stop cattle straying into front gardens.

Left: ROMFORD, ESSEX, THE CATTLE MARKET c1950   R52036

Aylesbury

AYLESBURY, BUCKINGHAMSHIRE, MARKET SQUARE 1921   70552P

THIS BUSTLING SCENE shows a thriving market in a typical country town square, complete with its civic buildings. We are looking from the north end of the market place, where a cattle and sheep market is in full swing in the early 1920s. To the left of the Clock Tower and County Hall is the Jacobean-style Town Hall and Corn Exchange building by Brandon, dated 1865. Much of this was destroyed in a fire in 1962, but fortunately the triple archway supporting the upper hall with its mullioned and transomed windows and shaped gable above survives.

The south side of the square is dominated by the Georgian County Hall which was designed by Thomas Harris; work started in 1722, but it was not completed until 1737 – local government has always been strapped for cash. There was a balcony across the centre at first floor level from which public hangings took place until 1845.

Livestock was sold here until 1927. After that date the stock market moved to a site off Exchange Street, now built over by a multi-screen cinema complex. Until 1866 there was a Market House and other buildings in the foreground which were all swept away to re-open this part of the market place.

ONE EVENT that has made Barnstaple famous throughout Devon is its fair. This has been held since time immemorial. It started off as a celebratory event after the huge annual market which lasted for a week. Horses, other livestock and produce were traded, and even farm labourers found new positions here. Today, the livestock market is held every Friday and the Pannier Market – so called because the original stallholders would bring their produce to

market by horse in panniers – every Tuesday and Friday. The fair, meanwhile, still takes place, but is essentially an event within the modern meaning of the word with roundabouts and dodgems.

Since this 1923 photograph was taken, there have been wholesale changes to the area. The Angel Hotel (offering 'Good Stabling and Garage') was knocked down and replaced by a cinema. This in turn has become a nightclub. A pub built next door – the Bell – is now derelict. The chimney in the background is at of the electricity works.

In the distance is the gorgeously ornate early 18th-century Queen Anne's Walk, once called the Exchange, with its statue of Queen Anne, given by Robert Rolle of Stevenstone in 1708.

Barnstaple

Top: BARNSTAPLE, DEVON, THE STRAND 2004 B25710K
Above: BARNSTAPLE, DEVON, THE STRAND, THE HORSE FAIR 1923 75164P

GLASTONBURY, SOMERSET, THE CROSS AND GEORGE INN 1904
52046

Glastonbury

GLASTONBURY LIES in eastern Somerset in the flat Somerset Levels, between the Mendips and the Polden Hills and beside Glastonbury Tor, a spectacular landmark that can be seen for miles around. Glastonbury is linked in legend with Joseph of Aramathea and with King Arthur, and is supposed to be his Isle of Avalon – and in an area prone to flooding, the Tor and Chalice Hill must have looked like an island in the Levels. Glastonbury Abbey was founded in the early 8th century, and a settlement grew around it. Glastonbury has always been a market town. Market Square lies beside the abbey. Its centrepiece is the market cross, erected in 1846 and designed by Benjamin Ferrey – it replaced a medieval one. Behind it are the Crown Hotel and the George Hotel, a rare survival of a medieval inn; it was built to house pilgrims to the abbey in c1450.

The ancient splendour of the architecture [of Glastonbury] survives but in scattered and scanty fragments, among influences of a rather inharmonious sort. It was cattle-market in the little town as I passed up the main street, and a savour of hoofs and hide seemed to accompany me … The little inn is a capital bit of character, and as I waited for the 'bus under its low archway (in something of the mood, possibly, in which a train was once waited for at Coventry), and watched the barmaid flirting her way to and fro out of the heavy-browed kitchen and among the lounging young appraisers of colts and steers and barmaids, I might have imagined that the Merry England of the Tudors had not utterly passed away.

HENRY JAMES, 'ENGLISH HOURS' 1872

Malmesbury

MALMESBURY, WILTSHIRE, THE MARKET CROSS 1924 76145

THE OCTAGONAL limestone market cross in Malmesbury was built during the reign of Henry VII c1490; John Leland, writing in 1542, states that the market cross was 'for poore market folkes to stand dry when Rayne cummith'. As we can see in this photograph from the gentlemen gathered beneath the market cross, it was as good a place to meet in 1924 as it is today. The building behind the cars (right) is the Abbey Café, which was the Green Dragon Inn from 1803 to 1922.

The market cross has flying buttresses, pinnacles, and a vaulted interior, and it is surmounted by an octagonal turret. The turret has niches which contain various sculptured figures associated with Malmesbury's historical past. On the west face is the Crucifixion, and the other sculptures are reputed to be St Paul, the Madonna and Child, St Aldhelm, King Athelstan, Maildulph, St Laurence and St Peter. The market cross was restored in 1912 by Harold Brakspear FSA, and more recently in 1991, when conservation treatment was undertaken. The market cross had been damaged during the 1970s, when further pinnacles were repaired and replaced; one of the pinnacles which was not replaced is on display in the Athelstan Museum. Also in the museum is a fine drawing of the market cross by Thomas Girtin (c1790), featuring a market scene with people and trestle tables around the cross. The drawing also shows the timber-framed vicarage in Gloucester Street, which was demolished in the late 19th century; the land became part of the adjoining White Lion Inn. The town well and stocks were situated by the market cross.

Until the mid 20th century, Malmesbury was a market town, with a cattle market held on the third Wednesday of each month. During the early 13th century a Saturday market was also held, possibly near St Paul's Parish Church and later in Abbey Row. Between c1900 and 1940 a general market was held in the Cross Hayes. Various other markets and fairs were held here, notably on St Aldhelm's day, 25 May.

Bonsall

BONSALL is 'set in a romantic valley amidst abrupt limestone rocks, and watered by a beautiful trout stream', said Glover in 1833. We are in the centre of Bonsall, which is dominated by its 17th-century market cross encircled by 13 gritstone steps. The cross is said to be the tallest in Derbyshire; it bears the date 1620, perhaps the date of its first restoration. Here livestock and goods were sold, and here too farm workers were hired. During the Napoleonic wars, the farm workers included French prisoners of war. The steeply-sloping Market Place at this date of this photograph is surfaced with crushed stone rather than tarmac. In the background is the King's Head public house, one of a number which slaked the thirsts of generations of the lead miners who formed the majority of the population of this sleepy little limestone village.

Left: BONSALL, DERBYSHIRE, THE CROSS c1955   B485013

GUISBOROUGH is the ancient capital of Cleveland, and is mentioned in Domesday. A 19th-century gazetteer describes the town thus: 'Guisborough is pleasantly situated in a narrow but fertile vale, and consists chiefly of one main street, running nearly East and West. The street is very broad, and many of the houses being built in a modern style, the town has a neat and pleasant appearance. A handsome town-hall, of free-stone, was built in the year 1821, upon the site of the ancient toll-booth, in the Market place, erected upon projecting pillars and arches with four cast iron pillars in the centre, the lower part or area serves as a shambles, &c. for the market people, and the Magistrates hold their meetings on alternate Tuesdays, in the upper story. The markets are well attended'. This is a very early view of this ancient market place. At the end, Jackson's, which sold boots and shoes, must have been well-established, as they were still in business well over fifteen years later. Next to Jackson's was Metcalfe's Newsagents, and on the left is the National Provincial Bank.

Right: GUISBOROUGH, YORKSHIRE, MARKET PLACE
1891   29209

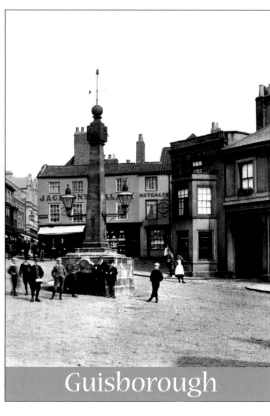

Guisborough

Guisborough joins the health spa bandwagon

It was in Guisborough that the first alum works in England was opened during the reign of Elizabeth I. The secrets of alum manufacture were smuggled from the Pope's alum works in Rome by Sir Thomas Chaloner, and for this act of industrial espionage the Pope declared an anathema against him. In May 1822, a mineral spring was discovered near the town, and Guisborough climbed aboard the spa town bandwagon. Those who took the waters were said to obtain relief from 'rheumatic, scorbutic and bilious complaints'; the water was a good diuretic.

SHEPTON MALLET, SOMERSET, THE CROSS 1899   44097

Shepton Mallet

FIVE MILES east of Wells in the eastern Mendips, Shepton Mallet was a prosperous wool manufacturing town, which declined when northern England's Industrial Revolution got under way. The fine market cross at the entrance to the Market Place has an elaborate medieval polygonal centre, with three storeys of arched niches; the crocketed pinnacle emerges from a plainer arched surrounding structure of about 1700 (all was rebuilt in 1841).

In the 19th century, various industries were established to replace the textile industry; these included brewing, with the splendidly named Anglo-Bavarian Brewery being established near Commercial Road, while Showerings brewery sold its beers and ciders for 200 years from its own pubs, the Black Swan and the Sun Inn. The town centre was demolished in the late 1960s and rebuilt.

BEVERLEY, YORKSHIRE, THE MARKET CROSS c1960   B80078

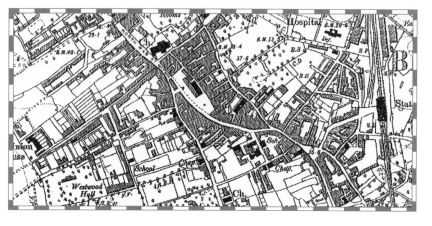

THE MARKET CROSS, sometimes still called the Butter Cross after the farmers' wives who traditionally sold their goods nearby, is a proud symbol of the town. Built between 1711 and 1714, it is an outstanding part of Beverley's 18th-century architectural heritage. It stands in the broad Saturday market place. Beverley has had two markets, the Wednesday market and the Saturday market. The Wednesday market was the original one, but it declined in importance in the 18th century and was closed. Once it held the town stocks and a cock-fighting pit.

In the Georgian period Beverley acquired the elegant houses, the fine public buildings and the fashionable promenade, New Walk, which gave it such a distinctive character. The Victorians had their own ideas of what constituted architectural excellence and in spite of the now regretted loss of neat buildings the 19th century made a further contribution to Beverley's appearance. In modern times the town's expansion as a popular residential area has been phenomenal. The town of small traders, each selling their specialist or home made goods, has virtually disappeared, and traffic has engulfed historic streets.

I was offered a large Codffish for a shilling and good Pearch very Cheape, we had Crabbs bigger than my two hands pence apiece wch would have Cost 6 pence if not a shilling in London and they were very sweete.
CELIA FIENNES
VISITING BEVERLEY, 1697

River and Bridge

SO MANY of our streets are connected with rivers. In a port town, the streets run beside the river and take on the character of quays. At an important or strategic river crossing, where the street once went through the river in the form of a ford, it now crosses it by a bridge; some river crossings are still made by ferry. Promenades and avenues follow the riverbank so that the townsfolk can enjoy the scenery.

Often the river itself plays the part of a street, with people travelling on it for business or pleasure.

As for the bridges, some are great works of architecture, and some are amazing examples of Victorian engineering ingenuity.

Bedford

THE RIVER OUSE rises on the Northamptonshire-Oxfordshire border and winds east through Bedford on its leisurely way to the Wash near King's Lynn. Bedford grew up at a ford over the river before the arrival of the Anglo-Saxons in the mid to late 5th century. It is certainly the river that gives the town its character now — it is probably its greatest asset. Its banks are laid out with public parks and footpaths; they are very popular for walking, and are thronged on a sunny summer or winter weekend.

In the 1880s, during the vigorous mayoralty of Joshua Hawkins, the river banks east of the bridge were converted into parks, the suspension bridge was built, and Bedford Park was laid out; virtually everything was opened by the Duke of Bedford or his sons. In the 20th century the industrial riverside disappeared, and more parks and walkways were developed along the western part of the river, including St Mary's Park on the south bank, while the north bank walkway has only recently been completed.

The rowing boat in this view is approaching the boat slide, the abutment of which is just visible on the far left. The huge weeping willow beyond is on a small island.

Left: BEDFORD,
BEDFORDSHIRE,
THE SUSPENSION BRIDGE
1921 70446

Crowland

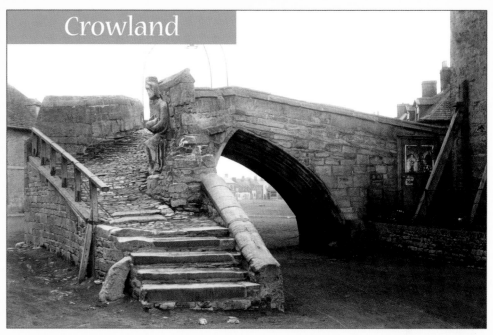

CROWLAND, LINCOLNSHIRE, THE BRIDGE 1894 34832

THE TOWN of Crowland grew up at the gates of Crowland Abbey, sited on a low island amid the surrounding marshes. This was a watery landscape, and the streets used to have streams flowing down them, which all had to be negotiated somehow. This beautiful and justly famous bridge, built in the 14th century, used to cross one of the streams; but now, with the marshes drained, the bridge is a redundant curiosity.

The abbey, in the Middle Ages the richest in Lincolnshire, was built on the site of the 7th-century timber hermitage of St Guthlac. It is now a fragment: the nave north aisle is now the parish church, with a monumental 15th-century tower capped by a squat spire. The remains of the rest of the abbey church are a tantalising glimpse of an opulent past, while all the monastic buildings have vanished.

I soon enter'd the little town [of Crowland], quite Dutch-looking (tho' not as to neatness) with a canal thro' it and many crossing footbridges. I was so eager for breakfast as to fancy it good, when the tea was, I believe, made of ash leaves, and the butter and bread intolerable.

JOHN BYNG, 'RIDES
ROUND BRITAIN', 1790
ED D ADAMSON, FOLIO
SOCIETY

PLYMOUTH AND DEVONPORT were served by a number of ferries, including these wonderful steam-powered, chain-guided floating bridges on the Torpoint service across the Tamar (known as the Hamoaze at this point), which were capable of carrying wheeled vehicles. Services operated were Ferry Road to Torpoint (fares 1d and 2d); the Barbican to Turnchapel and Oreston; Admiral's Hard to Cremyll (Mount Edgcumbe); and Mutton Cove to Cremyll. Before the construction of the Tamar suspension bridge, this was one of the few ways to cross the river.

The ferry still makes regular journeys across the Tamar, taking workers across to Devonport Dockyard and the City of Plymouth. The three chain ferries installed in the 1960s (the 'Tamar', the 'Tavy' and the 'Lynher') have in recent years been replaced by three new, larger ones, built on the River Clyde, costing £5 million each: the 'Plym II', the 'Tamar II' and the 'Lynher II'.

The first ferry here began in 1791, operated by rowing boats. In 1829 a steamboat replaced them, but it was not powerful enough to cope with the strong tides hereabouts, so a chain-driven floating bridge made of wood was installed in 1834. It was replaced in 1871 by a locally-built metal floating bridge, and her sister vessel joined her in 1878.

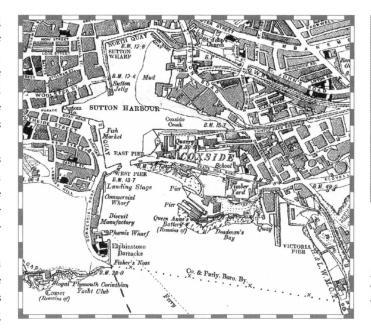

The chains that ran the ferry were a fatal attraction to one little boy. In 1884 Alfred Cheek managed to catch his foot in the chain. As the ferry moved, his leg was drawn into the mechanism. Although the ferry reversed to allow poor Alfred to be extricated and taken straight to hospital, his injuries were so bad that he died two days later.

Below: DEVONPORT, DEVON, TORPOINT FERRY, THE FLOATING BRIDGE 1890   22462

Devonport

Shrewsbury

THE BOAT HOUSE INN, opposite the Quarry bank of the Severn in the photograph on the left, began life as a tea room; then it became a landing stage for pleasure boats and then a boat house. Notice how the ferryman is pulling on the rope to take his passengers across the river. Each of his passengers will have paid $\frac{1}{2}$ d for the ride. Today there is a footbridge crossing the River Severn near this point – the ferry was replaced by the footbridge in 1923.

Left: SHREWSBURY, SHROPSHIRE, THE BOAT HOUSE INN AND THE FERRY 1911   63218T

Below: GREENOCK, STRATHCLYDE, CUSTOM HOUSE QUAY 1897   39814

AT THE TIME this photograph (right) was taken, the River Clyde was itself like a busy street, carrying goods and people near and far. Glasgow merchants travelled to their holiday villas in Rhu or Dunoon, while their workers went on pleasure trips 'doon the watter' to Rothesay. At the same time, great ships were steaming from the Clyde to trade all over the world, many of them built here in Greenock's shipyards. Greenock was a beneficiary of the River Clyde's industrial heyday. The first square-rigger to be built was launched here in 1760, and James Watt, the great engineer who pioneered the steam engine, was born here. Sad to say, most of the shipbuilding and heavy industry have gone into decline; however, sugar refining and textile works still keep Greenock's industrial traditions alive.

In this photograph, we can see that dense smoke from a distant inward bound steamer is being caught by strong winds and blown across the horizon towards the dockside shipping in this busy commercial port. The same breeze catches the starboard quarter of the paddle steamer approaching her temporary berth alongside the jetty, causing her to enter at an angle slightly more acute than perhaps would be usual, allowing the wind to assist berthing without smashing the boat alongside. Greenock Custom House (facing the camera) was built in 1818. In the distance are Cartsdyke mill and east yards, the Gravel graving dock, and the entrance to the James Watt Dock.

Greenock

Henley-on-Thames

BRABNER'S 'GAZETTEER OF ENGLAND AND WALES' of 1895 describes Henley's bridge thus: 'A fine stone bridge of five arches connects it with Berks, was erected in 1768, in place of an old wooden one, at a cost of £10,000, and has sculptures over the central arch representing by ideal heads the rivers Thames and Isis, which were executed by the Hon Mrs Damer.'

Most people's image of Henley in modern times includes the colourful regatta crowds swirling like peacocks along the banks of the River Thames or on crowds of small boats; champagne picnics, boaters and striped blazers; and for the rest of the year a comfortable middle-class market town with a number of speciality shops, including superior clothes shops, delicatessens, antique shops and art galleries.

In fact Henley, like Marlow some 8 miles downstream, grew up in the Middle Ages, its prosperity largely based on trading locally-grown commodities down river in barges to London along the River Thames; it was very much a workaday town, and its medieval wooden bridge, succeeded by the 18th-century stone one, was vital for good communications. The medieval plan is virtually intact, and there are quite a good number of medieval, Tudor and 17th-century timber-framed buildings lining the streets, many disguised behind later front elevations or encased in Georgian brick. Some timber frames, though, are modern facings and not to be trusted; these include the one to the north elevation of the Angel, or to No 40 Hart Street.

The riverside on either side of the bridge was lined with wharves, warehouses and inns until the 19th century. By the 1890s the leisure boathouses and boat builders had taken over, interspersed with inns and hotels catering for the visitors who flocked to the river in and out of the regatta season.

The event which serves to make the name of Henley famous is its annual regatta, which is universally admitted to take the first place among the amateur aquatic contests of England. It usually takes place about the beginning of July, and it attracts the best amateur oarsmen of England and occasionally some from the Continent, while it almost ranks with Ascot as a meeting-place of the fashionable world. The regatta course is just beyond the bridge in this photograph.

Left: HENLEY-ON-THAMES, OXFORDSHIRE, THE BRIDGE 1899 43016T

Maidenhead

MAIDENHEAD, BERKSHIRE, THE BRIDGE 1906   54099P

THE TOWN grew up on higher ground inland of the flood-prone River Thames, but its river crossing is the key to Maidenhead's growth and development. In the second half of the 19th century, just as at Henley, the river changed from a trade artery to one increasingly orientated towards leisure, and the town cashed in on this great boating boom. Development along the river itself and in the area between it and the town flourished: by the late 19th century the riverside was thriving with hotels, and boathouses where you could hire anything from a large steam launch to a humble punt

This view shows Sir Robert Taylor's superb seven-arch bridge, built between 1772 and 1777. Its arches are emphasised by massive, rusticated voussoir blocks, all crowned by a delicate balustrade. It is surely worth every penny of its £19,000 cost. The Edwardian ladies are enjoying a motor trip along the riverbank lane. Behind them is the side of Bond's boathouse, a long established boatyard with balconies to the river for viewing regattas. Sadly, the building is today utterly derelict and virtually beyond repair.

Rules for an enjoyable day out on the Thames

You must be prepared to pull and push, and struggle for your existence on the river, as in the vast city hard by men push and crush for money. You must assert yourself, and insist upon having your share of the waterway; you must be perfectly convinced that yours is the very best style of rowing to be seen; every one ought to get out of your way. You must consult your own convenience only, and drive right into other people's boats, forcing them up into the willows, or against the islands. Never slip along the shore, or into quiet backwaters; always select the more frequented parts, not because you want to go there, but to make your presence known, and go amongst the crowd; and if a few sculls get broken, it only proves how very inferior and how very clumsy other people are. If you see another boat coming down stream in the centre of the river with a broad space on either side for others to pass, at once head your own boat straight at her, and take possession of the way.

RICHARD JEFFERIES, 'THE MODERN THAMES' c1880

THE NEWPORT Transporter Bridge spans the River Usk in Newport, South Wales and is a Grade 1 Listed structure. Its historic importance stems from its very unusual design - there are only two others like it in the UK.

The Industrial Revolution reached Newport with the opening of the Monmouthshire & Brecon Canal in 1799; rich mineral resources could now be exploited. Coal and iron could be delivered to Newport Docks for shipment — most of the coal went to Bristol and Bridgwater. By the late 19th century rapid development was taking place on the east side of the River Usk some way downstream of the bridge in the town centre. A new crossing was needed, especially for the workers at Lysaghts steelworks.

The site was a difficult one because of the very high tidal range and the need to accommodate tall sailing ships. Mr R H Haynes, the Borough Engineer at the time, suggested that the engineer Ferdinand Arnodin should be consulted. He had previously designed an 'aerial ferry' at Rouen in France, and he produced a similar design for Newport: two high towers supported a track from which was suspended a platform which carried passengers and vehicles across.

The construction of Newport's transporter bridge started in 1902 and was completed by 1906 at a cost of £98,000. The towers stand 645 feet apart and rise 242 feet above road level. The platform or gondola is pulled across by a cable wound round a drum by an electric motor on the east bank at a maximum speed of 10 feet per second; it is capable of carrying six vehicles and 100 passengers.

In this photograph we see the bridge-house poised on the bank of the Usk. Attendants wait in readiness at the gate for passengers wanting to travel to the east side of the river. Notice the footbridge at the top of the photograph where pedestrians, if brave enough, are able to walk across 242 feet above the ground.

Right: NEWPORT, GWENT,
THE TRANSPORTER BRIDGE 1910   62513

Newport

Northwich

In 1759, the Earl of Bridgewater financed the building of the first proper canal – the Bridgewater Canal. When the first stretch of this canal opened in 1761, it totally revolutionised the transportation of goods and ushered in a frenzy of canal building projects all around the country; this was only to end when it was replaced by another, similar, frenzy when railways were introduced in the following century.

BELOW we see a fine example of Victorian engineering and ingenuity, which became known as 'the wonder of the waterways'. It was constructed so that boats could switch from the River Weaver to the Trent & Mersey Canal, just 50ft above the river and running parallel to it. Originally the lift operated on a hydraulic system with two counter-balanced water-tight tanks raising and lowering boats between the two waterways. The two tanks embodied in the lift, each containing 252 tons of water, were originally raised and lowered by a system of hydraulic rams, but in 1908 it was electrified so that the tanks could be operated independently. Despite the fact that some 570 tons of water and metal were moved when the lift was operated, the whole system was powered by a tiny 30 horsepower electric motor. The lift worked well until 1983, when severe corrosion of the main support legs forced British Waterways to shut it down. A renovation programme has now returned the lift to full working order, and people can now take a trip on the lift and visit the nearby Visitor Centre.

THERE IS one industry that has been of major importance to Cheshire since Roman times – the salt industry. This industry was based in the towns of Northwich, Middlewich and Nantwich – 'wich' in Old English meant 'salt works' – and the salt would have been taken all over the country. One has to remember the importance of salt for the preservation of food in the days before canning and freezing, not to mention the many other industries associated with it.

The salt was transported along rivers; Northwich stands on the River Weaver. Salt was brought down to the river on pack-horses to meet the tide, and sailing barges would load at high water and depart for Liverpool and other ports on the ebbing tide. This was labour-intensive, and the Weaver was sometimes impassable owing to floods or drought. Therefore, in 1721 work began to construct the Weaver Navigation. The river was straightened and deepened, so that cargo boats of 100 tons could be accommodated. Northwich had become an inland port, and the Weaver Navigation was a virtual street.

The photograph on the left shows Northwich's Town Bridge over the Weaver. There has been a bridge on this spot since medieval times; this bridge was built in 1899, probably the first electrically powered swing bridge in Britain. The man on the left wearing a peaked cap was the bridge operator, ready to open the bridge to let ships through.

Left: NORTHWICH, CHESHIRE, THE SWING BRIDGE 1900   45422T

Above: NORTHWICH, CHESHIRE, THE ANDERTON BOAT LIFT c1960   N43026

Wealth from the sea

As an island nation, overseas trade has always been essential to our survival, and the streets of many of our coastal towns lead alongside the quays and harbours. Here we can see evidence of the industries allied to shipping, including ship building and rope and net making, and the warehouses and offices of merchants and wholesalers. Our fishing fleets, too, once brought untold wealth to the streets of places like Hull and Fraserburgh.

Poole

Truly did old Leland write that 'it standeth almost as an isle in its haven' … Its almost land-locked harbour, guarded by encircling heights, is perhaps best seen from Constitution Hill, where we look down on the little triangular peninsula containing the old port.

The red roofs of its Queen Anne and Georgian houses are grouped at the edge of the quay in vivid contrast to the inland lake and the blue waters of the Channel, with the Purbeck Hills beyond … When the tide is full it has the appearance of a vast lake studded with islands. It owes much of its beauty to the phenomenon of the tides. Poole has two tides every twelve hours with about three hours between their high water marks, and the dreary wastes exposed at low tide in so many of our estuaries do not spoil the landscape here.

ARTHUR MEE,
'THE KING'S ENGLAND
– DORSET', 1939

MOST OF Poole's industries were directly related to its seaside location, and its quay was always busy. Boats, ships, sails, nets, rope and salt were all among the port's traditional products. While Bridport, also in Dorset, was the capital of the rope and net industry, Poole also had at least three ropewalks, situated at Hamworthy, Baiter and on a site now occupied by the bus station. Ship and boat building is an age-old Poole industry which continues to this day. Fifty ships' timbers discovered in 1987 date from about 1500, and were probably from a boat-builder's store. By the early 19th century there were five ship-building yards at Hamworthy.

In 61171T (opposite), the Custom House is in the background, and we can see the railway line running along the quay (railway trucks are standing ready to load the ships in 52814T (above). The railway lines, laid along the quay in 1874, became redundant in 1960, and within two years they had disappeared. On the left of 61171T a coal cart awaits its horse outside H &A Burden's, who advertise themselves as 'Coal Stores and Ship Chandlers'; the firm owned two small steamships. Two doors away is the Poole Harbour Office; it dates from 1727. The first floor was extended over the pavement on columns in 1822 to allow for a fire and chimney in the Ballast Master's office above.

These photographs were taken less than a century ago, yet sailing ships still dominate the quay. Among them are sailing barges – until the 1950s these barges brought clay from the Purbecks for the potteries not only in Poole, but in Seville and Stockholm.

The Custom House was built in about 1788. Its officials would have worked around the clock checking vessels arriving from foreign ports for contraband and diseased passengers or crew. Outside is the Town Beam, which was used for weighing. HM Customs has now relinquished the building, and it has become a wine bar and restaurant.

Opposite: POOLE, DORSET, THE CUSTOM HOUSE 1904 52814T
Below: POOLE, DORSET, BARGES AND THE QUAY 1908 61171T

Grimsby

GRIMSBY GREW from a declined medieval port into the fifth largest in England after a new dock was built in 1800; this was followed by the arrival of the railway in 1848, and further docks came in the 1850s. Grimsby was once the world's largest fishing port. The first fish dock opened in 1856, to accommodate the trawler fleet, and the Royal Dock was built between 1849 and 1852. Photograph 33272P shows a magnificently busy scene with all types of fishing and trading vessels, large and small, and cranes on the quayside. The Victorian Dock Tower stands 309ft tall, rising majestically over the busy port. The tower was built in 1852, and can be seen for many a mile.

World events such as wars affect trade, and Grimsby has had to make great adjustments since the Icelandic Cod War. The town had claimed to be the world's busiest fishing port, and it probably was; but when the cod ceased to be landed at the fish docks things had to change. By diversifying, Grimsby has now become one of the fastest growing towns in Europe. The Royal Dock remains Grimsby's premier commercial dock, and is capable of accepting vessels up to 475 ft long, carrying 6,000 tons of cargo.

Above: GRIMSBY, LINCOLNSHIRE, THE ROYAL DOCK c1955 G60019T

Right: GRIMSBY, LINCOLNSHIRE, THE DOCK 1893 33272P

Falmouth

FALMOUTH, CORNWALL,
THE LANDING STAGE 1904 53032

COMPARED TO many Cornish towns, Falmouth is not old – it began life as a port built by Sir John Killigrew in 1613, and it grew steadily, encouraged by the granting of a charter by Charles II in 1661. In 1688 Falmouth became a Royal Mail packet station: ships left from here to go all over the world, and Falmouth was now an important town. Fishing was the main industry here – the first fish dock was built in 1790. The Royal Mail packet ships ceased to use Falmouth in 1852, but the passing of the Falmouth Docks Act in 1859 enabled the building of the docks. In 1860 the first stone was laid, and the arrival of the Great Western Railway in 1863 allowed quick and easy handling of cargoes. Falmouth was kept busy with ship repairs and trade – cargo ships brought in corn and coal and exported clay, stone and salted pilchards. Ships called at the rate of 20 a week, providing business too for the victuallers and chandlers, and Falmouth continued to thrive. The railways brought holidaymakers too – today Falmouth's main industry is tourism.

FALMOUTH, CORNWALL, THE QUAY 1908 61059

The air was calm and mild – the sky of a very pale blue – a light mist hung over the landscape – and the general impression was peaceful and agreeable: on the surface of the water twenty or thirty ships, mostly packets, and two or three Dutch vessels with licences – a strange sort of trade! The custom-house officers mustered in crowds about the ship, ransacking every corner – barrels and bags, boxes and hampers of half-consumed provisions, empty bottles and full ones, musty straw and papers, and all that the dampness of a ship, pitch and tallow, and the human species confined in a narrow space, can produce of offensive sights and smells, were exposed to open day.

LOUIS SIMOND, 1810

FALMOUTH, CORNWALL, THE BAY 1908 61041P

SCARBOROUGH, with its two glorious bays and fascinating, busy harbour, developed into the premier resort of the east Yorkshire coast. Grand hotels and genteel terraces rose above the beach, and its streets rang with the sound of trippers determined to have a great day out.

Here we see a typical harbour scene, taken at the height of Scarborough's Victorian heyday. The paddle steamer 'Comet' loads up with passengers for an excursion trip round the headland. These small steamers were a feature of both the Scarborough and Bridlington holiday trade; they survived until they were replaced by screw vessels in the 1930s. This lighthouse was built on St Vincent's Pier in 1810, but it was destroyed during a German raid on 17 December 1914. A replacement was erected in 1931.

Below: SCARBOROUGH, YORKSHIRE, VINCENT'S PIER 1890   23471T

A famous literary visitor to Scarborough

Anne Bronte, the youngest of the supremely talented Bronte sisters and the author of 'The Tenant of Wildfell Hall', loved Scarborough, and visited the town for long holidays between 1840 and 1844, staying in the luxurious Wood's Lodgings on St Nicholas Cliff. Anne explored every corner of Scarborough and its bay, visiting the castle grounds, and enjoying constitutionals across the South Cliff. Upon her death from tuberculosis, she was buried in St Mary's churchyard; her grave is visited by hundreds of people every year.

Scarborough

Whitby

DATING BACK to Roman times, this is the only natural harbour between the Humber and the Tees, and is an important shipping haven. In the year of this photograph, Whitby is poised for a summer influx of new visitors via the new Scarborough to Whitby Railway, which opened on 6 July 1885. Down in the harbour, the tall ship is moored just in front of the Angel Vaults, still here as a waterside inn. The parish church of St Mary and the abbey ruins on the horizon are reached by the 199 steps from the old part of town.

Long tradition has meant that the employment sought by the menfolk means that they have to work away from the town. In earlier times, they went to sea in whaling and fishing vessels, and latterly in nearby developing industries, largely in Teesside, but also on oil rigs in oceanic isolation. This has meant that over the years the womenfolk have been left to run their homes, families and even the town. The matriarchal tradition remains.

Another old tradition is not now so widespread. The sea-going fraternity endeavoured to invest their hard-earned savings in houses bought in their wife's name so that she would have an income should they be drowned – a not uncommon event in those days before the welfare state.

Whitby Abbey was founded in the 7th century. The ruins that remain, dating from the 11th century, stand high above the harbour as a reminder of the great wealth of the church at that time. In AD644 the date of Easter was fixed here in a meeting between the Celtic and Roman churches – the meeting was known as the Synod of Whitby.

Bram Stoker, in his 1897 novel 'Dracula', describes the magnificent setting of the abbey: 'Right over the town is the ruin of Whitby Abbey ... It is a most noble ruin, of immense size, and full of beautiful and romantic bits; there is a legend that a white lady is seen in one of the windows. Between it and the town there is another church, the parish one, round which is a big graveyard, all full of tombstones. This is to my mind the nicest spot in Whitby, for it lies right over the town, and has a full view of the harbour and all up the bay to where the headland called Kettleness stretches out into the sea.'

Above left: WHITBY, YORKSHIRE, THE HARBOUR 1885 18168

SWANSEA, WEST GLAMORGAN, SOUTH DOCK 1906 54952

SWANSEA'S maritime tradition has always been vital to the town, as can be seen from the many old drawings and paintings of the port, which all show large numbers of ships anchored in the Bay. The port, and the various extensions of it to accommodate ever bigger ships and greater volumes of cargo, drove the vigorous economic development of the town.

    The South Dock opened in 1859, serving cargo vessels for regular services to London, Bristol, Liverpool, Dublin and Cork. The ship pictured here is the 'Talbot'. The large shed survived the blitz, and now houses the Maritime Museum. The rail carriages that we can see between the shed and the ship travelled on a spur line that linked the port facilities to the GWR network.

BARROW was the home of the huge Vickers shipyard, and the bridge in 60048 (below left), built in 1908, was a vital route for Vickers workers and their families. The Isle of Walney Estates Company, an auxiliary arm of Vickers Ltd, embarked on an ambitious and widespread housing scheme to provide homes on Walney Island for the shipyard workers. Vickerstown was created as two housing estates.

    At the outset the tenants of Vickerstown found that the only way to gain access to Walney Island was to ford the channel at low tide, or to use the Furness Railway Company's Walney Ferry. Some Vickers workers even swam across at the end of their shifts. The residents of Walney found this situation unsatisfactory; against the strong (and to be expected) opposition from the railway company, a bridge was eventually completed – the public opening took place on 30 June 1908. Mr & Mrs Anderson, born in the 1920s, remembered that you had to pay to cross the bridge – or you had to pay a penny to cross on the ferry. During the summer holidays schoolchildren in Barrow were given free passes to cross the bridge. They also remembered that in 1935, to celebrate the Silver Jubilee of King George V, the toll was removed, and the bridge acquired its name of Jubilee Bridge.

    Vickerstown was described as 'A Marine Garden City'; there are great similarities between it and Bourneville in Birmingham and Port Sunlight on Merseyside, which were both built later, suggesting that Vickerstown was a prototype. The Isle of Walney Estates Company acquired a notorious reputation at this time for their strict adherence to the allocation of housing according to the tenant's status in the shipyard regardless of ability to pay. Included in the tenants' rules were strict instructions about not changing the original colour scheme or the external appearance of the houses.

    Barrow took a battering from the German bombers during the Second World War. They used to pass out to sea, and then turn in for their bomb-run, hitting the shipyard, the steelworks and then the station. After the war, the 1950s brought about a time of growth and prosperity to the people of Barrow-in-Furness. The town enjoyed a period of almost full employment and its shipyard quickly returned to building liners and merchant ships as well as warships and submarines.

    The materials needed to outfit the ships in Vickers shipyard, some of which would have weighed tons, were transported from the manufacturing sheds all over the Barrow Island complex by trains, which were used by the shipyard right up to the 1970s. In photograph B26006, below right, the huge crane dwarfs the workers on the quayside and the steam train bringing in the necessary materials.

Above: BARROW-IN-FURNESS, CUMBRIA, WALNEY BRIDGE 1908 60048
Right: BARROW-IN-FURNESS, CUMBRIA, DEVONSHIRE DOCK C1950 B26006

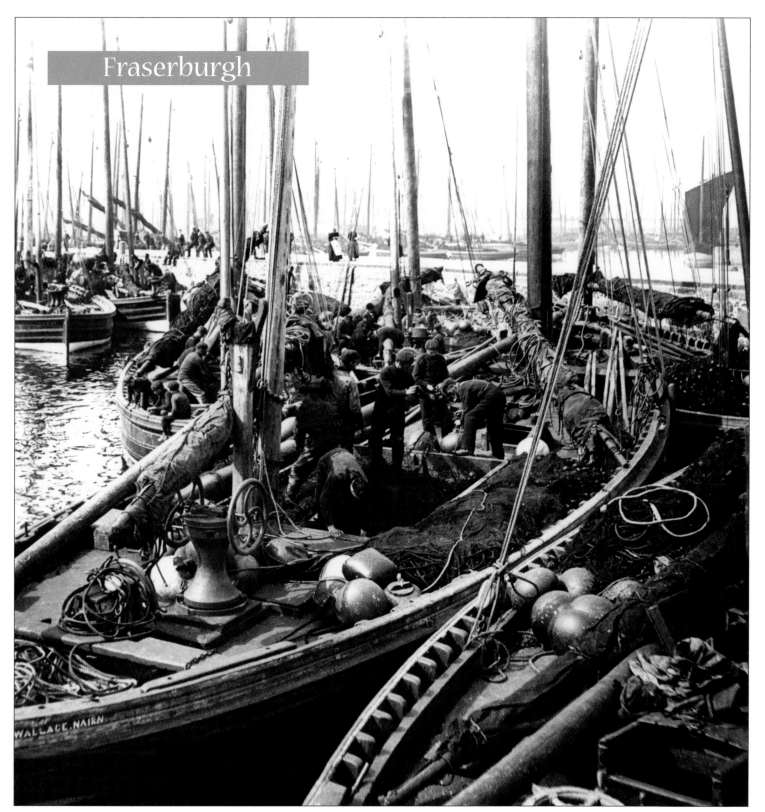

Fraserburgh

HUNTING THE HERRING was a perilous business, but when the drift nets were hauled and were near bursting with fish, it was a time for rejoicing. The Scottish poet Hugh Macdiarmid, born in 1892, expresses the fisherman's deep passion for his calling:

O it's ain o' the bonniest sichts in the warld
To watch the herrin' come walkin' on board
In the wee sma' 'oors o' a simmer's mornin'
As if o' their ain accord.

Chasing the 'silver darlings' (as the fishermen called the herring) began as an industry in Scotland during the 17th century. In 1808, when Fishery Officers first branded barrels of Scotch herring with a crown, the symbol of assured quality, expansion was rapid. A few years later there were also significant improvements in the methods of curing: herring shoals were pursued in deep seas far from the harbour, and the journey home was too long for the fish to be sold and eaten fresh. Some method of preserving them was essential, and the herring were normally salted and dried. Herring were particularly nutritious, and were sought after as a staple part of the Victorian diet.

The number of boats drifting for herring increased, and gutting and curing houses sprang up in the ports of the northeast and Scotland. The combined industry of the region was the greatest in the world.

In Scotland, drifting for herring was particularly hazardous, for the Scots fishers were wedded to their open boats. In this photograph of Fraserburgh, a major port on the northeast coast, the harbour is packed solid with open boats from ports around the region. The scene here is frenzied and boisterous: men are arranging the tackle ready for sailing, and folding and stowing the huge drift nets with their floats. The vessel in the foreground is from Nairn, further west along the Moray Firth. Though she is broad in the beam, her decking is shallow, and would offer scant protection in the violent storms that are common in the North Sea.

Left: FRASERBURGH, GRAMPIAN,
THE HERRING FLEET C1900 F63002P

Smoke and terraces

BEFORE THE 18th century, many industries, especially textile production, had been cottage industries: weavers, for example, would work in their own cottages, and bring the finished cloth to a local centre to sell it. Then came the invention of steam power, the Industrial Revolution, and the building of the canals and the railways. Workers migrated from the country to the new industrial towns, where a new kind of street scene developed of small terraced houses dominated by smoky factory chimneys.

Halifax

SET IN the foothills of the Pennines, at its height in the 19th and early 20th century, Halifax was the greatest of the textile towns of West Yorkshire, a centre for woollen manufacture and clothing. Weaving had been going on here since the 13th century.

Halifax is also where English toffee was invented, and it was here in 1934 that Percy Shaw produced the first cats' eyes, or to give them their proper name, reflecting road studs.

The railway cuts a swathe through Halifax, yet given the town's importance, there was a sense of outrage when the Manchester & Leeds Railway bypassed the town with no connecting branch line built. A branch line was promised as early as 1841, but until July 1844 the only way manufacturers could get their products to a rail-head was by horse and cart to Elland station.

Left: HALIFAX, YORKSHIRE, GENERAL VIEW c1955 H9070

Above right: BLACKBURN, LANCASHIRE, THE INDUSTRIAL AREA c1955 B111004

Blackburn

IN 1933 J B Priestley made his 'English Journey', and visited Blackburn. Handloom weaving as an adjunct to small-scale farming had been practised in the area for centuries, and quite extensively since the 18th century. With the invention of the power loom, the warehouses, which had been used to store the cloth pieces brought in by the handloom weavers, were converted into mills. Power looms were installed, and the formerly independent handloom weavers became employees. Their remote cottages had to be given up, and new homes, long rows of terraced houses, were built near the mills.

There was plenty of coal to be had fairly locally, and the damp climate suited the spinning and weaving of cotton fibres; and so the cotton industry boomed in Blackburn. The population had soared to a peak of 133,000 by 1911. At the time of Priestley's visit, however, the industry was in decline. It was a world-wide slump, but Blackburn, having relied heavily on just one industry, was hit particularly badly. Priestley described Blackburn as 'a sad-looking town', but added: 'The streets are not filled with men dismally loafing about. You do not see abandoned shops, which look as if they are closed for ever, down every street. Everything that was there before the slump, except the businesses themselves, is struggling on. In nearly every instance, the whole town is there, just as it was, but not in the condition it was. Its life is suffering from a deep internal injury'.

This photograph is taken from the viewing platform on the water tank at Revidge. How many chimneys are there in this shot? The one in the centre, which belonged to the refuse destructor, was the tallest one in town.

Macclesfield

Above: MACCLESFIELD, CHESHIRE, THE PARISH CHURCH AND CENTRAL STATION c1955 M2021   *Below*: MACCLESFIELD, CHESHIRE, CHESTERGATE 1898 42600p

MACCLESFIELD is tucked in against the Pennine slope, densely packed with houses and mills and punctuated by church towers. By 1850 it was an overcrowded, filthy, lively, inventive mill town. It was the centre of the silk trade, full of little terraced cottages and clacking mills. It had grown so fast that social care, medical care, schools and even space to be buried in had fallen far behind the need.

After 1850 there was something of a slump in the silk trade and the growth rate of the town slowed down considerably, so Macclesfield never became another Manchester. This was when Macclesfield caught up with itself. It was the age of public building and social improvement, when churches, technical and art schools, hospitals, parks, the museum and the cemetery all came into being.

The c1955 view is quintessential Macclesfield, photographed in the dog years between silk town prosperity and south Manchester boom town affluence. The old church stands on its hill, and Victorian houses cluster around. Waters Green is below, ringed with pubs and silk mills. A brief appearance by the River Bollin from under Central Station is indicated by the square of bushes, centre foreground. The scene is now much softened by trees. Waters Green has lost its animal sales, but the fair still comes here twice a year as it has done since the town got its charter in 1262.

Tiverton

Above: TIVERTON, DEVON, THE LACE WORKS 1890 23734P

INCREASING UNEMPLOYMENT, rising food prices, town fires, floods, disease – Tiverton in the early 19th century was in sore need of a saviour, and found one in 1816 in the shape of John Heathcoat, although to be strictly accurate it was John Heathcoat who found Tiverton. He was a lace manufacturer from Leicestershire who suffered greatly at the hands of Luddites when he tried to introduce machinery to his factory: he had invented the bobbin net machine which revolutionised lace production. The move south has almost become the stuff of legend. Those employees from his Loughborough factory who had chosen to follow Heathcoat left their native town to trudge the 200 miles through the English countryside on foot, bringing with them what machinery could be salvaged from the factory.

His purchase of the now redundant cotton mill at West Exe was to change the face of Tiverton forever. The mill was converted, local hands were trained, model housing was built for the workers, and production got under way – not a moment too soon. With the arrival of John Heathcoat in West Exe, Tiverton's fortunes seemed to take a turn for the better. There was a renewed optimism as the town hauled itself into the modern world.

Today, there is a thriving mill shop here selling an extensive range of fabrics, very popular with seamstresses from miles around. It is housed in what was the factory school, opened in 1841 and the first in the west.

Rochdale

ROCHDALE'S INDUSTRY has long been woollen weaving. The Rochdale Annals record that 8,000 pieces of flannel were produced here in 1825. The woollen-weaving hamlets were largely self-contained with their halls, folds, corn mills and coalmines clustered around the brooks, and Rochdale has mainly developed around them – many weavers' cottages still remain. Many of the merchants employing the handloom weavers went on to build their own steam-powered textile mills, Henry Kelsall and James Royds being among them.

During the Industrial Revolution, the River Roach and its tributaries provided water power for textile mills. The town's population increased fourfold during the 19th century, as people from rural areas moved in seeking work. Dwellings, shops and warehouses sprang up in Rochdale town centre on either side of the river. There were corn, dyeing and fulling mills (the fulling mill had a leat for fulling wool in the Roach), and also a forge.

In this photograph, we see how the mills crowd in towards the town centre, following the course of the River Roach and its tributary the Spodden. Textile mills reached their peak of prosperity at this time. Their pollution has blackened the Yorkshire stone of the Library, Museum and Art Gallery, varying according to the order in which they were built! Trinity Presbyterian Church, opened in 1869, is even darker. It was a familiar landmark until the early 1980s, when the disused building was demolished following a fire. St Chad's School on the left became the Gymnasium in 1897, and the Nurses' Home is to its right.

Rochdale is one of very few modern-day industrial towns to be mentioned in the Domesday Book of 1086. A market charter was granted in 1251, and in 1586 Rochdale was described as a well-frequented market town. It prospered largely through its handloom weaving, which was usually linked with local farming. The Annals of Rochdale record a large number of sheep on its moors in 1800 at the peak of the handloom weaving era.

Above: ROCHDALE, GREATER MANCHESTER, THE VIEW FROM THE PARK SLOPES 1913 65604

Swansea

Left: SWANSEA, WEST GLAMORGAN, GENERAL VIEW 1893   32719

A dense canopy of smoke and a peculiar lurid glare

In 1801 the first census gave the population of Swansea as 6,099, and in 1848 Charles Cunliffe wrote: 'The Swansea Valley forms no bad representation of the infernal regions, for the smell aids the eye. Large groups of odd chimneys and rackety flues emit sulphurous, arsenical smoke or pure flame. A dense canopy overhangs the scene for several miles, rendered more horrible by the peculiar lurid glare. All vegetation is blasted in the valley and adjoining hills. On a clear day the smoke of the Swansea valley may be seen at a distance of forty or fifty miles and sometimes appears like a dense thundercloud'.

SWANSEA, WEST GLAMORGAN, WIND STREET AND VIVIAN STATUE 1896   38754P

TO THE casual visitor, Swansea appears to be a very modern town, but it has a history stretching back many centuries. Its feeling of modernity is mostly attributable to the extensive rebuilding programmes of the 1950s and 1960s after the wartime blitz of February 1941 which laid waste much of Swansea. As a southern port, it was an obvious target – docks, industry, flour mills and the large grain stores were considered vital to the war effort. The German High Command obviously agreed. Swansea was attacked forty-four times during the war, but the worst moments came on 19, 20 and 21 February 1941 when thousands of bombs and incendiaries were dropped on the town. These incendiaries caused the majority of the damage, claiming some notable victims, and the fires acted as a homing beacon for successive waves of German bombers to locate the town and deliver still more mayhem. The fires could be seen from as far away as Pembrokeshire and North Devon. The death toll was 230, with 400 injured. Much of the city's architectural heritage was destroyed, and there are now only two remaining medieval buildings still surviving (the Castle and the Cross Keys Inn). It has to be said that the Victorian town planners also played their part by comprehensively demolishing entire streets to make way for developments.

In 1717 the first copper works were established in Swansea. The tempting combination of water, coal and iron ore was responsible for this. Swansea was once humorously referred to as 'Copperopolis'. By the 1880s, over 6,000 ships were visiting Swansea every year. Copper, zinc, steel and iron were all smelted in the town.

This view looks out into the hills behind the town, which play such a part in defining Swansea. Notice the factory chimneys and their puff-ball smoky emissions. The long lines of terraced workers' cottages tell the tale of Swansea in its heyday as a major industrial town.

Abertillery

Aylesbury

INDUSTRY DOES not have to be confined to industrial towns, as this somewhat rural picture shows. Aylesbury had long been a small agricultural market town, but the coming of the canal, the Aylesbury Arm of the Grand Union Canal, in 1815 and of the railway in 1839 heralded some new growth. This view is taken from the meadow beside the canal (the meadow is now occupied by 1990s housing, Hilda Wharf). The factory was built by the Aylesbury Condensed Milk Company in 1870, taking advantage both of the canal and of the rich cattle pastures hereabouts. The factory now belongs to Nestlé; the left-hand bay's top storey has gone, and the ground floor windows are mostly blocked, but the building remains in use.

HERE, EVEN more clearly than in the photograph of Swansea, we can see how industry shaped the streets of so many Welsh towns. Abertillery was almost completely formed and defined by the production of coal. Like many of the towns in Wales that grew because of the extractive industries such as coal and slate, Abertillery expanded at an astonishing rate from 6,000 in 1881 to over 40,000 in 1921. This massive increase came from those seeking work in the town's coal mines, both from other parts of Wales, industrial and rural, and from the west of England, particularly Somerset and the Forest of Dean. The new housing built for the workers can be seen rising up the hill like a tide, the streets planned in long, regular rows.

Above: ABERTILLERY, GWENT, GENERAL VIEW C1955 A279024

Top: AYLESBURY, BUCKINGHAMSHIRE, THE MILK FACTORY 1897 39640

Above: AYLESBURY, BUCKINGHAMSHIRE, THE CANAL 1897 39642P

Luton

LUTON, BEDFORDSHIRE, THE PRODUCTION LINE, VAUXHALL MOTORS c1950 L117046P

AFTER THE INDUSTRIAL REVOLUTION, Luton grew enormously, from 2,986 in 1821 to 36,404 in 1901. Its streets were busy with the public transport that its increasing population needed. A tramway opened in 1908; it was noisy and took up much of the road. The system was made obsolete by improved motor buses in the 1932, but at the time it provided cheap transport for a growing army of workers. More new businesses were coming to Luton: they included British Gelatine, whose product was used to stiffen hats, Laporte Chemicals, who found a market for their dyes in the local hat industry, Davis Gas ovens, Skefko ball bearings, Commer trucks, and also Chevrolet/Bedford trucks following the GMC takeover of Vauxhall in the late 1920s. GMC executives came over from the US to get work back to normal after the war.

People were clamouring for private transport too, and Vauxhall did much to supply the need. Much of the firm's success was due to David Jones, the industry's longest-serving design executive. In this photograph we see the L-type body shape, available in 4-cylinder Wyvern or 6-cylinder Velox versions. Both had the revolutionary rear hinged bonnet replacing the split bonnet. The Velox reached 75mph; the model ceased production in 1951 when it was replaced by the Detroit-influenced E-type.

Lutonians have also shown their mettle with some rather forceful responses to Vauxhall car management. Historically the company was hostile to the unions. Scottish newcomers during the depressed 1930s brought some passionate spirits. The management underestimated how much people expected from the post-war new order when they got involved in a bonus dispute in 1945. Trouble in the car industry reached new heights during the 1970s with a 3-month strike in 1979. This was a time of increasing Japanese competition; as Vauxhall was a fairly small design and manufacture unit within Europe, it was going to have a struggle to survive. A new agreement on working practices offered hope for the future.

BURNLEY, LANCASHIRE, DUKE BAR 1906 54183T

THE MOST important highways that serve the eastern part of Burnley can be seen in this photograph of Duke Bar. The road to the left is Colne Road, and the one to the right is Briercliffe Road. In the centre is the Duke of York public house (c1882), and it is from this building that the first part of the place name is derived. The second word, 'bar', is because these roads once formed part of an important turnpike. A toll bar, with gates across both roads, once stood here; hence the name Duke Bar. The roads lead the traveller in the direction of Yorkshire.

The pedestrians going about their daily business enliven this photograph. Notice the policeman near the lamp, in the centre, the men near the Duke of York, and the children on the left. Also there are two vehicles visible, a coal cart on Briercliffe Road and a tram on Colne Road. The open-topped tram is quite a rarity for Burnley, because only a small number operated in the town. Notice also the stone setts, which make up the road surface, and how they merge into each other at junctions.

The tip of a spire can be seen just off centre. It belongs to St Andrew's Church, which dates from 1867.

As we can see from its sign, Thomas Bate's general store (on the left) sold the Burnley-brewed 'Grimshaw's Sparkling Ales and Stout', which were also supplied to the Duke of York. Mr Bate's shop has several interesting signs on the walls: Sunlight soap, Bovril and Fry's cocoa. Later the shop became the local office for the Burnley Building Society.

In the days when few people could afford a watch, there were many more public clocks. In Burnley they were placed at strategic locations across the town, and this one at Duke Bar certainly fits into the pattern. The same is true of the large gas lamp to the left of the public house. Burnley people call these lamps 'gormlesses', because like this one they were always found in the middle of the road! If we look carefully, we can see the more usual and smaller lamps on both Colne and Briercliffe Roads.

PERHAPS NO OTHER settlement in England has seen so much change and fought back against depression in such a victorious manner as Corby.

It is difficult to imagine that the modern thriving industrial town of Corby was once an obscure Rockingham Forest village. An important Roman road passed through the southern area of the village, running from Huntingdon to Leicester. What attracted the Romans were the vast ironstone deposits in the area, much of which lay close to the surface, and was therefore easily extracted by hand or with a minimum of digging.

The coming of the railway in 1875 laid the foundations for what would eventually be a new era in Corby's history. During the railway's construction, the vast ironstone deposits of the area were rediscovered. In 1880 a Birmingham industrialist, Samuel Lloyd, sent an agent to the Corby area and began to look into the possibility of commercial ironstone quarrying and processing. In 1910, Lloyd began the commercial production of iron. Stewarts & Lloyds (formed by amalgamation with a Scottish tube-making firm in 1903) went from strength to strength in the following years until November 1932, when the startling news came that Corby had been chosen to be the site of one of the biggest iron and steel making complexes in the world, with unlimited job prospects.

With the coming of the steel works, Corby was transformed from a village into a modern industrial town. Swarms of newcomers arrived here for desperately needed employment, many of them walking or cycling a considerable distance, mainly from the north of the British Isles. Accommodation was at a premium: many slept rough in barns and hedges, or stayed in surrounding villages, until a place became available. When it did, it was not uncommon for a worker to share a room or a bed with one or two other people over a period of twenty-four hours: the bed became vacant when one man came home from his (mainly) eight-hour shift, and another left for his stint at the works.

This view is taken from the bridge over Rockingham Road, and shows (from left to right) the four blast furnaces, the Brassert towers (gas cleaners), and the cooling towers. A Barclay saddleback engine can be seen on the right, heading in the direction of the tall floodlight in the foreground. Everything in this scene has since been demolished, and much of the surrounding area has been redeveloped as a retail park and industrial estate.

CORBY, NORTHAMPTONSHIRE, STEWARTS & LLOYDS STEEL WORKS c1955 C337004

Efficacious in every way

DOWN THE centuries people have retained a firm and unshakeable belief in the curative and beneficial properties of natural springs. Bubbling from ancient rocks, these mineral waters have seemed to many to be imbued with a holy or supernatural force. Most wells had none of the direct associations with saints enjoyed by wells in the Celtic west; however, custodians of ancient springs often found it both convenient and diplomatic to make a saint responsible for the cure. It is not surprising that many springs and wells grew to become places of pilgrimage – and by the 18th century, smart spa towns had arisen, whose streets were full of the wealthy seeking a healthier lifestyle.

Right: GREAT MALVERN, HEREFORD & WORCESTER, HOLY WELL 1904 51153

Great Malvern

HOLY WELL, the source of J H Cuff's mineral water factory (51153, left), sits at the foot of the imposing Malvern hills. It houses an ancient spring that trickles out of the bare granite, and has been in use since medieval times. In 1654 John Evelyn reported how it was said 'to heale many infirmities, such as king's evil, leaprosie, sore eyes etc'. The water from Holy Well was renowned in particular for its special efficacy in treating eye problems. Bottling began as early as 1622 – a contemporary song records that a thousand bottles were shipped weekly to London, Berwick and Kent. By 1747 there were houses and apartments here for visitors, and business continued to be brisk.

The cottage ornée-style factory in the photograph was built in 1843 at a cost of £400 – note its somewhat eccentric battlemented detailing and imposing Norman-style doorway. In 1850 the famous bottlers Schweppes sub-leased the supply, and it was not until 1895 that J H Cuff took over the business. The bottling plant was run successfully for many years, but by the 1950s the building had fallen into dilapidation. In the 1970s John Parkes bought it and set about a thorough restoration. Bottling began again in earnest – one regular client was said to be Buckingham Palace – and only stopped again in 1990.

Fashionable society and many 19th-century celebrities and worthies, including Gladstone, Macaulay, Dickens and Carlyle – even Florence Nightingale – came to Malvern to take the cure.

Patients took cold baths, spent hours bandaged in wringing wet sheets, suffered icy douches, and stood naked under fierce cascades of freezing cold water. Douches were considered beneficial for painful joints and for the circulation. The pounding of the falling water and its icy coldness restored the circulation, and keeping the affected joint wrapped in flannel afterwards would bring back mobility. These curious treatments can be compared to today's alternative health therapies.

GREAT MALVERN, HEREFORD & WORCESTER, FROM THE CHURCH TOWER 1899   43988

The wells around the town of Malvern attracted visitors throughout the Victorian period, and it gained a reputation as an important spa town. In 43988, above, we can see carriages waiting patiently for passengers. Soon the streets were filled with bath-chairs containing pale men and women wrapped in shawls. Doctors Wilson and Gully set up a hydropathic establishment in the town with a course of treatment based on the spartan Czechoslovak method.

Rheumatism, gout, scrofula and affections of the liver

At spas like Bath and Harrogate the mineral waters were said to have a slightly unpleasant taste on the palate owing to their organic content. At Malvern the water was particularly pure. Dr John Wall claimed that it would 'pass through the vessels of the body' better than other spring waters. Malvern water was advertised as 'a table water of the highest class. Remarkably pure ... it has long been celebrated for its curative properties against rheumatism, gout, scrofula and affections of the liver and kidneys. Its methodical use is calculated to prevent the formation of morbid concretions and deposits'.

BATH, SOMERSET, ' PRINCE BLADUD DISCOVERING THE HOT SPRINGS' 1903   50744

THE DISCOVERY of spa water in 1571 led to Harrogate's long history as a spa town. For centuries, visitors have flocked here in the hope that the sulphur springs would bring them well-being. It was in 1898 that Dr Black first put forward proposals that Harrogate should build a Kursaal that would include a concert hall, a newsroom and games rooms. Plans were drawn up in 1900 following a visit to the continent by a deputation; R J Beale and the great theatre architect Frank Matcham were commissioned to design the building, and we can see from the photograph of the Kursaal interior that the result was rich, ornate and festive.

The Kursaal attracted world-class musicians, and though it was subsidised for a number of years, by the eve of the Great War it was operating at a profit. In 58656 (opposite, right), posters give notice that a sacred concert is to be held. These were a regular feature in spas and resorts around the country, as were open-air religious services. There is also a poster mentioning the daily concert given by the Municipal Orchestra. Formed in 1896 under J Sydney Jones, the orchestra survived until 1930 when it was disbanded as an economy measure.

The Pump Room (81527, below), was constructed in 1842 over the sulphur wells. In Bog Field, Valley Gardens, an astonishing total of 36 different mineral springs come to the surface, prompting it to be hailed as 'a wonder of the natural world'. Along with the Crescent Gardens which are situated between the Pump Room and the Municipal Offices (Victoria Baths), the Valley Gardens offer visitors a garden walk of nearly one mile in length from Low Harrogate to the heights of Harlow Moor.

Despite the decline of the spa trade in the 1920s, visitors continued to come to Harrogate, as we can see here. The fashion for health spas might have been on the wane, but Harrogate still had plenty of genteel pleasures to offer.

Harrogate

Right: HARROGATE, YORKSHIRE, THE KURSAAL 1907 58656

Photo courtesy of: David Peta

Photo courtesy of: Tom Curtis

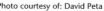

Opposite left: HARROGATE, YORKSHIRE, THE PUMP ROOM FROM VALLEY GARDENS 1928 81527

Above: HARROGATE, YORKSHIRE, THE KURSAAL INTERIOR 1911 58657

A stream of the halt and lame and the hale and hearty

The attraction of Harrogate centres, of course, in its springs and baths. With the exception of two springs – Tewitt and John's – these are all in Low Harrogate. Hither the visitors flock with automatic regularity every morning, those from the more distant hotels being conveyed by omnibus free of charge. In one season some 300,000 water-drinkers and 60,000 bathers have been numbered.

By seven o'clock it is time to be stirring, and from that till the breakfast hour there is a stream – not only of halt and lame, but also of hale and hearty visitors – to the old Royal and new Royal Baths Pump Rooms, where 'bumpers' of sulphuric and chalybeate waters are dispensed at a charge of 6d a day. After the first glass a mild constitutional is recommended, and this is usually taken up the prettily laid-out Valley Gardens, a little beyond which, 1 mile from the Pump Rooms, is the Magnesia Spring, under cover (charge 1d a glass).

The gathering-point is the Royal Pump Room, an octagonal dome-covered building containing the Old Sulphur Well – the strongest spring of its kind – sulphurous and saline and magnesian – in the kingdom. Subscription, 6d a day; Is 6d. a week.

There is a free tap of the same ingredients outside.

BADDELEY'S GUIDE TO YORKSHIRE 1902

Buxton

BUXTON in the High Peak of Derbyshire has been an inland resort for more than 2,000 years. The town sits in a bowl at 300 metres above sea level surrounded by hills which rise to 500 metres. Nowadays the immediate hills around the town are heavily wooded, but this was not always so; early travellers found a barren and inhospitable terrain which had to be traversed before reaching Buxton. Dr Hall, writing in 1863, said: 'A few generations back, the country for many miles round Buxton still remained so bleak and, with a few exceptions, so dreary that but for the rheumatic invalid seeking benefit from its waters, and the comforts of its inns and numerous boarding-houses, it possessed comparatively few attractions for strangers'. But reports of miraculous cures caused early travellers to brave the hardships in search of relief from the warm medicinal waters which rise from springs located in the present Crescent at a constant temperature of 82°F (27.5°C).

The Crescent was designed by John Carr of York and built for the 5th Duke of Devonshire between 1780 and 1784. The warm springs emerge in the area of the left-hand side of the picture and the Crescent was built in a low-lying grove of trees. The River Wye flows underneath the outer rim of the building. The Quadrant can be seen on the extreme right, the Palace Hotel behind the Crescent and the Devonshire Royal Hospital with its domed roof to the left. The streets and paths are remarkably empty; was this photograph taken in the early morning?

Poor John Byng

Buxton is a most uncomfortable, dreary place; and the Grand Crescent might be better named the Devonshire Infirmary. Snug lodging-houses, with adjoining small stables, were more necessary and comfortable than useless, ill-contrived grandeurs: but the Duke, I suppose, was made prey of by some architect, a contrast of his Grace, as having some genius and no fortune.

I spy'd about for some time, unknowing and unknown; till I return'd to our coffee room, where I subscribed and breakfasted. To people obliged to fly hither for relief, Buxton, as furnishing hope or health, may be tolerable; but it will not do for my plan; so that tho' I may make it my headquarters for some time, yet I shall skirt the country round: and this I began to do today at eleven o'clock, and upon Blacky for the first time, as Pony is going to be shod … My trunk not arriving is very vexatious; and now they say it cannot come till Monday. I pass'd this gloomy evening very gloomily in my bedroom: nor would I sup in company but had it, as last night, in my bedroom.

JOHN BYNG, 'RIDES ROUND BRITAIN', 1790
ED D ADAMSON, FOLIO SOCIETY

Opposite left:
BUXTON,
DERBYSHIRE,
THE VIEW FROM
THE SLOPES 1932
85213

Right:
BUXTON,
DERBYSHIRE,
DEVONSHIRE
HOSPITAL 1896
37855

Cheltenham

CHELTENHAM, GLOUCESTERSHIRE, THE PROMENADE 1931
83807

THREE CENTURIES AGO, Cheltenham was just one of the stone villages on the edge of the Cotswolds. Its fortunes changed in 1715 when a mineral spring was discovered. Within a few years, fashionable society had begun to arrive to take the waters.

The Promenade was designed for the convenience of pedestrians: here the pavements are much wider than the roads, allowing the genteel residents and visitors to the spa to walk in safety away from the traffic, which was contained in narrow carriageways. Trees provide welcome shade, and benches the opportunity to stop and rest. Similarly, the buildings in avenues such as the Promenade are much more spacious and elegant than the original dwellings and lodging places in the High Street. It was for the building of the Promenade and the surrounding crescents and terraces that many of the quarries were opened in the neighbouring hills.

Cheltenham soon became a retirement home for military officers and colonial administrators who occupied the spreading Regency terraces, such as the ones seen here along the Promenade. Others lived in purpose-built villas elsewhere in the town. But not every visitor was impressed by the elegance of Cheltenham Spa. William Cobbett (1763–1835) described the town as a 'nasty ill-looking place', full of 'East India plunderers, West Indian floggers, English tax-gorgers, … gluttons, drunkards and debauchers of all descriptions, female as well as male'.

Pier and promenade

THE CONCEPT of taking a holiday by the sea is a comparatively recent one: the idea that sea air and sea bathing might be beneficial to the health only arose in the late 18th century. Then the narrow lanes of little fishing villages suddenly became the broad streets and esplanades of smart seaside resorts – the transformation of Brighton by the patronage of the Prince Regent is a prime example. Later in the 19th century, increased prosperity and Bank Holidays encouraged the development of the less refined resort, complete with pier, prom, ice cream and charabanc trips.

'Hereabouts, they begin to talk of herrings ... and here also they cure sprats in the same manner as they do herrings in Yarmouth', noted the very observant Defoe during his famous perambulation in the early 18th century. Southwold invested furiously in this trade, and herring 'busses', 70-foot square-rigged sailing drifters, brought wealth to the town – but only temporarily. Southwold's harbour was incapable of the kind of expansion which would put it on the same scale as Lowestoft or Great Yarmouth. Now Buss Creek embraces the town on the landward side, a nod to the vessels of old, or perhaps a hint of what might have been.

Southwold

SOUTHWOLD IS a town of character and characters; its history, so closely tied to the sea, abounds with glorious adventures, mysteries and disasters, and some extremely fishy tales. But its fishing success did not last, and a new role for Southwold's beaches emerged in the Victorian era — sea bathing and general leisure use. The town council drew up by-laws to regulate behaviour on the beach, and there were steep fines for misuse of these public places.

The town has a number of greens, grassed open spaces that were intended to reduce the threat of fires. It is said that after a disastrous fire had devastated the town in 1659, the townspeople decided that to prevent it happening again, they would group the houses around these open spaces. We can see from photograph 38624 that the greens became a valuable amenity for Victorian holidaymakers, who are enjoying a stroll and a chat — and note the boy on a donkey.

The gleaming white lighthouse (45137) was first lit in 1889 and completed in 1890; it stands amid some of the finest Georgian houses in the town, safely positioned away from the cliff edge but not too centrally, where the smoke from coal fires might have obscured the light, which can be seen about 17 nautical miles away. The building is Southwold's trademark, and is topped by a golden weather vane, making it a landmark for miles around. The lighthouse inevitably dominates many of the street vistas, not the least of which is East Green. The Wesleyan chapel (left) is an intimation of the strong non-conformist tradition in Southwold. By 1933 the Methodists had added a contemporary facade to their chapel.

Opposite above: SOUTHWOLD, SUFFOLK, EAST GREEN 1900   45137

Opposite below: SOUTHWOLD, SUFFOLK, THE GREEN 1896   38624

Aldeburgh

ALDEBURGH, SUFFOLK, THE PARADE 1909   62011

The maltings

The former maltings at Snape, near Aldeburgh, have become famous for the annual Aldeburgh Music Festival established by the composer Benjamin Britten and the singer Peter Pears in 1948 – they lived in Aldeburgh. Today the festival attracts internationally-known artists and admiring and appreciative audiences to the magnificent converted Victorian red-brick buildings. The festival has vastly increased Aldeburgh's popularity as a fashionable place to enjoy a cultural break or a seaside holiday.

ALDEBURGH HAS long been a little fishing town, and from Victorian times has been popular with holidaymakers. William Camden (1551–1623), the antiquary and historian, described Aldeburgh's situation as 'right safe and very pleasant within Slaughden vale, where from the East the sea and from the West the river beateth. This name Aldburgh is by interpretation The Old Burgh, or, as others would have it, The Burgh upon the river Ald. Now it is an harbour verie commodious for sailers and fishermen, and thereby well frequented, and acknowledgeth the Ocean sea to bee favourable unto it, how spitefull soever and malicious it is to other townes in this coast'. In this photograph we see that only a flimsy wall protects these stately villas from the waves. A proud dad, a sailor home from the sea, takes his daughter for a stroll along the sandy path, and a rather bored pony meanders towards the camera. By the 1960s a more solid wall had been built to protect the town against the North Sea storms.

The esplanade is dominated visually by two lookout towers — this one is the southern lookout. Rival companies manned these towers to pick up the lucrative pilot trade into the Thames Estuary. They were nicknamed 'Up-Towners' and 'Down-Towners'; they raced to supply pilots and land cargoes, almost running errands to the passing ships. Then there was the bounty of salvage as the stormy seas battered vessels into submission.

Clacton-on-Sea

CLACTON-ON-SEA, ESSEX, PIER AVENUE 1907   58948T

BLUE SKIES, informal clothes, banners and awnings fluttering in the breeze – this street scene sums up all that is carefree about summer holidays by the sea. The Public Hall, the prominent building on the right with its wrought iron colonnade and large arch in its central gable, cost £7,000 and was one of the main features of the town. By the time of this photograph it had ceased to be a Public Hall and instead belonged to Lewellen's, an ironmonger's and cycle store. To the right of the hall is Henry Foyster's Restaurant, a prominent business in Clacton from the 1890s until the 1950s. Next to Foyster's is W Mann, a chemist's, and between Mann's and the Royal Hotel is Ubsdell's library, stationer's and fancy goods.

The Public Hall was destroyed by a fire in June 1939. The fire, generally known as Lewellen's fire after the shop which had taken over the main part of the hall, also destroyed a large part of Pier Avenue, from the Castle Restaurant at the north almost to the Royal Hotel at the south.

HERE we see a British seaside scene in its full glory, at a time just before the advent of cheap foreign holidays heralded the decline of seaside resorts. Here the street beside the pier is busy with cars, strollers, and of course that essential of a sunny day out – an ice cream van.

During the First World War, the owner of the pier, the Coast Development Company, went into liquidation and was bought by Ernest Kingsman. Being a shrewd businessman he took the view that Clacton Pier could become a big money spinner, but only by changing the whole concept of the pier. He immediately set about turning the pier from what was still basically only a landing stage into the biggest pleasure pier in the country. To achieve this ambition he promoted a Private Bill in the House of Commons aimed at widening the front of the pier to 90 feet by the compulsory purchase of land owned by Clacton Urban District Council. The Bill was vehemently opposed by the Council, but Kingsman was successful and thus able to continue his policy of building Clacton Pier into a major tourist attraction.

By the late 1930s Kingsman had spent about £200,000 on the pier. He added many attractions such as Britain's first open-air pier swimming pool, the Crystal Casino Amusement Arcade, the Blue Lagoon Dance Hall, the Cresta Run helter-skelter, and the Steel Stella roller-coaster.

But the decline of Clacton as a major seaside resort in the 1960s, with more and more people going abroad for their holidays, also saw the decline of Clacton Pier. In 1971 Barney Kingsman, Ernest's son, sold it. In 1973 the Steel Stella burnt down, and in 1978 the Ocean Theatre closed. By 1980 practically all the major entertainments had closed, although there were still a number of rides, such as the dodgems, as well as amusement arcades. The pier has recently undergone a small revival, but it is doubtful if the glory days will ever return to Clacton Pier.

Above: CLACTON-ON-SEA, ESSEX, THE PIER c1960 C107051

Tenby

TENBY HAS a long history: Castle Hill has a commanding view of both its landward and seaward approaches, and was almost certainly the location of an Iron Age promontory fort. The beaches, caves and rock pools around Castle Hill and especially St Catherine's Island have been a favourite haunt of the serious and amateur naturalist for generations. Above, the old fort, having never fired a shot in anger, remains a reminder of the threat posed to Pembrokeshire by Napoleon III.

TENBY, DYFED, FISHWIVES, 1890 28091

Fishing and especially dredging for oysters was an important part of Tenby's economy. Oysters from the Caldey Island beds were so large that a single specimen was considered too much for one person. A common sight in the harbour was the shallow-drafted clinker-built Tenby lugger, peculiar to the town, a three-masted open boat used mainly for drift-net fishing and oyster dredging. However, over the years the oysters declined, and subsequently Tenby depended more and more on the new industry of catering for seasonal visitors.

Children playing on boats and beach evoke a scene reminiscent of the fascination of British people from an early age with 'matters maritime'. Sailing trawlers were part of a major fleet in this port until 1888, when the Great Western railway opened its large fish dock in nearby Milford Haven. Since then Tenby's role became that of a seaside resort.

TENBY, DYFED, THE HARBOUR 1890 28041

Bognor Regis

BOGNOR REGIS, SUSSEX, THE BEACH FROM THE PIER 1890 22624

THIS VIEW shows a typical busy seaside resort beach scene with paddling children and pleasure boats. Until the 1920s these bathing machines were ready for business at 6am with 'the conductor waiting', and were 'drawn (by a horse) to any depth required; at low water the bather may even go as far as the rocks; the ladies will find a female guide'.

Bognor acquired a sea wall and promenade partly for the benefits of promenaders but mainly to protect the land from the rapidly encroaching sea. The 1,000-foot pier, from which this view was taken, opened in 1865, and became a favourite spot for photographers; here we are looking at the seafront buildings before the ornate Royal Hotel was built. We can see the east side of Waterloo Square with, behind the flag-flying Beach Hotel, the cupola'd bell tower of the old fire station, which moved inland in about 1900.

SITUATED west of Marine Parade, Park Terrace is a wonderful example of the kind of street built in the Victorian era for those wishing to take the Bognor sea air. It dates from the 1870s, and was popular with the nobility and well-to-do, including the Duke of Portland, who owned one of the houses. These houses carry the Regency love of first-floor Waterloo balconies over into the context of the more stolid High Victorian architecture.

This town is Worthing's twin sister – a quiet, mild, healthy watering-place, situate on a level in the face of the ever-restless Channel … Bognor is remarkably quiet, but it will doubtless commend itself to some people on this account.
VICTORIAN GUIDEBOOK

Left: HASTINGS, SUSSEX, VIEW FROM THE PIER c1955 H36052P

BOGNOR REGIS, SUSSEX, PARK TERRACE 1890   22635

Torquay

DURING THE first decades of Victoria's long reign Torquay enjoyed the epithet 'Queen of Watering Places', as most of her visitors were, as one account put it, 'of the highest class'. Just before this photograph was taken, the emphasis on encouraging invalids to come to Torquay was at its height. One guidebook reported: 'This watering place … is much resorted to by invalids with delicate lungs … The general effect of the white houses, the grey limestone cliffs, and the foliage and greensward … is unusually pleasant and picturesque, and calculated to soothe, as far as scenery can soothe, the lassitude and depression of ill-health'.

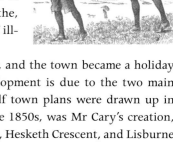

Soon afterwards, in 1892, through trains came to Torquay, and the town became a holiday resort as opposed to a retreat for invalids. Torquay's development is due to the two main landowners of the time, Sir Laurence Palk (on whose behalf town plans were drawn up in 1805) and Robert Cary. This elegant terrace, built in the late 1850s, was Mr Cary's creation, which attempted to emulate the grander efforts – The Terrace, Hesketh Crescent, and Lisburne Crescent – of Sir Laurence. It has an ornamental centre, matching bays and end pediments. At the date of this photograph it is little changed since it was built.

Left: TORQUAY, DEVON, ABBEY CRESCENT 1896   38598

Morecambe

Eastbourne

MORECAMBE, LANCASHIRE, THE PROMENADE 1899 42860

THE SEASIDE TOWN of Morecambe, situated on Morecambe Bay, has wonderful views of the hills of the Lake District. The brine-tinged air from the bay, softened by the fresh air flowing in from across the Lake District, produced what Morecambe does best – a relaxing and exhilarating environment for a break or holiday. The whole area has been designated one of Outstanding Natural Beauty, and the bay itself is one of Europe's best habitats for migrating birds. Central Morecambe has always had a pebble beach, especially at high tide. The pier, the sea, bracing air and excursions to Heysham and the Lakes – that was what the holidaymakers wanted, and that was what Morecambe provided. Because of its closeness to the northern border, it always had a 'Scotch Week' when workers from Glasgow and the surrounding area would descend and 'let loose'. It was a sort of Wakes Week, Scottish style; it was always in mid-July.

This lovely view of the crowded Promenade looks north towards Hest Bank, with the Central Pier in the background. An open-topped horse-drawn tram drives along, with happy holidaymakers enjoying the sea breezes.

The Central Pier reacted in grand style to the opening of the West End Pier by building a pavilion at the end. It soon gained the nickname 'the Taj Mahal', and indeed it did resemble that famous building. The Lancashire-style Indian pavilion burnt down in a fire in 1933; it was rebuilt in 1935, but it was not as grand and ornate as the original.

MORECAMBE, LANCASHIRE,
THE CENTRAL PIER 1906 56106

IN THIS photograph of Eastbourne on the south coast, charabancs are touting for business at the pier. The nearest is bound for Pevensey Bay, where the passengers will marvel at the Martello towers, circle the battlements at the castle, and then retire to the tearoom for some welcome refreshment. Meanwhile, passengers in the other charabanc will be enjoying the fresh air of the South Downs. Those with strong stomachs will peer dizzily down from Beachy Head at the matchstick-sized lighthouse hundreds of feet below. Then, holding hats firmly down with two hands, they will be up and over the downs, heading back to Eastbourne.

The Victorians invented the seaside. Many of the attractions that they enjoyed are still being enjoyed today – the piers, promenades, fairground rides, and trips round the bay. We have them to thank for the Great British Holiday that so many of us continue to look forward to today.

Left: EASTBOURNE, SUSSEX, THE PIER 1925 77946T

BOURNEMOUTH, DORSET, THE SQUARE 1923 74782

IT IS hard to believe that only 200 years ago there was nothing to be seen on this spot except miles of wild heathland. Had Mr Lewis Tregonwell decided to build his holiday home elsewhere in 1810, there is a possibility that Bournemouth might never have existed. No doubt seeking peace and quiet, other wealthy people followed Tregonwell's example; but even by 1841 there were still only about 30 houses scattered around the heathland. It was not until the arrival of the railway in 1870 that Bournemouth finally opened its doors to the mass invasion of tourists.

By the 1920s Bournemouth had become a major south coast resort, rivalling Brighton and Torquay. It used to be said that if you lingered in Bournemouth's square for long enough everyone you knew would pass by sooner or later. The traffic in the Square increased accordingly, with private motor cars competing with the charabanc for parking spaces. The latter would take trippers to the many beautiful localities nearby, such as Purbeck and the New Forest.

Bournemouth had the first electric trams in England, though it eventually gave them up in favour of electric trolley buses. The old tramlines were eventually torn up and used to reinforce the concrete of the sea wall.

Seaside piers began life as landing stages for steamers offering trips round the bay. Soon they became popular places to promenade, where holiday-makers could savour the bracing sea air and look back to enjoy exhilarating prospects of the coast and townscape. Piers were masterful feats of engineering, elegant and exotic, thrusting far out into the sea with characteristic Victorian aplomb. The Victorian entrepreneur was never slow in recognising commercial potential: modest piers were enlarged to make space for seats, kiosks, bandstands and pavilions. They became fashionable places to see and be seen. By the early 1900s they were the focus for seaside fun, and thousands pushed through the turnstiles to enter a world far removed from their workaday lives.

EASTBOURNE, SUSSEX, THE PIER 1906 56687P

Stilton and Shakespeare

THE CHARACTER of some of Britain's streets is formed by the one particular thing the town is famous for. It can be for a foodstuff – certain cheeses, like Stilton or Cheddar, for instance, or certain recipes, like the Bath bun or the Eccles cake. In this chapter, we learn that Bakewell Tart (or more correctly Bakewell Pudding) came about by happy accident, whereas the Melton Mowbray pie was an almost inevitable product of rich farming country. We will also see towns famous for sport, literature, and education.

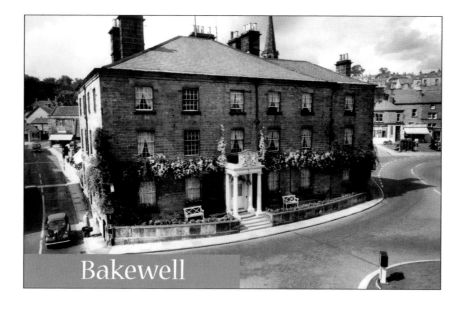

Bakewell

IF BAKEWELL is known for nothing else, its fame is for ever assured by a small item of pastry: the Bakewell Tart. Sadly, this nomenclature is incorrect. The item concerned is a Bakewell Pudding and was actually created by mistake.

It was at the elegant Georgian coaching inn the Rutland Arms in the 1850s that the mistress of the hotel, Mrs Greaves, gave instructions to her cook to prepare a strawberry tart. But the cook left the eggs and sugar out of the pastry, instead making a plain pastry case, putting strawberry jam in the bottom and then adding the egg mixture to the top. Despite the error, the resulting product turned out very nicely, and the recipe was preserved. Subsequently, it became very popular, especially when a shop was opened in The Square in 1859, selling puddings made to the original recipe – this is a secret one, handed down only to members of the family.

The Rutland Arms is also noted as the place where Jane Austen stayed when she visited the town in 1811. Whilst here, it is believed that she was at work on her novel 'Pride and Prejudice', which was published in 1813. It is suggested that the town of Lambton in the novel is actually Bakewell.

Above left: BAKEWELL, DERBYSHIRE, THE RUTLAND ARMS HOTEL c1955 B6086

Below left: BAKEWELL, DERBYSHIRE, THE OLD ORIGINAL BAKEWELL PUDDING SHOP c1965 B6100

Bakewell Tart – a rich dish for those special occasions

As with any traditional recipe, there are bound to be many different versions, especially if the original recipe is a well-guarded secret. The famous authoress Alison Uttley, who lived in Lea, a village near Bakewell, wrote in her book 'Recipes from an Old Farmhouse':

'Cover a wide shallow dish with thin puff paste. Put in it a layer of jam, preferably raspberry, but any kind will do. It should be half an inch thick. Take the yolks of eight eggs and beat the whites of two. Add half a pound of melted butter and half a pound each of sugar and ground bitter almonds. Mix all well together, and pour into the pastry case over the jam. Bake for half an hour and serve nearly cold. This was one our favourite dishes, but it was a rich dish for special occasions only.'

ON THE banks of the River Eye in North Leicestershire stands Melton Mowbray, an historic market town renowned for its rural tradition and its world-famous Melton Mowbray pork pie, which originated in Melton in 1831. Edward Adcock, who ran a bakery adjacent to the Fox Inn in Leicester Street, recognised the popularity of his cold meat pies among visiting huntsmen. Adcock decided to market his pies in London, which proved to be a huge success. By 1840 the increased demand allowed Enoch Evans to set up a rival business in the Beast Market, which is now Sherrard Street: the popularity of the Melton Mowbray pork pie began to grow. These hand-raised pies are uniquely rounded, made from the finest British uncured pork and encased in rich and crunchy pastry. Messrs Dickinson & Morris founded Ye Olde Pork Pie Shoppe in Nottingham Street (seen here in this photograph) in 1851; this is the last remaining firm in Melton to bake the authentic pies on their shop premises. The bakery has since become a huge tourist attraction, with as many as 250,000 visitors each year. They can enjoy sampling the pies, watch baking demonstrations or even, on specially organised evenings, try their hands at baking their own pie.

Below: MELTON MOWBRAY, LEICESTERSHIRE, NOTTINGHAM STREET c1960 M60114

Pigs, whey and Melton's prized delicacies

It is no coincidence that Melton's two most renowned delicacies (pork pies and cheese) originated in the same region. Pigs thrive on whey, which is the chief by-product of cheese making, and so Stilton cheese and pork pies were made side by side.

To make the pies, fresh pork, from pigs killed in the winter, was stuffed into the hot crust pastry. The pies were baked free-standing and came out bow shaped.

The creamy, blue-veined Stilton cheese was named after the Cambridgeshire village on the Great North Road where it was sold for delivery by stagecoach to London.

Stilton cheese is actually made in Leicestershire, Derbyshire and Nottinghamshire, but with three main producers in the town, Melton Mowbray can claim to be the Stilton capital.

Melton Mowbray

NEWMARKET is a thriving, busy town. Besides being a market town, it is the headquarters of horse racing and is establishing itself as a tourist centre. Close proximity to the A14 enables it today to serve as a dormitory town. A 1945 map would have shown only a quarter of the development we find here today. The old part of the town is mainly late Victorian, although it expanded rapidly after World War II as an overspill for London.

NEWMARKET, SUFFOLK, HIGH STREET 1929 81955T

Newmarket's connection with horse racing dates back to the time of Charles II, although it was not until the reign of Victoria that the sport received its biggest boost, promoted by her son the Prince of Wales.

The scene in 71918 is a daily sight around the capital of horse racing – stable lads exercising racehorses on Newmarket Heath. These racehorses are heading up to the gallops. One horse, in the distance on the right beyond the fence, is crossing the Bury Road to join the others on the heath. The large building behind the second horse in the string is the Drill Hall on the Snailwell Road. The lads are all dressed formally, wearing caps, jackets and neckties. The first horse has started to trot; his tail has swished up into the air. The second horse in the row is well protected by a blanket under the saddle, and his face and ears are covered.

Unsaddled horses are being led down the street. Could they be going to a Tattersalls sale? A man, a window cleaner and two children watch the horses from beneath the awning of Jessie Blyth, milliner; next door is William Parker, jeweller and optician. Further on a restaurant serves luncheons and teas to those walking to the races.

Above: NEWMARKET, SUFFOLK, RACEHORSES ON EARLY MORNING EXERCISE 1922 71918

Below: NEWMARKET, SUFFOLK, HIGH STREET 1929 81958

Newmarket

Being come to Newmarket in the month of October, I had the opportunity to see the horse-races; and a great concourse of the nobility and gentry, as well from London as from all parts of England; but they were all so intent, so eager, so busy upon the sharping part of the sport, their wagers and bets, that to me they seemed just as so many horse-coursers in Smithfield, descending (the greatest of them) from their high dignity and quality, to picking one another's pockets, and biting one another as much as possible, and that with such eagerness, as that it might be said they acted without respect to faith, honour, or good manners.

DANIEL DEFOE, 'A TOUR THROUGH THE WHOLE ISLAND OF GREAT BRITAIN', 1725

STRATFORD'S streets will always be remembered for its famous son, William Shakespeare. This historically important photograph (right) shows his birthplace before its restoration, which began in 1857. Shakespeare's birthplace was really two houses, one for the family, the other where John Shakespeare, William's father, worked as a glover and wool merchant.

The restoration was directed at bringing the appearance of the property into line with the earliest known illustration of it; the buildings either side were demolished to reduce risks from fire. Since Shakespeare's day the house had gone through a number of incarnations: at one point the family home became a butcher's shop, and the other part became an inn. The restorers were lucky in that the timber framework, stone floors, cellars, and several internal walls were original early 16th-century.

By the 1890s tourists were flocking to the house, around a quarter of them Americans. Many guidebooks stated that the house contained relics 'more or less authentic' to Shakespeare. In the room where Shakespeare was said to have been born, some visitors even scratched their names on the panes of glass in the window. Among the signatures are those of Sir Walter Scott, Thomas Carlyle, Robert Browning and William Makepeace Thackeray.

STRATFORD-UPON-AVON, WARWICKSHIRE, SHAKESPEARE'S BIRTHPLACE c1850 S21601

It has been greatly – perhaps over-much – restored; but extensive repairs were absolutely necessary, and all sorts of excrescences – fungoid growths, as it were, of plaster, wood and brickwork – had to be removed. A narrow, awkward staircase leads to the upper floor, where, in a small, low room overlooking the street, he was born. It is now almost unfurnished. The walls are covered with graffiti, where clown and peer, fool and genius, shoulder one another. SHAKESPEARE'S HOUSE, VICTORIAN GUIDEBOOK c1890

STRATFORD-UPON-AVON, WARWICKSHIRE, MEMORIAL THEATRE 1922 72392P

In the 1920s punts could be hired from a couple of locations at Stratford. The weir at Lucy's Mill marked the southern limit for boating, though it was possible to go up river as far as the barrier at Charlecote Park; those wishing to pass through the barrier and continue further had first to obtain the consent of the Charlecote estate office. The girls in this photograph are relaxing opposite the theatre.

The idea for a national Shakespearian theatre in Stratford dates back to December 1820. Comedy actor Charles Mathews was in town with his new play 'Country Cousins and the Sights of London', and he invited the audience to stay on after the performance so that his proposals could be given an airing. Though his idea was well received, and a theatre opened in Chapel Lane in 1827, the proposal for a national theatre remained dormant until 1864, when the town celebrated the tercentenary of Shakespeare's birth.

The Memorial Theatre was at last built at the end of Chapel Street between 1874 and 1879 in red brick and stone. Even as late as 1906 the Baedecker Guide said of the theatre that 'time has not yet brought it into harmony with its venerable surroundings'; indeed, judging by contemporary photographs, it was too determinedly picturesque, and the end result was raw and almost aggressive. However, by 1922, the date of this photograph, the theatre had blended into its surroundings; the tower, from which the view was highly recommended, is now ivy-clad, and the nearby trees have grown to veil the building.

ETON IS famous for Eton College, today a school for the rich and privileged. When Henry VI founded Eton College in 1440, it was intended that there would be ten priests, four clerks, six choristers and a school for 25 poor scholars. Almost immediately the number of scholars was raised to 70. Today there are well over a thousand pupils. During the mid 19th century, the curriculum was widened - up to that time only the classics had been taught there. Eton College schoolboys, with their tail-coats, have been, and still are, an integral part of the daily life in the High Street. In photograph 67007p we see a number of Eton College schoolboys in top hat and tails crossing Barnes Pool Bridge. The long tail-coats are still worn today, but not the top hats. Near the entrance to the College there is an interesting street lamp, known as the Burning Bush. It was originally installed as a gas lamp in 1864, and was later converted to electricity. Because of its dangerous position in the middle of the road, it was moved to the west pavement in 1965.

If you have never been in an Eton boy's room, you do not know how snug and cosy it is. The bed folds up very neatly and takes no room, the washing apparatus and the brushes and combs are put out of sight, a large cupboard contains table-cloths and tea-things, together with such supplies of additional dainties as the pocket of the occupant can afford. The table is covered with books and adorned with flowers; the mantel-shelf has a fringe of his sister's work, and a few choice ornaments which remind him of home … This is his castle, where no one may intrude.

PICTURESQUE EUROPE c1880

Eton

ETON, BERKSHIRE, THE COLLEGE CHAPEL,
FROM BARNES POOL BRIDGE 1914 67007P

MARLBOROUGH is another town made famous by its school. In this photograph, pupils and staff pause at the magnificently Baroque entrance gates designed for Marlborough College between 1876 and 1877 by G E Street. Hidden in the shadows of the equally ornate Porter's Lodge is perhaps the porter himself. We can just glimpse C House through the trees.

Hidden from the town, but with entrances only a short distance from St Peter's Church, Marlborough College was founded in 1845. The core of the college was C House, formerly the seat of Francis, Lord Seymour, who built it in the early 18th century. He must have cleared away the remains of the former royal castle, which were still quietly decaying in the early 17th century.

In 1751 the mansion became a prestigious coaching inn named after the castle. Its reputation was legendary on the London to Bath road, with forty coaches changing horses there daily. As with so many towns, the inn suffered with the coming of the railway and trade declined, so it was fortuitous that the Reverend Charles Plater was at that time searching for suitable premises in which to start his school for the sons of impoverished clergymen. The original intake was 200 boys and staff, of which one third were the sons of laymen, who paid extra, but within 5 years it had become so popular that it was second only in size to Eton.

Marlborough

MARLBOROUGH, WILTSHIRE, THE COLLEGE 1901 47658

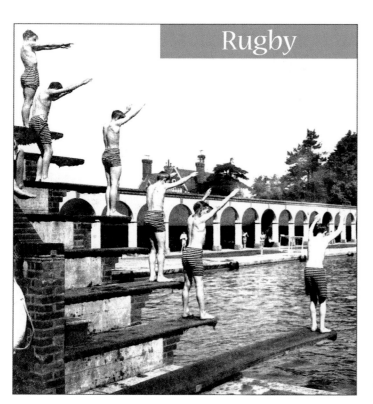

Rugby

IN 1876 the Rev Jex-Blake, Dean of Wells and ex-Headmaster of Rugby School, donated £3,000 to build a large, heated swimming pool on the Close, on the site of an old plunge-bath shed dating from 1790. These baths closed in the early 1900s, and in 1928 the baths we see in this photograph were opened off Horton Crescent. They were replaced in 1991 by the new school Sports Centre. Notice the standard school swimming trunks, known to the boys as 'bimbags'.

It was under Dr Thomas Arnold, who was headmaster from 1828 to 1842, that the face of the English public school was to change. It was his influence that led to public schools becoming places that trained character. Under his guidance, Rugby grew to become one of the country's leading public schools. Arnold became famous thanks to two books which proved influential in educational circles. They were Arthur Stanley's 'Life and Correspondence of Dr Thomas Arnold' and Thomas Hughes's 'Tom Brown's Schooldays'.

Left: RUGBY, WARWICKSHIRE, THE SCHOOL, THE OPEN AIR SWIMMING BATHS 1932 85188

Life at Rugby School had been positively dangerous in the 18th century. Dr Henry Ingles was known as 'The Black Tiger' for the severity of his rule. His headmastership is best remembered for the Great Rebellion of 1797. Dr Ingles was walking in the town when he heard pistol shots. A boy from the school, Astley, claimed that Mr Rowell, a grocer, had supplied him with gunpowder for a cork gun. Rowell denied this, and Astley was flogged as a liar. Astley, with his friends, retaliated by smashing Rowell's windows. Dr Ingles ordered that the Fifth and Sixth Forms pay for the damage. This provoked a riot in which Dr Ingles's door was blown off, windows were broken, and desks, benches and books were burned on the Close. Dr Ingles summoned help from the town. A party of recruiting soldiers and townsfolk advanced on the rioters, who took refuge on the Island (a Bronze Age tumulus on the Close, surrounded at this time by a moat complete with drawbridge). The Riot Act was read and the boys were called upon to surrender, but this was merely a diversion enabling the soldiers to wade across the moat at the rear and take the whole party prisoner.

Cheltenham

OVER THE past two centuries Cheltenham has become a byword for the excellent quality of its public school education. The buildings of the two major colleges and the several smaller schools are spread around the city and are fine examples of Victorian architecture – though not without their critics. The academic atmosphere is rather like that of a university town, and pupils from one establishment or another are a familiar sight on the city streets. Even in our modern age, Cheltenham's public schools continue to thrive, much as they have done since the boys' college was founded in 1841. Cheltenham College was originally a private concern with shareholders able to nominate potential pupils. Many of the early pupils were the sons of army officers, who intended to follow a military career after leaving school.

Apart from the clothes worn by the spectators in this evocative photograph (opposite left), this scene would look much the same today. The college still holds an annual summer cricket festival in the best public school tradition. This view from the playing fields shows the range of architectural styles adopted by the builders of the Victorian college.

Cheltenham College Museum was converted from an old racquets court in 1870 at a cost of £700. It aimed at arousing in the pupils 'an interest in the study of science and natural history'. This important collection was finally dispersed in 1976, many of the exhibits being sent to the Merseyside Museum. Early exhibits at the museum included, according to the museum catalogue, 'skins of grass snakes, some flint implements, a bandolier, a Mauser carbine, a flag, a Boer hat, three stuffed bears, two stuffed heads of elk, four cases of birds, an elephant's foot, a human skull, a grasshopper in a bottle and some Indian coins'.

Opposite: CHELTENHAM, GLOUCESTERSHIRE, THE COLLEGE PLAYING FIELDS 1907 59038P

Below: CHELTENHAM, GLOUCESTERSHIRE, THE COLLEGE MUSEUM 1907 59043

SHERBORNE, DORSET, THE KING'S SCHOOL, THE LIBRARY 1900 46075

FOR CENTURIES the town of Sherborne has been famous for its schools and especially, of course, for Sherborne School, known locally as King's. There is evidence that schooling here was in existence as early as the 12th century, and possibly as far back as the early 8th century, and the school even continued through the trials of the Reformation. In 1550 came the grant of its charter and endowment by Edward VI, from whence came its title, King Edward VI Free Grammar School, by which it was known until 1922. The school was largely centred around Sherborne Abbey, but later various buildings were acquired around the town.

This view gives us an interesting glimpse inside the school library: row upon row of orderly volumes line the shelves, which are arranged in bays, with the side windows providing plenty of light for reading and studying. The volume at the extreme right lying on its side is a facsimile of John Milton's minor poems.

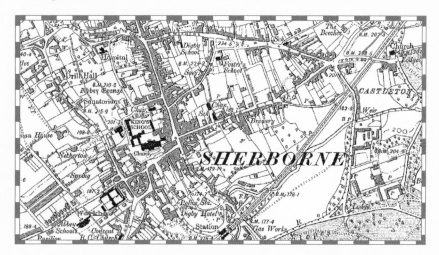

The shock of the new

THE TWO world wars destroyed great swathes of our towns. London's streets in particular suffered very badly during the Second World War, and so did many port towns and industrial towns. Hundreds of thousands of people needed to be rehoused, so in 1946 the New Towns Act was passed, and towns like Basildon and Harlow were created almost from scratch. In the 1950s and 60s came the trend for wholesale redevelopment of our towns, which often meant the destruction of the kind of historical building that would be conserved today. This era also saw the coming of the housing estate and the tower block.

Basildon

EAST LONDON suffered badly during the bombing raids of the Second World War. 20,000 people lost their homes in East and West Ham alone. Something had to be done for them: new starts, and – if necessary – new towns. The New Towns Act was passed in 1946, and the search began for suitable locations, including Stevenage, Crawley, Harlow, and Basildon.

At Basildon, the Development Corporation spent the next 37 years building homes for 33,600 people. The new town could not be built overnight. With an original target of 50,000 people living in 15 self-contained 'neighbourhoods', it would take time. It was not until 1986 that the Development Corporation was disbanded.

An area between Laindon and Pitsea, not far from the old village of Basildon, had been selected as the centre of the New Town. But how could business and industry be attracted to an as-yet non-existent town? How could the freeholders be integrated with the incoming population? The town centre was constructed on a plateau. The state of the art market place opened on 6 September 1958. It was typical of the stark angularity favoured by architects of the period, intent on constructing a 'brave new world'. The caravan on the left of B438040T is the Basildon School of Motoring's mobile office; the one on the right is a fish stall, offering skate, crabs, live eels and 'new season Scotch kippers – full of oil'. The ladies' calf-length, wide-collared coats are typical of the era.

Work on the town centre had begun in 1956. Again, as we can see from B438066, a somewhat bleak angularity was the order of the day. The shops at Laindon, Vange and Pitsea – the old centres – tended to suffer as new business was drawn into the precinct. In the 1930s, Laindon High Road had consisted of 120 shops; only one of the old buildings now remains.

Basildon's original target was that 16,000 people should be employed on its industrial estates. Built on the site of the Old Rectory, the Basildon tractor plant was finally completed on 20 February 1964. It covered 60 acres of the 100-acre site, and had 1,360,000 square feet of buildings. Its most recognisable feature was its distinctive 125ft-high water tower holding 600,000 gallons (seen on the right of photograph B438031); nicknamed 'the onion', it is still regarded as a local landmark. The tractor plant was followed into the town by the Ford Engineering Research Centre at Dunton. When it was taken over by the New Holland Machinery Company in 1994, the plant had manufactured 1,347,000 tractors.

Trapped in nowhere land?

Several of the sites earmarked for development were saved by conservationists, much to their credit. There were mistakes, naturally. The wholesale demolition of many of the area's ancient houses and farms now seems scandalous. There were human problems, too, such as the 'Basildon blues' that afflicted some of the new settlers when they found themselves on half-built housing estates in the middle of nowhere. Where were the shops? The entertainments? Why did this New Town have no hospital or central railway station?

Left: BASILDON, ESSEX, MARKET PLACE 1961 B438040T

Top: BASILDON, ESSEX, THE VIEW FROM FREEDOM HOUSE c1965 B438066

Above: BASILDON, ESSEX, THE INDUSTRIAL ESTATE c1965 B438031

CORBY, NORTHAMPTONSHIRE, THE SHOPPING CENTRE AND THE STRATHCLYDE HOTEL c1960   C337123

IT IS remarkable that Corby suffered relatively little damage during World War II, despite its steelworks being a strategic target for enemy aircraft. The post-war years saw expansion of the town, and a demand for even more housing and services. In 1950 another milestone in Corby's development took place with the town being granted New Town status under the 1946 New Towns Act.

These views date from the middle of the 20th century at the height of Corby's prosperity; at this time the town was undergoing its post-war outward expansion. Dominating the scene in C337123 is the three-star, 41-bedroomed Strathclyde Hotel, a substantial building standing on a podium, which provided welcome accommodation for business visitors to the town. It no longer functions as a hotel; now called Grosvenor House, it is occupied by Corby Borough Council. The photograph was taken from the roof of the newly-opened theatre complex.

Sited on the Earlstrees Industrial Estate to the north of the town, the Golden Wonder Crisp Factory (C337136) occupied a vast area – 266,000 sq ft. It was destroyed by fire in 1988, whereupon the business was transferred to nearby Princewood Road. Only the distinctive brick pillars at the entrance to the forecourt remain, and the site is now occupied by TNT.

The Phoenix (C337103) was one of sixteen new public houses built to serve the estates of Corby. Although the pub pre-dates the closure of the steel works and its traumatic effect on the town, the name symbolises Corby's nadir and subsequent recovery.

Left: CORBY,
NORTHAMPTONSHIRE,
MARKET SQUARE c1965
C337154

Below left: CORBY,
NORTHAMPTONSHIRE,
THE GOLDEN WONDER
CRISP FACTORY c1965
C337136

Above: CORBY, NORTHAMPTONSHIRE, CORPORATION STREET c1965 C337060T

Below: CORBY, NORTHAMPTONSHIRE, THE PHOENIX, BEANFIELD ROAD c1965 C337103

From disaster to new prosperity

*The nationalisation of the iron and steel industry in July 1967 led to Stewarts &
Lloyds becoming part of the newly-formed British Steel Corporation, but in 1979,
following a Government White Paper, Corby found itself in a similar disastrous
situation to the one it had experienced with the weaving industry slump in
the previous century: the closure of the steel works. Mass redundancies took
place, and a general mood of despondency prevailed. Yet the town refused to
be beaten – it had bounced back before, and it would do so again in the coming
months. The EEC provided funds, and the town received Assisted Area status,
and later, acceptance into the Enterprise Zone scheme in 1981. Hundreds of
new jobs were created as other industrial companies came to Corby, and in
1995, Corby gained a major advantage with Eurohub, Britain's first operational
road and rail interchange, being set up in the south-east of the town.*

Harlow

HARLOW was another of the new towns begun in the 1940s to house some of the bombed-out population of London. In 1946 Sir Frederick Gibberd was appointed to design Harlow New Town by the Development Corporation. Harlow was chosen because of its good position, good communications, and quality of landscape. Plans for the new town centre were simple. There was a rectangular layout, with the shops in the middle, and the bus terminus along one side. The market square was at one end, and the library and civic square at the other, and there was a walkway to the Bus Terminus opposite West Walk.

By 1956 the town centre had started trading. National multiples such as Boots, Marks & Spencers, Sainsbury's, the Co-op, Dolcis, WH Smith and many more (H22083), attracted people from surrounding villages and towns as well as all the young families in Harlow New Town. Note the many prams and push-chairs parked outside the shops; they were a typical sight in Harlow, leading to its nickname 'Pram Town'. One of the busiest shops in Broad Walk was Bellmans, selling wool and patterns for babies and young children.

The new houses were to be allocated only to people working in Harlow, preferably those with required skills, with 10% of the houses to be built for sale. Harlow was to consist of several neighbourhood clusters, each with its own centre containing a shopping area, a community centre, a school, and a church. Each of the thirteen neighbourhoods was to be individually designed, with houses suitable for all ages and circumstances. Some of the designs were very advanced for their time, and they have since become very popular. There was an emphasis on quality, both in the design and the materials. Sharpecroft (H22034) was started in 1955 and finished one year later.

A decision was taken that the village of Harlow should be known as Old Harlow and be left as it was, and that the new town of Harlow should be built on the old hamlets of Latton, Little Parndon, Great Parndon and Burnt Mill. Wherever possible, the old names of people and places were to be used, and ancient tracks, lanes and bridleways between the hamlets would be kept to link neighbourhood clusters in the New Town, providing safe and easy ways to cycle or walk to work or the shops. The natural landscape was to be kept as linear parks, so that everyone was within walking distance of the countryside. Harlow will always be protected from urban sprawl by Epping Forest, Queen Victoria's gift to the people of East London.

Above left: HARLOW, ESSEX, BROAD WALK c1960 H22083

Below: HARLOW, ESSEX, SHARPECROFT c1955 H22034

Tiverton

THESE TWO photographs are a fascinating and vivid example of the kind of picturesque streets and cottages (albeit inconvenient and unsanitary) that were swept away all over Britain in the post-war years and of the streets of solidly built council houses that replaced them.

Much of Tiverton before the middle of the 20th century would have been what we today would consider to be a slum. The cramped and squalid living conditions undoubtedly contributed to the ease with which fires took hold, as they also did to the spread of disease – it has been reported that a 'pestilence' added to the misery of the townsfolk during the 18th century. Fire was a regular, constant threat. There were significant conflagrations in 1762, 1785 and 1788, and in 1741 Tiverton suffered an epidemic of what was called 'spotted fever' which accounted for over 600 lives.

These houses in the Little Silver area of town at the lower end of St Andrew Street would be worth a fortune today (69893P). They were demolished after the last war when slum clearance was the watchword. Restoration was eschewed: down everything came. The post-war years saw Tiverton go through something of a revival. Over a 25-year period the slums were torn down and replaced with around 500 new council houses. The ones we see in T55015 are The Walronds, off Exeter Road.

Above left: TIVERTON, DEVON, OLD COTTAGES, LITTLE SILVER 1920   69893P

Below left: TIVERTON, DEVON, THE NEW COUNCIL HOUSES c1955   T55015

Scunthorpe

ONE RESULT of the success of the iron and steel industry in this area in the 19th century was that five villages gradually joined together to form the town which is now called Scunthorpe. One of these villages was Crosby. It expanded rapidly in the early 20th century after new housing was built for the workforce of Lysaght's steelworks between 1910 and 1912, and as we can see from this photograph, a great deal of new housing was built in the 1960s. It seems that the planners of these streets did their best to keep cars and people separate – the low blocks of flats are arranged around 'greens' with footpaths, and bollards stop the cars impinging on the greens.

The tower blocks in the background of S78112 were built using the Bison wall frame system. This was the same system that was used to build the Ronan Point tower block in London that so spectacularly collapsed in 1968, killing five people. After the disaster, the flats in Scunthorpe were inspected, and judged to be structurally sound. However, in 1983 the National Association of Bison Tenants petitioned Scunthorpe Borough Council to demolish the flats owing to fears for their safety. In response, the council said that despite some problems with rain leaking through the roofs, the flats were safe. In the 1990s the flats were refurbished.

Opposite: SCUNTHORPE, LINCOLNSHIRE, CROSBY FLATS c1966 S78112

Banbury

BANBURY, OXFORDSHIRE, MOLD CRESCENT c1960   B13086

BUILT ON a gracefully curving street with wide pavements and plenty of patches of grass, each with its garden, these semis must have seemed a vast improvement on cramped cottages. From the 1930s onwards, country towns were expanding, and Banbury was no exception.

In the Neithrop area on the edge of Bretch Hill council housing was set down alongside inter-war properties constructed by R W Messenger. He had advertised the Orchard Way area as part of drier and healthier Banbury where you could secure your home for as little as £5 down payment. Mold Crescent was an offshoot of Orchard Way, which stretched across the unfinished Neithrop housing estate. These houses were probably both cheap and quick to build: the walls are pre-fabricated units, and it costs less to construct a roof than a wall – hence the mansard-style upper storeys.

AYLESBURY is another example of an expanding country town. Here, mainly after 1870, speculators built housing estates beyond the old town centre for the first time – they first had to drain the marshy ground. After World War I Aylesbury began developing along the arterial routes into the town. Along the Tring Road the late 19th century saw the arrival of the factories and cemetery, and also housing developments such as the Edwardian Queen's Park or the 1890s Victoria Park. This took development as far east as the old main road which had turned south to Walton, now marked by King Edwards's Avenue. From the 1920s speculative semi-detached and detached villas sprang up further east: this is a typical post-war example. Again, these houses would probably have been cheap to build, but each has its front garden and boundary wall.

Right: AYLESBURY, BUCKINGHAMSHIRE, NARBETH DRIVE c1965 A84068

Aylesbury

Market stall to chain store

SHOPS BRING character and life to a street, and what varied characters they have. Shops probably began as little more than stalls open to the street, and in this chapter we will see an old-fashioned open-fronted butcher's. We will see tiny shops in ancient premises, and vast Victorian emporiums. Exuberant window dressing, sign writing and advertising signs are well to the fore. Victorian and Edwardian streets were rich in individually owned shops, but by the end of the 19th century chain stores such as Boots, Woolworth's and the Co-op were coming to the town centre. This chapter also shows examples of typical suburban parades and an archetypal corner shop.

Above: KNARESBOROUGH, YORKSHIRE, MARKET DAY 1921 71687T

Knaresborough

THE ANTIQUE-LETTERED signboard over the shop announces that it is 'The Oldest Chymist's Shop in England. Established 1720'. It has had over two hundred and fifty years of dispensing medicines to the people of Knaresborough.

In the early 20th century, when these photographs were taken, the apothecary was Mr Lawrence. His family had been selling patent liniments and corn eradicators in this picturesque Yorkshire town for two generations. Inside, we can see the various pestles and mortars in which he ground his potions and medicines. The giant pestle with its marble mortar was turned by dogs in a cage until 1840. Behind is Mr Lawrence's 'bleeding couch', where he pulled teeth – possibly a little too public an exhibition for modern tastes. Today we prefer to suffer in private. Many of the glass-stoppered drug bottles on the shelves and the spectacular bottle tree on the counter have been preserved.

Lawrence's was noted by the discerning for its Knaresborough Old English Lavender Water, which was sold in the fancy cut-glass bottles on the counter on the right. The special lavender water is still a much sought-after gift item, packaged in wicker-covered bottles. On the counters and shelves are early Box Brownie cameras, boxes of Colgate dental cream, oatmeal soap, aromatic pine inhalations, numerous packets of pills, potions and cures, retorts, scales and weights, and shaving brushes for gentlemen. Mr Lawrence's leech jar has been preserved. The fine old shop front remains almost unchanged, and Mr Lawrence's brass plate is still in position. Mrs Dorothy Merrin ran the shop until recently and did a brisk trade in his patent Pino-Creo Inhalent and Corn and Wart Eradicator.

Left: KNARESBOROUGH, YORKSHIRE, THE OLD CHEMIST'S SHOP INTERIOR 1914 67279

Above: KNARESBOROUGH, YORKSHIRE, THE OLD CHEMIST'S SHOP 1911 63543

PAIGNTON, DEVON, CHURCH STREET 1912 64719

CHURCH STREET in Paignton had a good selection of shops. The projecting property with the Georgian sash windows was Mrs Martin's Drapery, long since lost to road widening. Opposite is the New London Inn (1766). Next door to Macdonald the baker (right) are Evans Engineers, who successfully drained the marshes in 1867. Pook Bros, family butchers, are still trading as butchers did in the days of market shambles. There is no glass window and rabbits and carcases are hanging from hooks in the open air. The shop was built on the site of the old Crown and Anchor Inn. The courthouse and the magistrates' room were above, and so too almost certainly was Paignton's first theatre!

Church Street (64719), originally Fore Street (the Anglo-Saxon name), was known in the 18th century as Culverhay. The name almost certainly refers to pigeons. Certainly, behind the present day Coach House Inn (New London Inn) there is a 16th-century pigeon-house. However, it has also been suggested that the word Culverhay possibly relates to a Christian cross once situated at the top of Church Street, or even to the huge culverts the bishops used to redirect the Westerland stream in the 13th century, which are still buried beneath the street. But the most likely definition is a dove enclosure or pigeon loft. Near the pigeon house was a skittle alley and possibly a bear pit.

LOOKING AT this photograph of Shepton Mallet (44843, right), it is hard not to believe that shopping used to be a far richer experience than it is now. It was not enough to cram the shop windows with wares – clothes and shoes are bursting out of the shops and hang outside too. Notice the wonderfully ornate signwriting on the extreme left pointing the way to the drapery, millinery and readymade clothing departments; men's coats surround the door. The 'Dairy Utensil Manufactory' next door advertises itself with a huge kettle for a shop sign. Beyond it, Frisby's is an early example of a boot and shoe chain store. The well-dressed passers-by are good advertisements for the outfitters – note the children's smart knickerbockers suits and Eton collars, and the beautiful hats worn by the woman on the left and the little girl on the right. A postman, complete with bulging sack, poses in the centre.

Shepton Mallet

Banbury

THE ROBINS BROS ironmongery business in Banbury had been located on the corner with Butchers Row since Victorian times. It was housed in a fine late 15th-century timber-framed building, stuccoed at this time, with a fragment of arcaded pargetting visible along the side. Above the shop numerous rooms and passageways were indicative of extensive family accommodation. The windows are packed with goods, and on the pavement are more wares, including a good selection of lawn mowers.

The taller property beside Robins's shop was built in the 1850s as one of two rival Corn Exchanges both opened on the same day in 1857; the other was in Cornhill in the north-western corner of the market place. This building, known as the Central Exchange, was not given its main front until around 1880. The curious fact is that until 1860 the façade could not be seen because of the presence of an earlier town hall at that end of the Market Place.

Above: BANBURY, OXFORDSHIRE, MARKET PLACE, OLD HOUSES 1922 72090P

Barmouth

THIS VIEW shows a classic stationer's shop during the Edwardian era. The display of stock cascades over the frontage – there are local prints and postcards, and maps for the walker and tourist. It is also a circulating library, offering the latest novels and bestsellers to discerning visitors in exchange for a small lending fee.

The well-known holiday resort of Barmouth, which has an excellent sandy beach, stands on the west coast of Wales at the mouth of the Mawddach estuary. Both Darwin and Ruskin enjoyed stays here. The old harbour stands on the shores of the Mawddach estuary, and was formerly of some importance. The old town clings to the steep hillside. Nearby, the viewpoint of Dinas Oleu was the National Trust's first property.

Left: BARMOUTH, GWYNEDD, HIGH STREET 1908 60215T

Padstow

IN 1906 you couldn't get much further away from Fleet Street than the remote Cornish fishing village of Padstow. Yet what do we see clipped to the end of Williams the Stationers' window? A display of the latest comics, with the ink hardly dry.

There are names here to bring back the memories: 'Puck', 'Home Chat', 'Titbits', 'Forget-Me-Not' ...... all waiting to be carried back to the fishermen's cottages, and then passed around and swopped month after month.

Proper books were usually out of reach of most children's pockets: many cost up to 6/-, a third of the working man's weekly wage. It's no wonder that 'penny stinkers' and 'penny dreadfuls' grew so popular.

At the foot of the magazine tree you can see a copy of 'Puck', packed with 'jokes and pictures for the home'. It ran from 1904 up to 1940. Above it is a woman's magazine, 'Handy', and above this 'Photo Bits'.

Behind is an issue of the notorious 'Ally Sloper's Half Holiday', which ever since its beginnings in 1884 had encouraged a 'Dennis the Menace' mentality in children all over the country.

Social critics thought these comics nasty and socially disruptive, believing that they led children into theft and lives of crime. Some comics were doubtless lacking in moral uplift, but much of the criticism was little more than a religious backlash.

PADSTOW, CORNWALL, MARKET PLACE 1906 56268

Oakham

OAKHAM, RUTLAND, MARKET PLACE 1932 85151XT

OAKHAM is the county town of England's smallest traditional county, Rutland. This excellent view has Castle Lane to the right, with J E Smith on the corner selling all manner of goods from Players, Wills Star and Gold Flake to local view postcards, wooden hoops, newspapers, magazines and toys. Next door, F W Hart the grocer is still in business – note the errand boy's bike outside. Some years later Glaziers and Harts moved into the High Street. This whole scene is a rich jumble of posters, placards, and shop wares – not forgetting the parked delivery van.

Song of the birds, rhythm of the anvil

The Ellingworth family were well-known in Oakham; they were music dealers and photographers and ran a chemist's shop. Dulcie Ellingworth, one of the daughters, interviewed by A R Traylen in the 1970s, gave a very evocative picture of the old Oakham. 'We crossed and re-crossed the road to each other's homes to our hearts content, not having to fear traffic, save for a few horses'. The sounds of the day were 'the song of the birds, the rhythm of the anvil at the blacksmith's shop next door and the Angelus'. She said there was never a need to lock the doors, and spoke of the pageantry when the judge came for the Assizes at the castle. The May Fair, the Flower Show, and the Horse Show were all important celebrations. The opening up of the big houses or hunting boxes for the hunting season was a time of activity and evening entertainments; after this, Oakham 'settled down to its summer siesta'.

East Grinstead

ACCORDING TO the 1965 edition of 'East Grinstead – The Official Guide', the High Street has a distinct charm of its own, containing Tudor and Jacobean buildings, the 'cathedral -like' parish church and the 'peerless' Sackville College. The street provides a shopping centre 'in which may be found the dignity of a past age'. Edwin Tooth's stationer's shop was located in the 15th-century Tudor House at Nos 22-24. It sold books and art materials too. On display inside Tooth's are some children's books including 'A Nursery Alphabet', 'Animal Friends', 'A Merry Heart' and 'Neddy'. There are also art materials; stationery; and a fine range of local view cards, all by Francis Frith & Co. Recognisable views include the High Street, Sackville College, the Dorset Arms and Brambletye Castle.

    East Grinstead is a North Sussex town founded in the 13th century. The name itself is even older, referring to an area known as 'grenestede', meaning a clearing in the forest or green place. In the 11th century, then, the town was Grenestede, but by the 13th century it had become 'Estgrenested', to distinguish it from West Grinstead, a place south of Horsham.

'Dear Auntie Ada, Visiting East Grinstead. Nice town, good hotel. Wish you were here!'

The first photographs of the town were taken in 1855 by Joseph Cundall and Philip De La Motte. By the 1860s, one or two locally-based photographers had set up shop specialising in portraits and street scenes. Francis Frith & Co seems to have been the first national postcard-producing firm to photograph the town in 1890, when the population of East Grinstead was just 5,500. After 1902, the photographic postcard industry really took off in popularity, and coutrywide people were sending friends cards saying 'Wish you were here'. The national firms vied with local publishers for sales, and from 1902 to 1914, there was picture postcard mania and almost any subject could be, and frequently was, made into a postcard. After the First World War, when it cost one penny to send a card, their popularity declined somewhat, but production of views of East Grinstead continued unabated. Frith & Co photographers visited the town on 18 separate occasions from 1890 to 1937, focussing mainly on the High Street and London Road.

THE LIVELIHOOD of the small shopkeeper – such as the one-man baker, shoe repairer or tobacconist – was always precarious. Life was a constant battle to survive. He was in direct competition with the market stalls, and unlike the market traders he had considerable fixed costs. He had invested in a sizeable stock for which he had to pay cash. And there was the rent of the shop premises to pay. In most cases he was open for long hours and so had to employ extra staff to cope.

He was increasingly in competition with the powerful chain stores, who were offering goods and services at low prices – but strictly for cash. Like most other small shopkeepers he often had to offer credit, which reduced his working margins still more, and consequently he had to write off a number of bad debts.

One way the small man coped was by constant innovation and expansion. Here in Hounslow, we see that Mr West the tobacconist and confectioner is also a barber and shaving saloon. This must have brought a good number of extra customers into the shop to buy his lemonade, chocolate and cigarettes.

It was hard to expand a small shop beyond a certain point. It required capital and the will to invest and take a risk. So it is hardly surprising that many small shopkeepers shied away from the fight, and stayed uneasily on the fringes, unable to buy goods at advantageous prices from wholesalers or offer an attractive enough product range to potential clients.

Hounslow

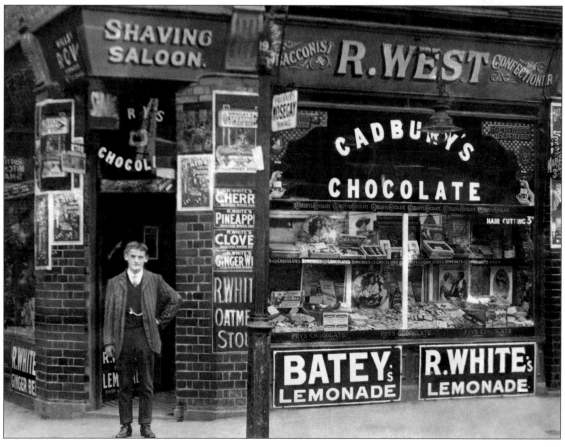

Opposite: EAST GRINSTEAD, SUSSEX, TOOTH'S SHOP, INTERIOR 1927 79594

Above: EAST GRINSTEAD, SUSSEX, HIGH STREET 1921 70619

HOUNSLOW, GREATER LONDON, HANWORTH ROAD 1910 H162301

Southwold

THIS SHOP in Southwold shows the resourcefulness of the Victorian shopkeeper. Not only is he a barber, but he offers the latest novels through a library service, and what's more he is a Frith postcard stockist. The window display shows tea sets and china, and outside there are racquets, balls, and walking sticks. Note too the flagpoles. This retailer is clearly capable of raising the flags to advertise the amazing variety of his wares.

Is there a small town in England more deserving of the attentions of the discerning explorer? Remarkable vistas await around each corner, and civilised greens abound, random dabs of green paint on an already colourful palette.

Left: SOUTHWOLD, SUFFOLK, HIGH STREET 1896
38628xp

Northwich

NORTHWICH is a town that has quite literally, as well as metaphorically, been built upon salt, with thick rock salt seams and natural brine streams underlying much of the land in the region. Salt has always been a valuable and vital commodity, and it has been panned and mined here since Roman times, bringing wealth to the town.

This 17th-century building stands at the bottom of Winnington Hill. At this time this shop was Jo Allman's second-hand shop. Its floors were soil tamped down – no tiles or floorboards – and it was full of all manner of bric-a-brac, with many of the more 'weather proof' items being stored on the pavement. Stories abound from that time of people alighting on valuable items amongst the piles of jumble. It looks as if the old thatched roof has been covered with a bitumen sheet or a tarpaulin. Soon after this picture was taken, the Council made Jo Allman leave, as they considered the house unfit for human habitation. The house next door was reputed to have been built by the navvies who had constructed the canal.

Left: NORTHWICH, CHESHIRE, THE OLD CURIOSITY SHOP c1950   N43002

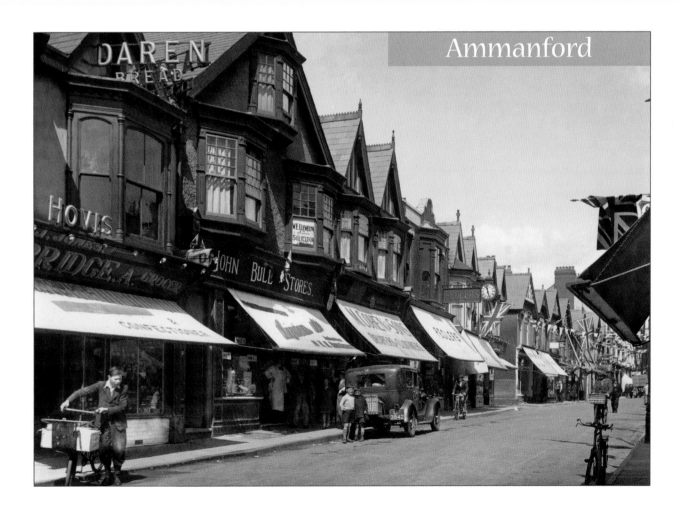

Ammanford

THE STEEP roofs and gables overlook a hive of activity in this street scene. The mass of Union Jacks indicates a royal celebration: this was for the accession of George VI, who was crowned in 1937. In the days before TV advertising, every shop blind played its part in announcing the shop

Photo courtesy of: Torridge Auctions

proprietor and his speciality. 'Service with a smile' is evident as the delivery boy sets off on his delivery bike from the premises of Mr Bridge. Above Mr Bridge's shop are the gilded signs of two of the great bread brands of the era – Hovis and Daren.

To the right is John Bull Stores, which would appear to be a branch of the chain store Lipton's – the Lipton logo is painted on the awning. Like Francis Frith, Thomas Lipton (1850-1931) became a millionaire at an early age – and by selling groceries too. As a teenager he went to America as a stowaway, and worked in a grocery store; he later returned to his native Glasgow, where he set himself up as a grocer, and soon had branches all over Britain. He specialised in quality teas. At his death, he left his considerable wealth to the city of Glasgow.

Left: AMMANFORD, DYFED, QUAY STREET 1937   87811

SEVERAL of these lovely old buildings remain, though the shop fronts have changed. This part of Fore Street in Taunton is now a pedestrian precinct with trees, flowerbeds and benches lining the side of the road where the Frith photographer would have stood to take this picture.

F C Halliday's antique shop Odds and Ends has a display of giant teapots and vases sitting above the shop window. The ornate timbered building is the oldest in Taunton, its Elizabethan frontage dating back to 1578. The passage on the left now leads to a shopping precinct. Today, Lewis & Lewis's frontage has been improved – the long signboard obscuring the upper storey has been removed. The Stores building (far right) was demolished and replaced by a modern building now housing a shoe shop. Its signage is now considerably more discreet!

TAUNTON, SOMERSET, FORE STREET, OLD HOUSES 1912   64506

Taunton

THE MARKET and racing town of Wetherby lies on the A1 between York and Harrogate. Ward & Sons were probably blacksmiths before they diversified into cars. They were established in 1868. At the time of this photograph they are the AA agent for Wetherby, repairing vehicles and selling cycle and motor tyres and Kodak film.

Many a blacksmith adapted his skills to become a motor mechanic. Before the days of the internal combustion engine, the horse was the universal method of transport, and cart and carriage horses, plough teams, hunters, hacks and cab horses all needed re-shoeing every few weeks. In addition, the smith would make and mend tools and farm vehicles and kettles and pots, and many a smith had wheelwright's skills too. But with the advent of the car, the smith had to adapt to survive. He learned the skills of motor vehicle repair, and swapped his hammers and bellows for acetylene welding equipment, and his forge for petrol pumps.

WETHERBY, YORKSHIRE, NORTH STREET 1909   61731

KETTERING, NORTHAMPTONSHIRE, NEWLAND STREET 1922   72235

THE NORTHAMPTON RUBBER CO'S shop (left of photograph 72235) advertises itself as a rubber merchant. Hanging from the display are rubber hosepipes. However, like so many businesses, they felt the need to diversify, and are advertising themselves as the 'finest house in the county for all sports'. In the window are tennis racquets along with cricket bats, pads and stumps. They also sold motorcycle tyres and tubes and waterproof capes. Ernest Woodcock's shop, on the right, extended down Montagu Street and was described as Kettering's leading department store for fashions, fabrics, furnishings, furniture and household linens. They were also funeral directors.

This junction of Newland Street with Gold Street, Silver Street and Montagu Street was sometimes busy enough to have policemen on point duty, as we can see. By the post-war period traffic had increased, so traffic lights were installed.

HARROW-ON-THE-HILL, GREATER LONDON, STATION ROAD 1914   66820X

Harrow-on-the-Hill

HERE WE SEE the beginnings of a familiar retail pattern: multi-nationals are taking over the high street (above). On the left is Home & Colonial, which by this date had several hundred branches. Their pricing policy was aggressive: signs in the window proclaim '2d in the shilling returned'. Two doors along is Boots, 'the largest chemist in the world'.

Note the parked delivery bicycle, the handcart, and the more capacious delivery tricycle: at this date, the streets are not choked by vans and lorries, and the smiling shop assistants are not choked by petrol fumes!

King's Lynn

CASH & CO (centre) supplied the footwear worn by the twin boys in the foreground. Trenowath Bros, general drapers (left), diversified into cab making, upholstery and removals because they could not compete with the early department store Jermyn & Perry. Alfred Jermyn (later Sir Alfred) established his first business in 1872, and was later joined by the draper Perry. The shop was burnt down in 1884 when an assistant set fire to the Christmas decorations: the fire took hold because the Lynn fire engine had broken down. There was another fire in 1897, started by a careless person lighting the 220 gas jets on Boxing Day. The store in the picture, rebuilt from the ashes, was in every respect well ahead of all its opposition.

After removing his sister from his cart, the boy will collect the horse droppings from this very respectable street.

Right: KING'S LYNN, NORFOLK, HIGH STREET 1908   60023T

Northampton

The Co-op principles

The principles of the Rochdale Pioneers, which are still the basis of all Co-ops today, were:

♦ *Open and voluntary membership*
♦ *Democratic control (one member, one vote)*
♦ *Fixed and limited interest on share capital*
♦ *A surplus allocated in proportion to members' purchases (the dividend)*
♦ *Provision for education*
♦ *Co-operation amongst co-operatives*
♦ *Political and religious neutrality*
♦ *No credit*

The Toad Lane shop flourished, and Co-op shops were opened all over the country, followed by wholesale groups (the CWS) and by Co-op banks and insurance firms. By the end of the 19th century there were over 1,000 retail Co-op societies in the UK.

BEDWAS, MID GLAMORGAN, NEWPORT ROAD c1960 B475019

NOTE THE rather fine and elaborate late 19th-century facade of the Northampton Co-operative Society store, which was replaced in 1938 by an Art Deco building – it still survives.

The UK Co-operative Movement is simply 'the Co-op' for most of us. The Co-op has its roots in the early 19th century, when the Industrial Revolution meant the exploitation of many workers and their families. The provision of shops did not keep up with the growth in population, so that existing shops had a monopoly; if the shopkeeper was unscrupulous, he might adulterate his products or charge huge prices.

But at the same time, political and social reform and the growth of the trade unions gave people the idea of acting collectively. The co-op shop where the Movement began opened in 1844 at Toad Lane, Rochdale; the 28 founders are known as the Rochdale Pioneers. They sold basic grocery items, treated their customers honestly, and made their customers members who shared in the profits, pooling resources and ensuring that everyone benefited.

Above left: NORTHAMPTON, NORTHAMPTONSHIRE, ABINGTON STREET, 1922 72171T

Godalming

GODALMING'S STREETS have been described as 'tortously twisting and narrow'. A more accurate description of the High Street is 'slightly sinuous'. It runs through the centre of the town like a spine, on a line which has evolved rather than been designed. The original line may have been a track first trodden over 1,400 years ago. Adequate for pedestrians and even horse-drawn vehicles, the street is certainly narrow, and was soon found woefully deficient when mass motor traffic arrived. This was part of the main road from London to Portsmouth, and with no rear access for most of the shops and no car parking to one side of the street, congestion was soon a problem. An early expedient was to restrict parking to one side of the street on even-numbered dates and the other side on odd dates.

The smaller of the two buildings occupied by Timothy Whites, on the left, was the scene of a double murder in 1817, when one night George Chennell and William Chalcraft, after drinking, returned to Chennell's father's home and bludgeoned the old man and his housekeeper to death, seeking more money for drink. They were publicly hanged on the Lammas Land.

Left: GODALMING, SURREY, HIGH STREET c1955 G23032

Above: GODALMING, SURREY, CHURCH STREET 1906 57050T

A POLICE OFFICER keeps a close eye on traffic at the foot of Preston Street (right), with the International Stores displaying its selection of groceries in its corner window, and the printers and stationer's shop of Voile & Roberson with its ornately carved entrance on the adjacent corner. Further along on the left is the hanging sign of the Prince Albert public house.

International Stores were another early chain with a branch in most towns in the south of England. Initially known as the International Tea Company, the firm was founded in 1878 by Hudson Kearly (he was later to become Viscount Devonport) and G A Tonge; their business plan was to sell tea direct to customers rather than to wholesalers. International Stores was a member of the FT30 index of leading companies until 1947.

Right: FAVERSHAM, KENT, PRESTON STREET c1955 F13019T

Faversham

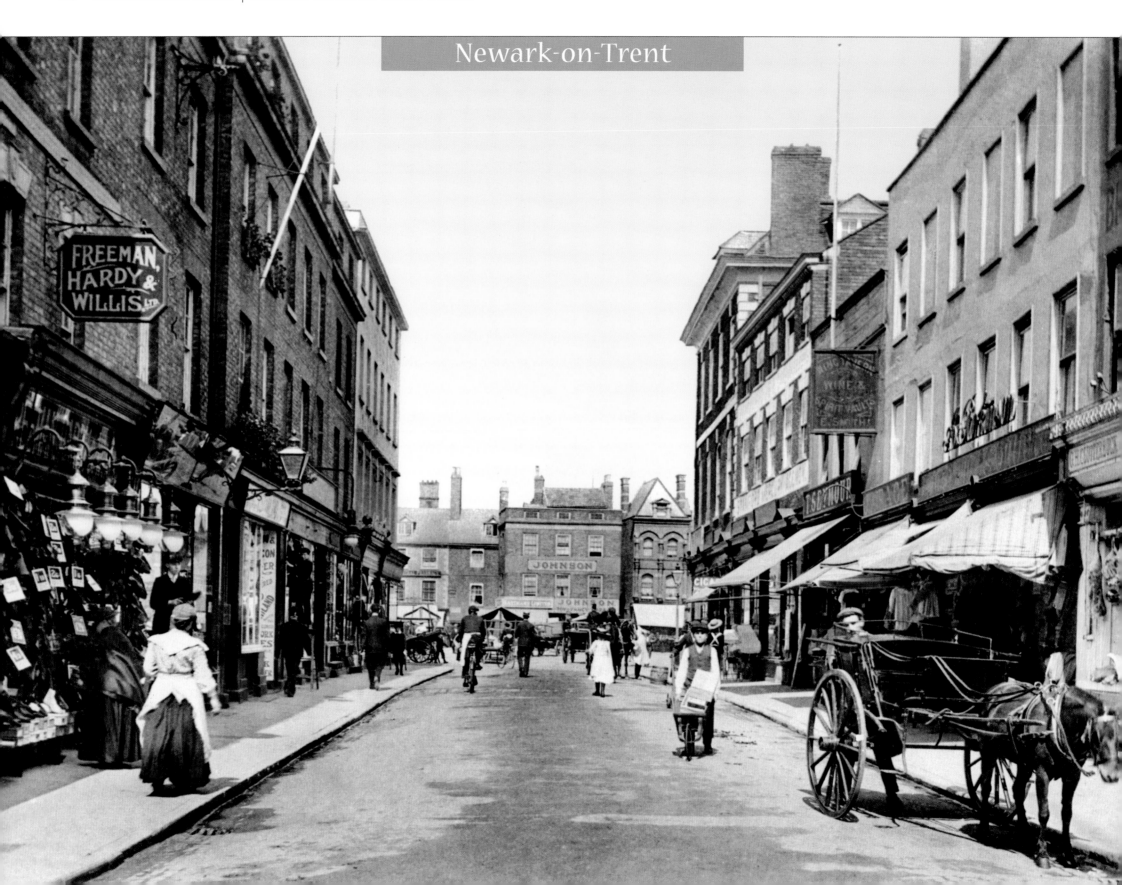

Newark-on-Trent

NEWARK'S GOLDEN AGE was during the Middle Ages, when it was a serious rival to Nottingham. The town grew rich on sheep and wool, especially during the reign of Edward III, who actively encouraged Flemish weavers and merchants to settle in England. Flemish immigration and the introduction of the spinning wheel into more rural areas were both factors in the significant increase in cloth woven in England. From Newark wool and cloth were exported to the Low Countries by way of Boston and Hull. Wool continued to play an important role in the commercial success of Newark, but there were other industries such as tanning, brewing and milling.

Clevedon

WH SMITH, a familiar presence on high streets and railway stations all over Britain, has its origins in 1790, when William Smith and Henry Everett joined forces to provide a newsagency service. The partnership ended when Henry Everett decided that he wanted to provide the service overseas, so in 1792 Henry Walton Smith and his wife established a newsvendor business in London. Their business was continued by their son William Henry, and in 1846 the firm became WH Smith & Son when his son, also William Henry, joined him. The coming of the railways helped the firm in their distribution of newspapers and magazines, and they opened newsstands on railway stations. The business was handed down through the generations, becoming a limited company in 1928, until the last family member left in 1996.

An early boot and shoe chainstore

Freeman, Hardy & Willis (seen in 56492t) must have been one of the earliest high street chains – the firm was established in 1875 – and there was a branch in large and small towns alike all over Britain. They appear to have been early exponents of the corporate image, both in the style of lettering used on their signs and in the way their premises were fitted out. Many feature the same design of outside lighting. In the 20th century Charles Clore bought the company to join his British Shoe Corporation empire based in Leicester, long a shoe-making town; the company's name became simply Freeman Hardy Willis to allow larger lettering on the shop signs.

Opposite left: NEWARK-ON-TRENT, NOTTINGHAMSHIRE, BRIDGE STREET 1906 56492T

CLEVEDON, SOMERSET, WH SMITH & SON 1925 77665X

A CLASSIC FORD CAR stands on the left beside Woolworth's. 'I believe that a good penny and sixpence store, run by a live Yankee, would be a sensation here'. So said Frank Woolworth on his arrival in Liverpool in 1890 – he had travelled to England to buy china for the American Woolworth's. On this buying trip he met a young clerk, William Lawrence Stephenson, who so impressed him that he offered him the directorship of the British company, F W Woolworth & Co Ltd, when it was founded in 1909. The first Woolworth's opened in Liverpool (the first customers were entertained by a brass band); the shop proved hugely popular because of its low prices. Branches spread rapidly throughout the country. One of the first major chain stores to populate our high streets, Woolworth's kept their traditional logo and shop style – gold lettering on a red ground.

The man in the centre of the photograph below is a chimney sweep carrying his rods on his back – he will do his job without the help of a powerful vacuum cleaner. Whilst food rationing introduced during the war ended in 1954, coal rationing did not end until 1958, so the sweep would have been much busier after this date.

Below: UTTOXETER, STAFFORDSHIRE, HIGH STREET c1955 U29005

NEWTON ABBOT, DEVON, COURTENAY STREET 1930 83105v

Newton Abbot

HERE WE SEE one of the most familiar and best-loved shops on British streets, Marks & Spencer. Affectionately known as Marks and Sparks, M&S has about 600 branches in the UK and 240 abroad. It is the largest clothing retailer in the UK. Its story began in 1884, when an immigrant from Minsk called Michael Marks set up a market stall in Leeds – the site in Kirkgate Market is marked today by a commemorative clock. Marks was joined by Thomas Spencer in 1894, and the pair rapidly expanded their operation, setting up Penny Bazaars all over the country. An original Penny Bazaar is still open in Newcastle.

Uttoxeter

Basingstoke

Uttoxeter

THE BRANCH of Dorothy Perkins shown below is typical of its time. Gone is the traditional shop front, to be replaced by floor to ceiling glass, a flat fascia, and a striking logo. There is now nothing to block the browsing shopper's view of the stock, which is strung imaginatively from wires to create an eye-catching display. The result is very different from the traditional women's outfitter, and a deliberate attempt to escape from the post-war depression and gloom – and to cash in on the 'never had it so good' prosperity. Next door but one is Melia's, a now-defunct grocery chain.

IT IS interesting to contrast Longley Bros the draper's in the photograph above with the Dorothy Perkins shop in U29058, right. Longley's is a typical old-style shop, its Victorian windows packed with clothes and underwear of all kinds, crowded so closely together that it is difficult to see – and choose – individual items. The three fancy lamps disguise the fascia signboard – hence the brash new first-floor painted sign.

Church Street is busy with shoppers and shopkeepers. Did the little girls buy their gleaming pinafores from Longley's? Note the sign on the right of the street in the shape of a dustpan.

Right: UTTOXETER, STAFFORDSHIRE, HIGH STREET c1965 U29058

St Neots

ST NEOTS, CAMBRIDGESHIRE, ROPER'S SHOP, CAMBRIDGE STREET c1968 S37060

ROPER'S SHOP started life as a baker's, but by 1968 it was stocking all kinds of attractive goods. Jars of sweets line the shelves, chocolate bars are displayed on the counter for impulse buying, the refrigerator is full of ice creams, and the glass case in front of the shop assistant overflows with cosmetics and household products. The aerosol cans of deodorant must be among the first to come into use, although disinfectant is still being sold in glass bottles. Many of the goods, including the Parkinson's sweets, would have been carefully weighed on the Avery scales by the immaculately coiffured lady assistant. Children would have opened their purchases and dropped the wrappers into the waste bin (centre) provided under a token scheme run by Fairy Soap. Today, Roper's has been split into two premises - Unwin's off-licence and an American Burger Bar.

Shirley

SHIRLEY, WEST MIDLANDS, THE PARADE c1965 S337051

STRATFORD ROAD was first recorded in 1322, though it was just a trackway known as Shirley Street at that time. Shirley developed along it in linear fashion, expanding hugely from the 1920s to the 1940s. It is administratively within the borough of Solihull, itself a suburb of Birmingham. This archetypal shopping parade was built for Shirley's growing commuter population in the mid 20th century, but today it is only part of a seemingly endless string of commercial premises along both sides of the road. This somewhat formless architectural jumble is set in the context of one of Birmingham's widest roads. Somehow there is room for several lanes of traffic, cycleways, pedestrian zones and even some planting.

Raynes Park

RAYNES PARK, GREATER LONDON, COOMBE LANE c1955 R355006

ARCHITECTURALLY SPEAKING, Raynes Park is a classic undistinguished suburb. This view looks northwest along Coombe Lane with the bus turning left into West Barnes Lane. On the right are 1930s and 1950s shopping parades, so typical of suburbs anywhere. The concrete plank fence on the left is still there – it screens a Thames Water depot. Elsewhere in the vicinity are semi-detached houses and blocks of 1930s neo-Georgian flats.

Rose Hill

MORDEN, GREATER LONDON, ST HELIER, BISHOPSFORD ROAD c1950 M359320

HERE AT ROSE HILL on farmland north of Sutton, Carshalton and Morden, the St Helier Estate was built by the London County Council between 1928 and 1936 to rehouse Londoners. A vast council estate of over 9,000 houses and flats, mostly in neo-Georgian style, replaced the old lavender fields. An exception was Rose Hill Court at the junction of St Helier Avenue and Bishopsford Road, flats over a parade of shops: this amazing and striking block was built in Art Deco or 'Ocean Liner' style. The

smooth brickwork and rounded corners give the building a streamlined look, stressed by the horizontal emphasis of the balconies. These shops would have seemed the height of modern luxury when they were built. The Gaumont cinema beyond is now the Mecca Bingo.

South of London is an area that was radically changed from farmland by suburban expansion between the two World Wars, filling in the gap between London and Sutton. The Victorian parts of Worcester Park, Raynes Park, and New Malden were all built over and expanded. This complex of suburbs grew up mainly as a result of the coming of the railway and the influx of commuters. The result is a melange of architectural styles. There are 1920s neo-Georgian houses and shops, and long terraces of late 19th-century buildings with terracotta bay windows. Mock timber-frames and gables jostle with 1950s and late Victorian styles.

Arcades and covered markets

SOME TOWNS have long had covered walks to protect shoppers and shopkeepers – the Butterwalk in Totnes is an example. But the large indoor shopping arcade and the covered market, essentially indoor streets, were Victorian inventions, which enabled commerce to continue whatever the weather. The large size and exuberant design of these arcades and markets made shopping far more than a mundane chore, and their descendants, the shopping malls and covered town centres of today, prove how well our forefathers understood that shopping should be enjoyable.

Bournemouth

Above right: BOURNEMOUTH, DORSET, THE ARCADE c1871 5511

Below right: BOURNEMOUTH, DORSET, THE ARCADE c1955 B163153P

BOURNEMOUTH, once in Hampshire but now in Dorset, did not exist two hundred years ago. In 1810, Lewis Tregonwell built a holiday home on lonely heathland, close to the mouth of the tiny River Bourne. Other wealthy gentlemen followed his example, but it was to be the middle of that century before the town achieved popularity as a holiday resort. Sir George Gervis, a rich landowner, added to Tregonwell's vision and founded Bournemouth as a fashionable resort. Advertisements of the day commented that 'enterprise has converted the silent and unfrequented vale into the gay resort of fashion, and the favoured retreat of the invalid'.

Space and light

THE SHOPPING ARCADE *was very much a Victorian concept, enabling the shopper to browse without getting wet on rainy days. As with so many seaside resorts of the 19th century, Bournemouth (opposite) attracted a wealthy and fashionable clientele – often not in the best of health – who expected the resort to provide every possible amenity, and they would have welcomed the grandeur, space and light of this arcade. The 1950s photograph (opposite below) shows that the Bournemouth Arcade's interior was as lavish as the exterior. By the time this photograph was taken it had served the town well for around a century. Today, the Arcade is as popular as it was then.*

Southport

LEYLAND ARCADE in Southport (now known as Wayfarers Arcade) is a wonderfully ornate example of what the smart late Victorian visitor expected to find in a superior resort. Its lofty glass roof, supported by ornate ironwork, floods the area with light, and makes the interior bright and airy. There is plenty of room for two storeys of 45 inviting shops - in 1899 the arcade even had a bioscope parlour. All is elegance and opulence here, and for Southport society this was the place to be seen. Entertainment was provided here too – we can see that chairs are lined up ready for a palm court orchestra, perhaps. In later years a group of ladies robed in white sang here twice a day.

Leyland Arcade lies just off Lord Street, the main shopping street of Southport. It was named after Sir Herbert Naylor Leyland, MP for Southport; it was designed by local architect G E Bolshaw and built between 1890 and 1898. This was an innovative design, and the architect even provided electric lighting and a hot water system throughout. The barrel-vaulted roof has a span of 13 metres – the arcade is one of the widest in Britain.

Southport had been a very different place to visit sixty years earlier. Ruth Manning-Sanders, in 'Seaside England', recounts Sir George Head's visit to the town in 1836: '[Southport] consists of one very wide, straight street, with but few shops … Woe betide you if you are not equipped with thick-soled, well-fitting shoes, for the street is paved with large stones and the side-paths with smaller ones "more acute than I ever remember to have walked on – except in a stable". And at the crossings the sand lies ankle-deep. "Many gardens are filled with mountains of sand that overtop the house, overwhelm the lower apartments, and which no one, from their size, thinks of removing"'.

Left: SOUTHPORT, MERSEYSIDE, LEYLAND ARCADE 1899 43327

Halifax

Opposite left:
HALIFAX, YORKSHIRE,
THE INTERIOR HALL,
BOROUGH MARKET 1896 38782

Near left:
HALIFAX, YORKSHIRE,
ENTRANCE AND ARCADE,
BOROUGH MARKET 1896 38777

MARKET HALLS and covered markets have existed for centuries, but it was in the Victorian era, that time of expanding population, that the most impressive market halls were built. Halifax had been a market town for many centuries, but unlike its close neighbours Bradford and Huddersfield, it had never enjoyed the benefits of a covered market hall. A Market Act in 1810 prohibited street trading, and anyone caught selling goods from a basket around the town could be arrested. A custom-built market hall had become a pressing priority.

The Town Council had been buying and setting aside land for such a scheme since the 1850s, but building did not actually begin until 1891. The design of the market was put out to competition, and the winning architects were Joseph and John Leeming of London, both Halifax-born. The new Borough Market was to be the magnificent centrepiece of the town and was eagerly awaited. Construction, however, progressed at a painfully slow pace, and the council was obliged to provide extra injections of funds more than once. The building was finally completed in 1896 at a total cost of £130,000. On 25 July 1896 the grand opening ceremony was carried out by the Duke and Duchess of York, who addressed the packed hall from below the imposing ornamental clock.

The market was set on a sloping site, and around its heavily rusticated perimeter walls were 43 small shops, originally all butchers. Inside, arranged in straight lines, were 20 small shop units and 33 stalls that on market days could accommodate almost a hundred traders. Would-be market traders could rent stalls weekly for between half a crown and eight shillings, and the shops in the arcades cost £100 per year. The fish market was originally in the main hall, but it was soon agreed by one and all that it would be better sited outside in Albion Street. Sixty feet overhead, supported on decorative iron pillars, was a spectacular octagonal dome of glass and iron. Directly below it was the renowned ornamental clock that soon became a favourite meeting point for visiting shoppers, and which was once visible from any point in the hall.

IN THE dim light is a sea of hats, caps and upturned faces. Business at the Barnstaple Pannier Market has been suspended for a few moments for the Frith photographer. As soon as he steps down from his platform the bargaining will begin again in earnest. Everyone in North Devon seems to have turned out: even the curate is there in the thick of the throng, searching for his favourite chutney.

Barnstaple Pannier Market was built in 1855. Its spectacular, lofty wooden vaulted roof is cathedral-like, exalting the proceedings below. On the fringes of the crowd stand the stall-holders - farmers' wives, country women and old men. They brought the goods they wanted to sell in baskets – panniers – hence the name of the market. For most, the shillings earned were a vital part of their survival, but for some the sale of a few vegetables and fruits helped pay the cost of tobacco and beer.

On the left is a woman in a white blouse and apron standing guard by her pannier. She would have been up before dawn, filling it with jars of home-made jams and marmalade, and with cabbages and cucumbers fresh-picked from her garden. Then there was the long journey on the carrier's cart through the twisting Devon lanes into town. Inside the market building each stall-holder had a numbered pitch. The cost of a year's stall rent in 1919 was just 6d. Today it is considerably more, but the Barnstaple Market Superintendent believes it is still a bargain, for on Tuesdays, Fridays and Saturdays the hall is filled, and you can pick over the produce of 400 stalls. Prices are low, and shoppers discover produce they would not find in High Street shops, such as rare cottage garden plants and forgotten varieties of apple.

Right: BARNSTAPLE, DEVON, THE PANNIER MARKET 1919 69324P

KENDAL, CUMBRIA, THE NEW SHAMBLES 1914 67400

Kendal

THIS IS not quite an arcade or a covered market, but today it is almost as smart as a Victorian arcade. However, Kendal's New Shambles has a long history, and it was not always as salubrious as it is now!

Animals were bought, sold and butchered on Beast Banks from an early date. A corporation bylaw made it an offence to kill a bull without first baiting it. The animal was secured to an iron ring and dogs were set on it to provoke it. The practice was a popular sport but was abolished in 1791. Butchers had moved from Beast Banks by 1785 into the newly built Old Shambles off Highgate. There were problems with the draining of blood and offal here, and although the slaughterers and traders paid to have the Old Shambles cleaned every week,

it was known as Stinking Lane. So the shambles moved again, this time to Watt Lane, an ancient route between Market Place and Finkle Street; it was converted into the New Shambles in 1804 (67400) – it then contained 12 butchers' shops. This soon became redundant with the opening of a municipal slaughterhouse and was changed into a delightful passage of shops, one of which remains as a butcher's to this day. There were also cattle sales in the Market Place, and a cattle fair was established on Beast Banks in 1816.

THE EARL OF DERBY'S market of 1839 was a forbidding building surrounded by high walls. It was not popular with traders, who were accustomed to the open spaces around the old Market Place, and for a time it was occupied by a company of foot soldiers. In 1867 a glass and iron roof was added. But over the years this became neglected and unsafe, and traders were obliged to move out and set their stalls up against the walls.

In 1901 a new market hall, with a distinctive dome (48562T), was opened across the road, together with a large open market covering much of the old fairground. It was a place of civic pride – the borough coat of arms was carved over the main entrance – and it was to prove very popular with the public. The Hall was open every day except Sunday and Tuesday, while the open market was open on Saturdays. It grew to be one of the largest markets in Lancashire, where all manner of things could be bought, not least the famous Bury black pudding. Within the Market Hall was a labyrinth of stalls, among them James Lawless, ironmongers, and Goslings, where treacle toffee was sold from trays.

Shops clustered around the outside of the building, including Berry's the florists and seedsmen, and Halsteads the grocers (centre), where the aroma of freshly ground coffee wafted temptingly through the door.

Bury's Market Hall was destroyed in a disastrous fire on a Sunday morning in November 1968, and the building was gutted. The dome survived, but it was unsafe and had to be demolished. By now a new Market Hall was under construction a short distance away in the new shopping centre, and a temporary structure was built within the shell of the old building to house the traders until the new one was complete. The site was then cleared, and a new train and bus interchange was constructed.

BURY, GREATER MANCHESTER,
THE MARKET 1902   48562T

Bury

Hitchin

Left:
HITCHIN,
HERTFORDSHIRE,
THE ARCADE 1931
84207

HITCHIN'S ARCADE has scarcely changed since this photograph was taken in 1931. The shops were once the outbuildings and stables of the large Swan Inn. The Swan, starting point for daily coaches to London and Hertford for so many years, closed in 1884; it had existed since at least 1539. The site became the Swan Ironworks, run by John Gatward who, by 1900, described his business as a 'complete house furnishers and general ironmongers'. In 1924, it became a shopping arcade, which it remains today.

Blackburn

BLACKBURN, LANCASHIRE, THE MARKET c1965 B111062

THE CANVAS-COVERED stalls in the market place provided little protection for shoppers in Blackburn's frequent wet weather. A cascade of cold water down the back of your neck was all part of the shopping experience. It was this, along with the time-consuming task of erecting and dismantling stalls and clearing away rubbish, that led to the building of a new market hall in Victorian times.

However, by the 20th century a new hall was needed, and work began on a new ultra-modern market in the 1960s – the course of the River Blakewater had to be diverted. The old Victorian market hall was demolished, and with it on 30 December 1964 the much-loved market hall tower.

Romford

COMPARED TO most of the markets and arcades we have seen so far, this arcade is comparatively modern. The L-shaped Quadrant Arcade stretching between South Street and the Market Place was formally opened on 23 September 1935. This view from the centre looking towards the market shows some of the 36 shop units which it provided. It was the pet project of Mr W Goodchild, who overcame considerable opposition to his ambitious scheme. Before the arcade could be built, the old council office building needed to be demolished; long negotiations had to be undergone before Romford Council would agree to pay for this. During the Second World War, the arcade suffered from incendiary bombs.

Left: ROMFORD, GREATER LONDON, QUADRANT ARCADE c1950 R52035

The battle of the signs

A STREET'S character can be made or marred by the quality of the signs, lettering and advertisements in it. In this chapter we see how the oversize lettering of the early 20th century was the visual equivalent of screaming; we also see some charming period signwriting and some fascinating advertising signs that enhance the buildings they adorn. And for us today, cinema posters of the 1920s and advertising posters of the 1950s already have period charm.

Photo courtesy of: Torridge Auctions

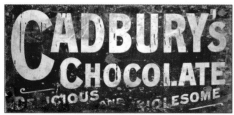

Photo courtesy of: Torridge Auctions

Frome

IT IS regrettable that the Georgians' good manners were rarely displayed in the Victorian era. In Frith photographs of the 1890s and 1900s, the high street becomes an arena for pitched battles between warring shopkeepers. The weapons are not picks and shovels – although one often feels if they could have used them they would – but letters and signs. The photograph of Frome depicts the quintessential small corner shop, almost cloying in its quaintness. Known locally as the 'pepper pot', Mr H R Hughes' shop, said to be the oldest in Frome, sits at the top of Cheap Street and Eagle Lane. His wares are well advertised in both windows. Mr Hughes's shop name is painted discreetly above the door and there are modest Rowntree's Cocoa logos on the windows. Yet even Mr Hughes could not resist the lure of a sizeable but unnecessary 'Grape-Nuts' enamel sign which he has placed high up on his wall, well outside the fascia of his shop. Today we find these old signs nostalgic and fascinating, yet they were the thin end of a very large wedge from which we have been suffering ever since.

Left: FROME, SOMERSET, THE OLDEST HOUSE 1907 58851P

Harrogate

IN THE picture of Harrogate (left), Boots the cash chemist's have installed their standard gilded wooden sign over their premises, which smothers the entire frontage from the roof downwards. Boots, it would appear, were determined to make an impact in the town. Opposite, Mr Taylor the chemist has risen to the challenge and has fought back with an even more gigantic sign with letters that would have each required three men to lift. The effect is the equivalent of having both managers standing facing each other on their respective pavements, screaming their sales messages through megaphones from dawn to dusk – for that they would be arrested, and quite properly. Yet they were permitted to assault us visually, and no-one could say a word.

Left: HARROGATE, YORKSHIRE, PARLIAMENT SQUARE 1907   58649P

TAUNTON, SOMERSET, FORE STREET 1902   48723

Taunton

IN 1902 in Taunton, The Stores, not content with cladding their building with fake timbering, have turned it into a gigantic and boisterous hoarding, a forty-foot street poster. Poor Mr Spiller's sign on the tiny shop next door is no bigger than The Stores' 'Price List Free' sign over the entrance. Once the process of gigantism was set in motion it was almost impossible to reverse – who would make the first move, you or your competitor?

Size is not everything in the High Street battle to get noticed

Modern research has proved that the battle of the signs was all in vain, and that any victory achieved was a Pyrrhic one. Tests have shown that shoppers rarely look up at any sign above the level of the shop window, for the viewing angle is too acute. In most town high streets it is impossible to step back far enough to read such massive letters without being run down by a car. It has also been proved that a tiny two-inch letter can be read perfectly well from across the street and that the most effective signs are those at eye-level.

The huge signs, it seems, were money wasted. But they clearly demonstrate the war that developed in the retail trade after the multiples moved into our towns near the end of the 19th century. It is a war that has never stopped being fought, for there are as many examples of excessive signage today as there were a hundred years ago. Many of us would welcome a return to the more sedate and better-mannered Georgian times.

STAMFORD, LINCOLNSHIRE, RED LION SQUARE 1922   72300T

IN STAMFORD in 1922, Freeman, Hardy & Willis, not content with emblazoning their name over their own shop, have invaded the houses next door. The people of Stamford must have ended up with eye-strain. Red Lion Square has always been at the heart of Stamford's commercial life; indeed, seven roads radiate out from the square, including the Great North Road itself until recently. The square lies on the site of the earliest Mercian settlement, centred on St John's Church to the west and the Danish burgh to the east. It is a natural market site, and by medieval times it had developed into the site of the town's sheep market. The large building housing the Freeman Hardy & Willis shoe shop is known to contain elements of a large 14th-century timber-framed building. It has been suggested that this may be the wool house of the Brownes, one of the town's most successful families of wool merchants.

Brawling, drunkenness and an almost unendurable noise, filth and stench

Markets and fairs had been held in Rugby for centuries. By the middle of the 19th century, in addition to the Saturday market there were some 13 horse and cattle sales each year, a large Martinmas horse fair, 3 hiring fairs and 2 cheese fairs. These fairs, the cattle markets in particular, caused almost unendurable noise, filth, stench and confusion. Horses were tied up in the streets, often to the churchyard wall; sheep and pigs were penned in the main streets; and cattle roamed everywhere, causing inconvenience and danger. Filthy streets were not the only problem. The 15 inns in and around the Market Square provided ale at 10d a gallon and Jamaica rum at 1s 4d a bottle. Gin was even cheaper. Brawling, drunkenness, singing and shouting made life almost intolerable for the respectable townsfolk. The first attempt to solve the problem was the creation of the Town Hall Company, a private organisation of wealthy townspeople, which in 1857 built Rugby's first Town Hall.

In the 1879s the market place was freed of livestock. It then presented a colourful, bustling scene, loud with the cries of the market-traders, the rumble of cartwheels over cobbles, the barking of dogs and the shouts and laughter of children chasing through the crowded streets. There might well have been an Italian street-piano player to entertain the crowds, a monkey or bright-plumaged parrot perched upon his shoulder. Country people would have brought their goods into town by cart, perhaps hiring a carrier if they had no cart of their own. Some, perhaps, used a handcart, or even a backpack.

IN THE VIEW of Abingdon (right), above Fisher's 'Old Bear' boot stores on the left is a boot sign – these simple pictorial signs were popular in the days before most ordinary people could read. This view looks along Stert Street towards the tower of St Nicholas's Church which faces the Market Place; the street still retains much of its character, despite the traffic.

Stert Street runs south towards the Market Place; in the 1890s, it was one of Abingdon's main shopping streets. On the right, W H Hooke's bookshop (now a jeweller's) is the start of the market place encroachment. Until 1883, only the church tower was visible from here; then two pubs which jutted into the street, one on each side, were demolished for road improvement.

Right: ABINGDON, OXFORDSHIRE, STERT STREET 1893 31693

RUGBY, WARWICKSHIRE, MARKET PLACE, HIGH STREET AND SHEEP STREET 1932 85179

HERE WE SEE another gigantic piece of advertising. The lavish gilded wooden sign with its elegant flourish is impossible to miss. Is it meant to suggest a needle and thread, or a bootlace, perhaps? Briggs & Company the boot makers (Peter Briggs today) has traded on this site for over a century. Durrant, a piano retailer, had previously held the site, one of at least three piano retailers in the town centre at the end of the 19th century. Today there are none.

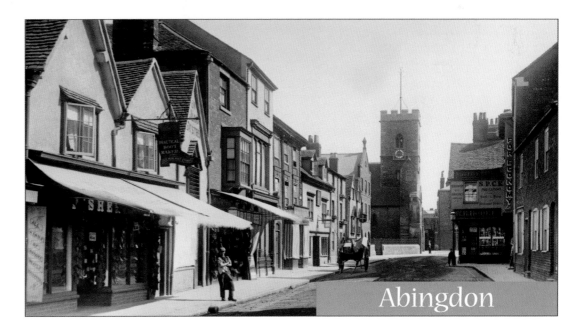

Carnforth

CARNFORTH, LANCASHIRE, MARKET STREET 1898   41032

ON THE CORNER is Woolstencroft's the chemist's. Notice the apothecary jars in the window and the mortar and pestle trade sign above the door, clear indications of what kind of shop this is. Look too at a sign etched on the glass of the door, 'Teeth Carefully Extracted'. The board behind the mortar and pestle boasts that they sell General Drugs and Patent Medicines, Horse & Cattle Medicines and Thorleys Cattle Spice, as well as being Oil & Colour Merchants. They were also agents for the Caledonian Fire & Life Insurance and Ocean, Railway & General Accident. They also sold sleeping powders, cures for influenza and butter colour.

Carnforth, six miles north of Lancaster, has a place in history as a railway town. The Furness & Midland Railway and the London & North Western Railway opened a station at Carnforth between them in 1880, and it was always an important junction. Already busy with turnpike traffic, the railway's arrival encouraged more hotels, such as the Royal Station Hotel at the bottom of the street.

CHICHESTER, SUSSEX, SOUTH STREET 1923   73655

Chichester

THIS SPECTACLES SIGN, with its pair of staring eyes, is somewhat alarming. It would surely put people off rather than attract. The optician certainly wanted his business to be noticed by people with sight defects! It seems to be above a cycle shop rather than an optician.

Wrotham

WROTHAM, KENT, HIGH STREET 1901   47636

THE NARROW high street leading to a small square boasted a varied selection of businesses at the turn of the last century. On the right hand side is Wagland's bakery, with the Wrotham Cycle Works and its hanging bicycle sign a few doors along towards the George & Dragon Inn. On the left-hand corner of the street, J Coleman's operation combined the service of local undertaker with that of grocer and draper.

THE VICTORIAN TRADER was not slow to diversify. The spectacles sign above this small shop in one of York's ancient and picturesque streets suggests that John Wharton is an optician. Yet the painted signs above his shop tell us that he stocks glass, glasses, china, earthenware, tin goods, brushes, lamps, wicks, and oil. Are the spectacles there just to draw attention to his shop and stock – a way of saying 'look'? Or did an optician use the attic room? This view is remarkable for its many large and diverse examples of the signwriter's art.

Left:
YORK, YORKSHIRE,
GOODRAMGATE 1892
30631T

Letters to arrest and strike the eye – trade tips from the Victorian signwriter William Sutherland

1. A sign should be legible, and capable of being read by all classes.
2. A sign should not be overcrowded with words … many signs are stultified by this fact alone, as people have neither the time nor inclination to stop and read a sign if it has too much matter upon it.
2. When writing or steting out a sign for business purposes, we should use only plain, readable types of letter.
3. The different lines of letters should always contrast with each other, either in size or shape, as we thus give greater distinctness and effect to each line.
4. In setting out a business sign, the name of the person and his business should appear the most prominent feature of the whole, and the other words be kept subordinate.

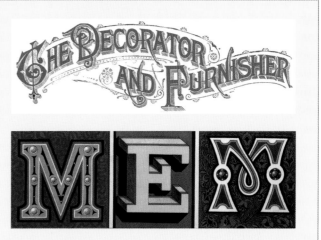

KIDDERMINSTER, HEREFORD & WORCESTER, TOWN CENTRE
1957 K16025

Kidderminster

IT WAS not just the Victorians who indulged in huge signs. The sign for the dry cleaning business on the right of this photograph spreads across the entire face of the building. Oddly, it does not explain the nature of the business. In fact, it is misleading. 'Your Zip Shop' suggests it is a supplier of zip fasteners. Notice the policeman on point duty in his pulpit.

Carmarthen

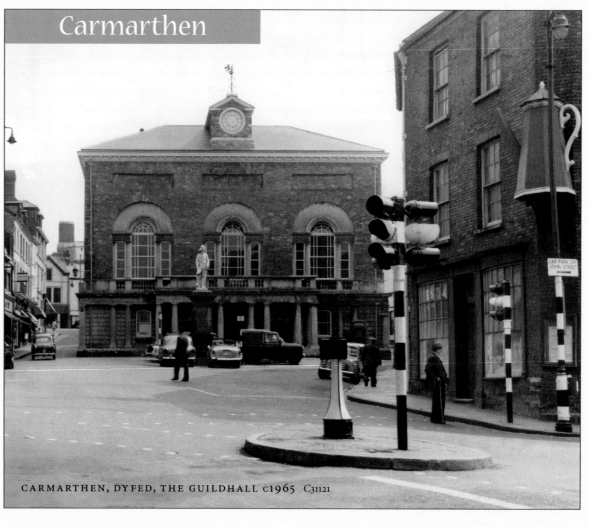

CARMARTHEN, DYFED, THE GUILDHALL c1965 C31121

IS THIS COFFEE POT (extreme right of photograph C31121) the biggest trade sign ever? It advertises Wonacott's Tea and Coffee Warehouse at the corner of Dark Gate and Guildhall Square. The history of the sign has been researched by a local historian, Mrs Edna Dale-Jones. The coffee pot was mentioned in a poem circulating around 1856:

'When first I was set up on high,
Some viewed me with a jealous eye,
With thoughts that I, an empty pot,
Would custom bring to Wonacott.'

In 1907 George Eyre Evans, Secretary of the Carmarthenshire Antiquarian Society, published the verse and asked who the author was. Mr Charles Finch, who ran a fishmonger's in Nott Square, lent or gave a copy of a book, 'Poetical Pieces' (subtitled 'Moral and Satirical Pieces'), to the society's library. The book, which is now in Carmarthen Museum, contains 33 poems including the one above; it was written by Alexander Aitkin, and published in 1856. It would appear that three pots have hung on the corner of the building. The original was made some time before 1856; the second was made between 1871 and 1883, and was constructed of wood by D M Williams; and a third, also in wood, was made by Ryan Joinery in 1975. The 1975 coffee pot was refurbished in 1992 by Gwyn Phillips and encased in fibreglass for protection.

St Ives

THE CORNER of Fore Street in St Ives is plastered with hoardings for the cinema on Barnoon Hill. Large posters advertise the film 'Suds', in which Mary Pickford plays Amanda Afflick, a London laundry woman who tries to rise above her station in order to capture the love of a wealthy young man and thus misses out on the truer love of one of her own class. The gaudy posters clash somewhat with the old cobbled street lined with slate-hung shops and houses.

Fishing and Painting

For centuries a celebrated fishing port, St Ives is today better known for its artistic community. Artists such as Christopher Wood, Ben Nicholson, Barbara Hepworth, Peter Lanyon and Patrick Heron all lived and worked here, making use of the unique quality of Penwith's light. Visitors flock to see the town's narrow twisting streets, which are a maze of fishermen's cottages and wynds and alleys.

Left: ST IVES, CORNWALL, FORE STREET 1922 72852

Pocklington

POCKLINGTON, YORKSHIRE, MARKET PLACE c1955 P186002

HAROLD KAYE the barber makes a direct appeal on a hoarding above his shop window: 'Your Haircut Sir!' An arrow points down at his premises. To the right, Fred Lee the tobacconist has painted his brickwork and is using the whole front of the building as an advertising hoarding, while to the left a large proportion of the building's façade is dominated by signwriting.

Pubs and inns

PUBS, INNS and hotels provide a welcome excuse to pause and restore ourselves – and their rich variety reflects the varied character of the streets on which they stand. They may be grand, ornate medieval masterpieces, or reminders of the heyday of the coaching age, or humbler neighbourhood pubs, or Victorian temperance hotels; they are as old as history, and as eternal as our need for refreshment.

The loveliest town in England

'The streets are lined with many quaint old houses, decorated with various devices, moulded in plaster, and set within crossing timbers of black oak. The town has an antique stamp, and suggests a prosperity that has in great measure passed away.'

Victorian Guide c1890.

'Probably the loveliest town in England'.
John Betjeman 1943

Close by the Feathers Inn was the entrance to Ludlow's market, with traders paying tolls at the nearby Tolsey (or toll booth), and refreshing themselves and striking their bargains over an ale in the Angel. The ashes of A E Housman, who wrote the above lines in 'A Shropshire Lad', are buried here in St Lawrence's churchyard.

Ludlow

IT IS generally agreed by those outside the profession that lawyers charge too much. This large, grand and ornately ornamented house is the evidence. It was built by a lawyer, Rees Jones, in the early 1600s. In a period when just about every fine building in the county was owned by a wool or cloth merchant, this house reminds us of the importance of the legal profession to the wealth of Ludlow. By the end of the century it had become an inn with stabling for 100 horses. Today the decorative carving is much as it was when first built, with the exception of the balconies, which were added in the 19th century. The main room on the middle floor on the left has a truly magnificent plaster ceiling. The house is described by Nikolaus Pevsner as 'that prodigy of timber framed houses'.

The name of the hotel is derived from the ostrich feather carvings on the three gables; ostrich feathers are the badge of the Prince of Wales, and the house was built just after celebrations in 1616 at the investiture of the future Charles I as Prince of Wales. The Feathers remained an inn for the next 200 years, and was occasionally the scene of cock-fighting and prize-fighting. Candidates for parliamentary elections would make speeches from the hotel balcony, then invite voters inside for a drink to help secure their votes.

Left: LUDLOW, SHROPSHIRE, THE FEATHERS HOTEL 1892 30829P

DORKING, SURREY, THE WHITE HORSE HOTEL 1905 53333

Dorking

'DORKING is one of those old pleasant little towns which have a special character of their own; one of those which are a blend of all that is home-like, lovely and beautiful in England.' So says the 'Rambler's Guide to Dorking and Environs' (c1930). 'Tales of Old Inns' (2nd ed 1929) adds: 'The White Horse at Dorking has always been a patrician among English inns, the great coaching house of the place with its dozens of bedrooms, its scores of servants, and its vast range of stables', and the book paints a vivid picture of what it must have been like in coaching days: 'You can almost hear to-day, echoing back from its white walls, the notes of the horn and the clatter of hoofs on the cobbles, as the Worthing Accommodation rattled in, five hours out from the Belle Sauvage on Ludgate Hill, or the Dorking stage from the Spread Eagle in Gracechurch Street pulled up at the end of its 23-mile journey.'

The White Horse is a very old inn. Its first name was the Cross House, referring to its former owners, the Knights of St John of Jerusalem, whose badge was a Maltese cross. They are said to have bought it from the Knights Templar in 1278; certainly the cellars, carved out of the sandstone on which Dorking stands, are very old, and from them a passage leads down to an ancient well. The building we see today dates from the 15th century, with the long street frontage probably built in the early 18th century. Through the old archway is the cobbled stable yard, and beyond is a large garden.

Sam Weller patronises the Marquis of Granby in Victorian Dorking

Dickens visited here often, and in his 'Pickwick Papers' it was in Dorking that Sam Weller descended from the Arundel coach and headed for the fictional Marquis of Granby, kept by Mrs Weller – Dickens's original for this pub was probably the King's Head.

'It was just seven o'clock when Samuel Weller, alighting from the box of a stage-coach which passed through Dorking, stood within a few hundred yards of the Marquis of Granby. It was a cold, dull evening; the little street looked dreary and dismal; and the mahogany countenance of the noble and gallant marquis seemed to wear a more sad and melancholy expression than it was wont to do, as it swung to and fro, creaking mournfully in the wind. The blinds were pulled down, and the shutters partly closed; of the knot of loungers that usually collected about the door, not one was to be seen; the place was silent and desolate.'

FROM 'PICKWICK PAPERS' 1837

THE WHITE HORSE has been an important inn in Romsey Market Place for many centuries. The present building, largely timber-framed, dates from Tudor times and has Tudor wall paintings, but there is evidence in the cellars of an even earlier building. It has always been used by the local inhabitants as well as by travellers. This was particularly so in the case of property auctioneers and the market fraternity in the 19th century.

In the heyday of the coaching era in the mid 18th century, the White Horse had 35 beds, six rooms, and stabling for 50 horses and room for four carriages. Although the much-enlarged modern hotel has 33 bedrooms now, 35 beds did not mean 35 bedrooms three hundred years ago. There were probably one or two dormitory-style rooms, and staff slept over the stables or where they worked.

There were differing opinions of Romsey amongst travellers. A Dr John Latham, writing about Romsey in 1820, said: 'This town is on a leading road to the west and a good thoroughfare with good inns viz the White Horse which is the principal one. The public is accommodated with post chaises and horses, besides which stage coaches pass daily to London, Portsmouth, Southampton, Salisbury and from the latter to Bath, Bristol and many other places westward.'

The traveller John Byng was not so complimentary during his journey to the west in 1782: 'No information of my road could be got here, so I must proceed by map as a mariner does by his compass; for neither ostler nor waiter knew a mile from the door, and a landlord would scorn to wait upon me.'

Romsey

ROMSEY, HAMPSHIRE, THE WHITE HORSE HOTEL 1903   49340P

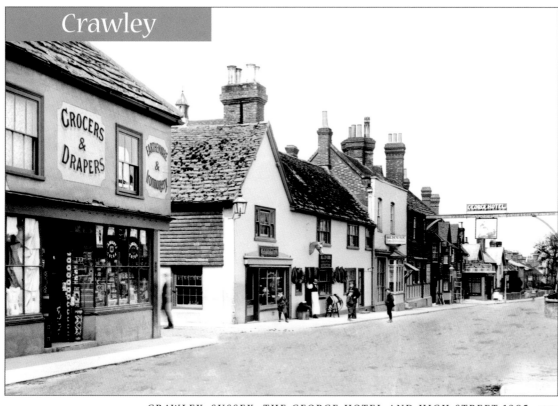

Crawley

CRAWLEY, SUSSEX, THE GEORGE HOTEL AND HIGH STREET 1905 53313

THE GEORGE HOTEL in Crawley (with its sign stretching across the road) was a famous coaching inn. One of the best descriptions of how it would have looked back in its Regency heyday can be found in Sir Arthur Conan Doyle's novel 'Rodney Stone' (1896): 'And then at last, we saw the formless mass of the huge Crawley elm looming before us in the gloom, and there was the broad village street with the glimmer of the cottage windows, and the high front of the old George Inn, glowing from every door and pane and crevice, in honour of the noble company who were to sleep within that night.' The hotel name derives from St George rather than the Prince Regent, who is said to have been a regular visitor en route to Brighton.

Crawley's George Hotel, which has existed for hundreds of years, has its own ghost haunting the corridors. The ghost in question is thought to be that of Mark Hewton, a night porter who liked to deliver wine to guests in the evening, regardless of whether they wanted it or not. Any wine left over when he collected it, he would consume himself. Unfortunately for him, one guest had put poison in some of this wine, which Hewton drank and promptly died. Staff insist they have unpleasant feelings in the locality of his room, now number seven, and say they have seen faint shapes. They have also had trouble with the corridor lights, which frequently turn themselves on and off!

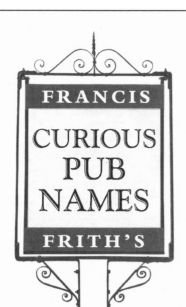

FRANCIS

CURIOUS PUB NAMES

FRITH'S

Babes in the Wood
The signboard shows two men in the stocks.

Bag o' Nails
Possibly a corruption of Blackamoor's Head, or Bacchanals (drinking revels).

Bird in Hand
A hawking reference to the falcon on a gauntlet.

Bucket of Blood
200 years ago the landlord was shocked at finding a man's head at the bottom of his well.

Bull and Spectacles
Once the Bull's Head, but renamed many years ago after an inebriated customer climbed up the wall of the pub and put his spectacles on the head of the bull.

Cat and Bagpipes
Refers apparently to the Caterans, war-like Scots who carried out raids over the border to the village of East Harlsey.

Cat and Fiddle
Possibly Le Chat Fidele (the governor of Calais) or Catherine la Fidele (Catherine of Aragon).

Duke Without a Head
Originally The Duke's Head, but at some time in the past the landlord applied to transfer his licence to a different building. The reply came from the authority: 'Permission is given to remove The Duke's Head'. And so the landlord did.

George and Cannon
A corruption of the name of George Canning, the 18th-century Prime Minister.

Goat and Compasses
Said to derive from 'God encompasseth us'.

The Nobody Inn
Named after a former landlord of the pub at Doddiscombleigh who refused to open the door to customers.

Pipe and Gannex
A pub at Huyton near Liverpool, the reference being to the pipe and Gannex raincoat worn by the former Prime Minister Harold Wilson, who was MP for the constituency.

Quiet Woman
Shows a woman carrying her own severed head, suggesting that women are only quiet after they're dead!

Round of Gras
From 'gras', a shortened version of asparagus, which is grown in the locality.

Turk's Head
Either a reference to a local rope industry (A Turk's Head is a kind of knot), or to the Crusades, when many inn names had references to Turks or Saracens.

The Why Not?
Refers not to the decision whether to take a drink or not, but to a Grand National winner at the end of the 19th century.

Abergavenny

NESTLING BETWEEN the Black Mountains and the Brecon Beacons, and near the beautiful Usk valley, Abergavenny is about half-way between London and Milford Haven, and has long been a stopping place on the road; the Angel is a fine early Georgian building, refurbished in coaching days, when it gained its dignified facade. The inn was busy in the coaching era. The coach from London to Milford Haven, the 'Champion', took 15 hours to reach Abergavenny, a difficult, gruelling journey, and its passengers were happy to receive all the hospitality the Angel could provide. The Royal Mail coach stopped here too. After 1858 the London service ceased, but the daily coach from Ross-on-Wye still stopped here.

Famous people associated with the Angel include the ironmaster Crawshay Bailey, who attended a fancy dress ball here in 1838; Walter Morgan, whose family lived here, who was Lord Mayor of London in 1905; Gregory Peck the film star, who stopped here in 1945 on his way to film 'Moby Dick', heavily bearded for his role as Captain Ahab; and Richard Burton and Elizabeth Taylor in 1963, who consumed steak and kidney pie and a bottle of claret.

ABERGAVENNY, GWENT, THE ANGEL HOTEL 1893   32596T

TENBY, a fishing and trading port from ancient times, and a medieval walled town, had become a seaside resort in the 19th century thanks to Sir William Paxton, a wealthy London banker, who recognised the potential of Tenby with its magnificent cliff-top setting. Fine, elegant terraces were built, together with hotels and lodging houses. Tenby was now a popular resort for the wealthy. This photograph shows Quay Hill in the old part of the town leading down to the harbour. The guests at Griffiths' Temperance Hotel may not be having anything very exciting to drink, but they will have a feast of seafood for their supper – note the basket loaded with shellfish and an enormous flatfish.

Tenby

TENBY, DYFED, GRIFFITHS' TEMPERANCE HOTEL 1890   28076

Knaresborough

KNARESBOROUGH STANDS above the River Nidd on a sandstone cliff, and it is said that Mother Shipton was born in a cave here in the 15th century. She was renowned as a prophetess; she wrote her prophecies in verse, and among other things foretold Sir Walter Raleigh's discovery of tobacco and potatoes in America:

> 'From whence he shall bring
> A herb and a root
> That all men shall suit,
> And please both the ploughman and king'.

The Mother Shipton Inn, which stands in front of her cave, was originally a 17th-century farmhouse. The Dropping Well is a petrifying well, similar to those at Matlock Bath in Derbyshire, where the limestone content of the spring water solidifies objects that are placed in it. At one time the star attraction here was a petrified mongoose!

KNARESBOROUGH, YORKSHIRE, THE MOTHER SHIPTON INN 1914 67264

The drive to keep the working man out of temptation

The temperance movement was a huge influence on 19th-century society. Indeed, it has been estimated that by 1900 about a tenth of the adult population were total abstainers from alcohol

– and if they were away from home, they needed somewhere free from temptation where they could stay. The temperance movement began in 1832, when Joseph Livesey and seven Preston working men signed a pledge that they would never again drink alcohol. By 1835 the British Association for the Promotion of Temperance was formed. Its influence grew until in some parts of Britain public houses were forced to close on Sundays, and permission was rarely granted to allow new ones to open. Lady Rosalind Carlisle (1845–1922), a prominent temperance campaigner, used her influence to close down pubs or convert them into temperance hotels or coffee houses.

Redhill

REDHILL, SURREY, THE MONSON ARMS C1965 R17039

A FINE EXAMPLE of a post-war pub, the Monson Arms – named after a local nobleman – advertises Double Diamond, a beer brand from the past that is still available, and has children sitting outside rather than in the bar as is so often the case today. Parked on the left are a Wolseley and a two-tone Ford Zodiac, now a much sought after classic car.

Civic pomp and pride

ALL STREETS lead to the town centre – and in the town centre can be found the public buildings where merchants, administrators, doctors, entertainers and educators carry on the varied activities that make up town life. Some towns have small, ancient market houses, town halls and lock-ups; larger towns have grand, pompous public buildings, monuments to the ambition of aspiring Victorian architects and engineers. Between these architectural extremes come the dignified customs houses and guildhalls of the 17th and 18th century – and the rather bleak public buildings of the new towns.

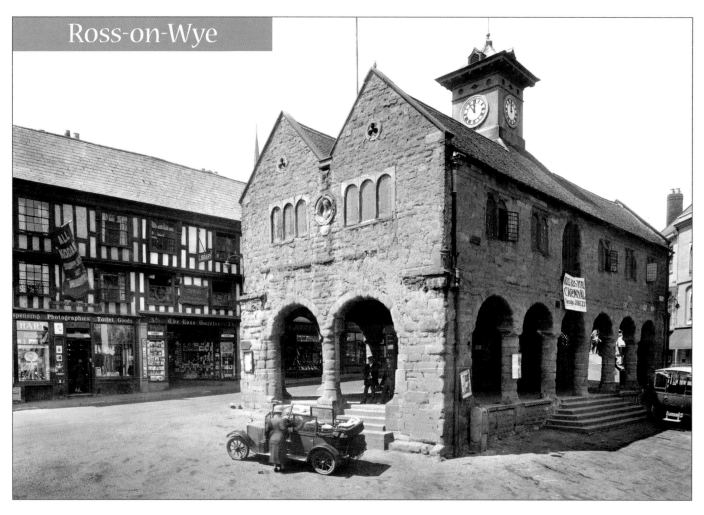

Ross-on-Wye

The medieval market place in the centre of Ross was much larger than the present one, and by the 16th century the Market Place contained a High Cross and a Boothall where the market tolls were collected. The Boothall was joined by a group of houses to a row of quaint tenements called Underhill, which were demolished in the 19th century, but in the 17th century the Boothall was considered to be unsatisfactory. The Boothall, High Cross and the adjacent houses were pulled down and replaced around 1650 with the existing Market House.

THE DIVERSE public buildings of our towns lend much character to their streets. Like other public buildings in use for over 350 years, Ross-on-Wye's Market House has undergone a number of changes and uses. It was built in local sandstone around 1650 to replace the medieval buildings in the market place, and was described thus by Thomas Bonnor in his 'Picturesque Views' of 1799: 'Ascending to it by several steps, semicircular arches spring from four-and-twenty pillars, with bases and caps, in the Saxon style of building: the pillars forming three rows, consisting of eight in each row, sustain a range of chambers, more constructed for convenience than ornament'.

Markets have been held here on Thursdays and Saturdays since the 12th century. The market was sited in a wedge-shaped site, roughly equidistant from the church, which stands at the highest point in Ross, and the mill, situated at the bottom end by the brook; the market thus effectively filled the gap between the two communities.

Above: ROSS-ON-WYE, HEREFORD & WORCESTER, THE MARKET HOUSE 1925   76888

Bridgwater

THIS IS the heart of Bridgwater, where Cornhill and Fore Street join. The origins of the noble Market House with its dome and lantern lie in the late 18th century, when a meeting of Bridgwater's citizens agreed to build a market house and to improve the street paving and lighting. By 1791 a market house had been built, financed by a trust and the corporation; then in 1825 the corporation ordered the trust to demolish part of the market house so as to widen the road. By 1826 the Market House had been enlarged and altered into the form we see it today, and the streets around it had been widened and improved. Since then they have seen many elaborate celebrations, including the unveiling of Admiral Robert Blake's statue in 1900. Built in hollow bronze, it cost £1,200 and was paid for by contributions from the Victorian public.

Above: BRIDGWATER, SOMERSET, CORNHILL 1901 47866T

In 1605, after the failure of the Gunpowder Plot, Bridgwater, along with other towns and villages, celebrated with the traditional bonfire and fireworks display. But in Bridgwater this tradition was to develop into what has now become the world's largest night-time carnival. The bonfire was the centrepiece at Cornhill until 1925, when tarmac was introduced on the roads.

King's Lynn

KING'S LYNN is lucky to have some immensely characterful public buildings to enliven its streets. The Guildhall, the building with the large window, was built between 1422 and 1428. Authorised by an ambitious official, the building on the left of the Guildhall was added in 1624. Above the arched door and the handsome square window are the remains of the arms of Queen Elizabeth I, which were removed from St James's Church on 7 August 1624. On top of the façade are the arms of Charles II, added forty years later.

The men seated on the benches in photograph 28754 are waiting to get a perfect view of sentenced prisoners being taken to the Town Gaol of 1784, which is on the right of the Guildhall. On top of its front door is a motif of fetters and chains identical to that of London's Newgate prison. On the far left is the notorious Town Arms pub, which was demolished in 1894.

Built in Ketton stone and opened in 1685, King's Lynn's famous Customs House (by Sir William Turner, based on a design by Bell) was shared by merchants, who did their dealing on the lower floor, and HM Customs on the first floor (see 40878P, bottom left). Outside the entrance, a strict-looking customs official is keeping his eagle eye on the photographer as well as on the fishing boats, which were often used for smuggling tobacco, wines and spirits.

Centuries ago the Wash was larger than it is today. Located on its south east corner, King's Lynn was built on the edge of the sea, probably with help from the Romans and later the Dutch, who were experts in cutting dykes. From ancient times it was always a populous and flourishing seaport, borough and market town. King's Lynn harbour provided an outlet for all the navigable rivers in the area. Trade in all commodities was developed with salt, furs, cloth, farm produce, fish, wine and wood bringing in merchants and buyers from home and abroad.

KING'S LYNN, NORFOLK, THE TOWN HALL 1891   28754

KING'S LYNN, NORFOLK, THE CUSTOMS HOUSE 1898   40878P

KING'S LYNN, NORFOLK, THE CUSTOMS HOUSE AND PURFLEET 2003   K28704K

HERE WE SEE a view of the Market Hall with its imposing front and large statues mounted over the entrance. There was a corn market in Accrington as far back as the 16th century. This Market Hall was opened on 23 October 1868 by Samuel Dugdale, chairman of the local Board of Health. It contained 80 permanent stalls and shops, plus 23 lock-ups in the basement, served by lifts, for the use of the stall-holders. Market days were Tuesday, Friday and Saturday. Early closing day was Wednesday.

This same building still stands – a monument to the foresight of the members of the Local Board. The clock, protected by cherubs and fruit, has been working hard since 1869.

Below: ACCRINGTON, LANCASHIRE, MARKET HALL 1897   40117
Right: ACCRINGTON, LANCASHIRE, MARKET HALL 2004   A19703K

Accrington

CAMELFORD, CORNWALL,
TOWN HALL 1895   36995

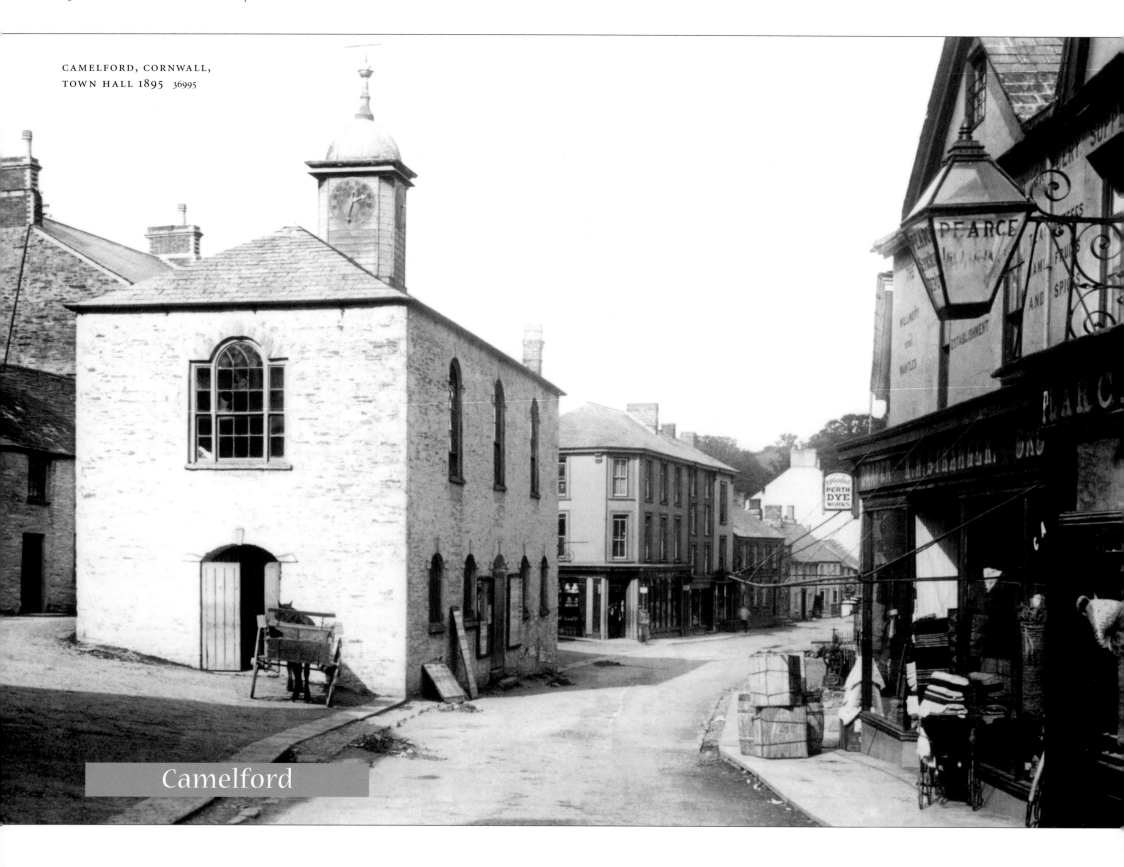

CAMELFORD, CORNWALL,
TOWN HALL 1895   36995

Camelford

THIS ATTRACTIVE TOWN of grey slate houses sits at the edge of Bodmin Moor on the banks of the Camel, and a camel weathercock wittily crowns the fine Town Hall; but in fact the name of the town has nothing to do with the ship of the desert. The name was probably originally Camalanford, which actually means 'ford over the beautiful (alan) crooked river (cam)'. In early times travellers did indeed ford the river, but a bridge was built in 1521.

The Town Hall was built by the Duke of Bedford in 1806. The ground floor was the market house, with its main entrance on the long side of the building. The first floor, reached from the other side of the building by granite steps, was the court house. Today the building serves as the library. Camelford is an ancient borough, and somewhat sleepy and forgotten. Behind the houses are long narrow gardens, remnants of strip cultivation.

An old bell hangs by the door of Camelford's Town Hall; it was given to the town by the then mayor in 1699, and it was rung to warn the people of the town of any danger or calamity such as fire or flood. It used to hang in the cupola.

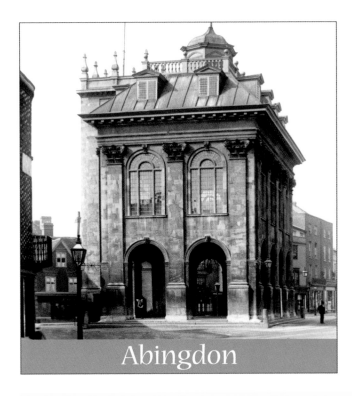

Abingdon

THE TUDOR red brick and half-timbered Moot Hall has dominated Aldeburgh's Main Street for 500 years, and is a reminder of the time of the town's greatest prosperity as a sea port, during the 16th century, before the River Alde was cut off from the sea by the growth of Orford Ness. The building was heavily restored in 1855, and the sundial, visible on the gable end, dates from 1650. It also served as a police station and jail. Today it houses a fine museum display. Little more than a shingle beach protects the Moot Hall from the waves. Once it was centrally placed in the town, but the sea has carried away a number of streets, finally pausing here.

Right: ALDEBURGH, SUFFOLK, THE MOOT HALL 1894   33360

FRITH'S VICTORIAN photographer was looking from the lane leading to the abbey gateway across the Market Place to what is now undoubtedly the finest building in Abingdon: the Town Hall, also (and probably more correctly) called the County Hall, as Abingdon sought to be the county town of Berkshire until the mid 19th century. The building to the left on the corner of Bridge Street, in 1890 a coffee tavern, was sadly demolished in 1938.

The Town Hall is a combination of up-to-the-minute Baroque grandeur and monumentality and the slightly old fashioned style of the stair tower with its almost Jacobean pinnacles and plain elevations. The main part of the Town Hall is superbly proportioned with giant order Corinthian pilasters supporting the cornice. Above it is a leaded top storey with dormers and a cupola. The flat lead roof has a balustrade, and from it there are fine views over the town.

Designed by Christopher Kempster (who was probably advised by Sir Christopher Wren – Kempster was one of the masons Wren used in rebuilding London after the Great Fire of 1666), the Town Hall was built between 1678 and 1685 at a cost of £2,772. Stone plaques record its erection by the Corporation in 1677, a restoration in 1853, and further restoration by the Ministry of Works in the 1950s; by then it was a Scheduled Ancient Monument. Nowadays it is a museum.

Left: ABINGDON, OXFORDSHIRE, THE TOWN HALL 1890   26995

Aldeburgh

POOLE, DORSET, THE QUAY 2004 P72741K

POOLE, DORSET, LIFTING BRIDGE 2004 P72715K

POOLE'S old town retains its fine setting, with the quay protected from the English Channel by its position inside Europe's largest natural harbour. (In world terms it is exceeded in size only by Sydney Harbour in Australia.)

The Guildhall, forming a climax at the end of Market Street, was built in 1761 with provision for a market on the ground floor. Poole Council continued to meet upstairs until 1931. The Angel to the left remains, but the grocer W Fagg has been replaced by award-winning housing. The Guildhall's backdrop has changed today. To the left can be seen the two long windows of the surviving Blue Boar on the corner of Dear Hay Lane, but the police station behind to the right was destroyed by fire in the Second World War.

Poole

The town sits in the bottom of a great bay, or inlet of the sea, which entering at one narrow mouth opens to a very great breadth within the entrance, and comes up to the very shore of this town. This place is famous for the best, and biggest oysters in all this part of England, which the people of Pool pretend to be famous for pickling, and they are barrelled up here, and sent not only to London, but to the West Indies, and to Spain, and Italy, and other parts. 'Tis observed more pearl are found in the Pool oysters, and larger than in any other oysters about England.

DANIEL DEFOE, 'A TOUR THROUGH THE WHOLE ISLAND
OF GREAT BRITAIN', C1725

Left: POOLE, DORSET, THE GUILDHALL 1904 52812P

Reigate

REIGATE, SURREY, THE TOWN HALL AND MARKET PLACE 1925   78937P

BY THE END of the 18th century, Reigate was one of the most prosperous country towns in Surrey. The Town Hall, built in 1729, dominated the Market Square which was lined with elegant old buildings and sufficient pubs and inns to mark it as a major coaching post. A weekly market attracted farmers and traders, and the town itself had a good range of shops and services.

Note the chimneys on each corner of the Town Hall: only one had a fire beneath it, while the others were for aesthetic appeal. The building on the extreme right of the photograph was demolished and replaced by a curious striped building that is a branch of Lloyds Bank, which bears no relation to the town's historical vernacular tradition. The banks were notorious for demolishing Georgian buildings and shops and replacing them with often outlandish structures that were designed to impress and even overawe. The omnibus, with its conductor leaning nonchalantly on the front mudguard, is en route to Kingston-upon-Thames.

Northampton

THIS IS a prime example of the kind of public building that Victorian civic pride erected in the larger industrial towns as they expanded. By the 1860s, the corporation of Northampton was feeling cramped in the 15th-century Guildhall on the corner of Abington Street, looking into the Market Place. Following an architectural competition, which was won by Edward Godwin of Bristol, the foundation stone was laid in St Giles's Square in 1861, and the building formally opened in 1864. Besides council chambers and offices there was a library, which was intended to raise the standards of the local workers' education.

This view shows the Guildhall after it was extended in the same style by Matthew Holding between 1889 and 1892, virtually doubling it in width. The seven bays to the right are Ernest Godwin's original 1861–64 building – the clock-tower was central then. Matthew Holding added the six bays at the left, and improved the building's scale and grandeur immensely. The result was a Gothic town hall to match many a medieval one in Flanders and northern France, according to locals.

NORTHAMPTON, NORTHAMPTONSHIRE, THE GUILDHALL 1922   72181

Northampton has long been a shoe making centre. Fuller wrote concerning the town 'that it may be said to stand chiefly on other men's legs'; and an old saying asserts that 'you know when you are within a mile of Northampton by the smell of the leather and the noise of the lapstones'. In 1895, Brabner's Gazetteer of England and Wales stated: 'Immense quantities of boots and shoes are still made for the supply of the army, the London market, and for exportation. A large trade is also carried on in the tanning and currying of leather.'

WARRINGTON, CHESHIRE, THE TOWN HALL, THE NEW GATES 1895   36688

Warrington

THESE ORNAMENTAL GATES had only recently been erected when this picture was taken. Warrington's Town Hall was originally Bank Hall, built 1749-50 by the world-famous architect James Gibbs as a home for a local businessman, Thomas Patten. (Gibbs had previously designed St Martin in the Fields Church in London and the Radcliffe Library in Oxford). Patten's wealth came from his copper works at Bank Quay. The building was bought from the family to become Warrington's Town Hall in 1872. The ornate gates replaced the brick wall which the Pattens had erected in Sankey Street to give them privacy from curious passers-by. Warrington's ratepayers demanded the right to see their new seat of government!

Probably the most interesting monument in Warrington is the altar tomb of Sir John and Lady Butler, who were murdered in 1463. One of the effigies is of their black servant, who managed to save the life of the murdered couple's infant son.

Southend-on-Sea

THIS BUILDING is a huge contrast to the dignified Georgian or ornate Victorian public buildings of most towns. Southend's Civic Centre is to be found in Victoria Avenue. Where once Prittlewell Church dominated the skyline, now this massive Civic Centre building has taken over. Steel and glass were used in the construction of these offices, opened by the Queen Mother in 1967. The complex includes the Town Hall, the law courts, police headquarters and the Technical College, all built close to the Civic Square. Victoria Avenue is on the left.

In Southend, as in many other towns, fine reminders of the Victorian and Edwardian ages were lost during the building boom of the 1960s and 70s. Victoria Circus was re-developed and a large shopping centre replaced Garons and the Talza Arcade. The High Street was pedestrianised, and Supa-Save, on the site of the Strand Cinema, was a pioneer of supermarket development. The old Olympia building on the seafront is now occupied by an amusement arcade. The beautiful bandstand, which formerly stood on Clifftown Parade and was so popular with the Edwardians, had to be removed after cliff slippage.

However, the bandstand has now been restored and resited at Priory Park; the grand reopening of the bandstand was celebrated on 20 July 2008.

Left: SOUTHEND-ON-SEA, ESSEX, THE CIVIC CENTRE c1967   S155191

Above: SOUTHEND-ON-SEA, ESSEX, THE BANDSTAND c1950   S155032

Harlow

THIS IS a fascinating example of how the 20th-century planners and architects of the post-war new towns tried to bring dignity and beauty to the surroundings of their new public buildings. This is Harlow New Town's Civic Centre, dating from the early 1960s; between it and one of the central car parks these water gardens step down in three levels planted with flowers and shrubs. From a canal at the top, water is delivered through seven lions' heads (designed by William Mitchell) to a central canal, then piped to pools in small enclosed gardens at the lowest level. 'Eve', a bronze by Rodin, was placed at the far end of one of the water canals (in the foreground of H22121), and 'Bronze Cross', by another famous sculptor, Henry Moore, was placed beside the Town Hall. Behind the car park is an uninterrupted view of one of the landscape wedges where the countryside had been preserved as a buffer between the neighbourhood clusters.

Left: HARLOW, ESSEX,
THE CIVIC CENTRE AND THE WATER
GARDENS c1965 H22121

DUNSTABLE'S CIVIC HALL was built during the 1960s, a period of civic pride and enthusiasm, often somewhat misplaced as keen borough surveyors happily authorised the demolishing of period buildings in so many of our towns. This building has a rather pleasing and unusual design, functional and yet futuristic. However, the facility suffered from being under-used, and in 2000 the site was sold to a major supermarket group.

Dunstable nowadays virtually merges with Luton, but it owes its origins to its location on the Icknield Way and to the effects of the Romans building Watling Street; this made it an important crossroads settlement. The stage coach brought steady through traffic and trade, boosting the fortunes of the inns. The rise of straw hat making really set things rolling, and the town became famous; but the population was still only 4,000 when it was incorporated in 1864, compared with Luton's 15,329. Like Luton, it grew apace between and after the wars. It shared in the fortunes of the motor trade as the home of commercial vehicle builders and AC Delco, who made carburettors.

Right: DUNSTABLE, BEDFORDSHIRE, THE CIVIC HALL c1965 D69029

Dunstable

Kendal

IN 1670 the philanthropist Thomas Sandes established a hospital or almshouses in Highgate in Kendal for eight poor widows where he employed a schoolmaster to read prayers to them daily and to teach poor boys until they were ready to attend the grammar school. He also set up a trust to pay £5 a year for seven years for a poor boy to be sent from the grammar school to Queen's College free of charge with an additional £1 a year to be given to the boy for his expenses. He insisted that the boy, chosen by the mayor and corporation, should not be a 'rich man's son'. The gatehouse of Sandes Hospital served as a schoolroom and library and the work of the schoolmaster led to the formation of the Bluecoat School in a tall building at the head of the almshouse gardens which, together with the gatehouse and almshouses, can still be seen. Only boys were taught at first, since only boys went to the grammar school, but in 1714 girls were admitted and were taught by Isobel Fisher. From that year the scholars were all dressed in a blue uniform. The school prospered and in 1886 merged with the new grammar school.

Opposite: KENDAL, CUMBRIA, SANDES HOSPITAL ALMSHOUSES 1914   67399

Above right: REDHILL, SURREY, THE HOSPITAL 1908   59627

Redhill

HOSPITALS ARE an essential component of our towns. This photograph shows typical examples of a cottage hospital and a convalescent home. In 1866 the Reigate Cottage Hospital opened in Albert Road North. It soon ran out of space and moved to new premises in 1871 in Whitepost Hill and took on a new name, Reigate and Redhill Hospital. It was the borough's main hospital until the 1930s. Here we see a young man pushing a perambulator to the door, there to be greeted by a nurse. Is he visiting his sick wife?

There was another, more famous hospital in Redhill, the Royal Earlswood. This dramatic Victorian pile was opened in 1855 as, according to its own literature, an 'asylum for idiots'. The driving force was the Rev Dr Andrew Reed who, before most, saw that the mentally ill needed special treatment. The Royal Earlswood was one of a number of hospitals Dr Reed opened in the south east. Earlswood, which cared for two of the Queen's cousins for many years, closed in 1997, and it has been developed into flats. A small display of artefacts from the Royal Earlswood is now on display in the Belfry shopping centre in Redhill.

Andover

ANDOVER, HAMPSHIRE, THE UNION WORKHOUSE 1906   54627

HAVING OPENED in 1836, the Union in Andover offered a harsh regime until the abolition of the Poor Law in 1930. In 1948 St John's Hospital for the aged and infirm came on site. A girls' hostel was added in 1972 and sheltered housing for the elderly was built in 1982. That year the hospital moved to Charlton Road, and Cricklade College took over the workhouse as classrooms. From 1998 the buildings were converted to private flats, and by 2001 a large number of private houses and flats had been built for sale on the rest of the site.

The first workhouses probably came into being in the 17th century, and it was at the end of Elizabeth I's time that parishes were made legally responsible for the care of their poor, funded by local taxes; relief might be given to the poor in their own homes, or they could be housed in the workhouse, where the able-bodied had to work in return for their keep. The parish workhouse might be an ordinary house converted, or purpose built. Life was not necessarily harsh in the workhouse in earlier times - some institutions were nicknamed 'Pauper Palaces'.

In 1834 the Poor Law Amendment Act formed every parish in England and Wales into a Poor Law Union, each with its Union Workhouse managed by an elected Board of Guardians. Relief would now only be given to those poor who entered the workhouse, where conditions were basic and work was hard (stone-breaking, for example). In many places the workhouse was one of the most prominent buildings in the area, but to enter it was the ultimate disgrace.

By the end of the 19th century conditions improved, especially for the sick and children (who might be sent to special Cottage Homes in the country). In 1930 the Union era ended when the duties of the workhouses were legally passed to the local authorities' social services and the NHS. The subsequent history of the Andover workhouse is a typical one, echoed all over the country.

Bradford-on-Avon

BRADFORD-ON-AVON, WILTSHIRE,
THE CHAPEL AND THE BRIDGE c1955
B174068

IN HIS 'Topographical Collections' of 1659–70, John Aubrey wrote: 'Here is a strong and handsome bridge in the middest of which is a little chapell as at Bathe, for Masse'. Possibly built for pilgrims, the building was later used as the town lock-up and sometimes called the blind house. Some amazing metal lavatories can be seen inside on Heritage Open Day each year.

This bridge and chapel must be one of the most photographed landmarks in west Wiltshire. The Frith photographers obviously found its appeal irresistible. Pevsner's description seems rather mundane: 'Nine arches, plain parapet, essentially c17, though there are still two c13 arches'. The chapel is 'in the middle set on a cutwater (the angular edge of a bridge pier) with its domed roof and bell finial'.

This view up St Margaret's Street shows two fine Georgian buildings: the one on the left has a Tuscan-columned doorway, and the one on the right is Westbury House. Just behind, at the entrance to St Margaret's Hall, we can see the petrol pumps of Stamper's Garages Ltd. The entrance to the public gardens and former swimming pool and baths is bottom left.

Castle Cary

CASTLE CARY, SOMERSET, THE OLD PRISON c1955 C611023

ALSO KNOWN as the Blind House from its lack of windows, and as the Roundhouse, this was the village lock-up. Built in 1779, it sometimes held children playing truant from school. The roof of Castle Cary lock-up is reputed to have inspired the design of the modern British police helmet.

Most small town lock-ups date from the 18th and early 19th centuries. In those days, there was no organised county police force, and each community had to deal with criminals themselves. Lock-ups fell out of use after 1839, when the County Police Act provided a paid police force in every county and local police stations, each with its own secure cells.

Cage, jug, bridewell, bone-house ...

Lock-ups have been given many nicknames, including blind house, bone-house, bridewell, cage, jug, kitty, lobby, guard-house, roundhouse, tower and watch-house.

Buckingham

THIS ROMANTIC ivy-covered Gothic pile was actually built in 1748 by Lord Cobham, the owner of nearby Stowe, famous for its landscape garden and Gothic and classical follies and temples. This building looks like another folly, but in fact it was the gaol, fittingly built in the style of a medieval castle keep. The rounded part of the building nearest the camera (the gaoler's house) was added in 1839; this was an early work by a local man, George Gilbert Scott, who went on to become one of the most distinguished architects of his age. Today the ivy has been removed, and the old gaol is a museum.

One renowned prisoner at Buckingham's gaol was Simon Byrne, a prizefighter, who in 1830 was tried at Buckingham Assizes for the manslaughter of fellow prizefighter Alex Mackay.

BUCKINGHAM, BUCKINGHAMSHIRE, THE OLD GAOL c1950 B280028

Herded together, cheek by jowl

Bodmin gaol was no doubt better than many of the smaller prisons … A writer (circa 1799) states that he found the male prisoners here employed on regular tasks, such as gardening and 'polishing moorstone for chimney pieces', and the females in spinning and weaving, and making rugs, in the profits of which they were allowed some small share. Even so, however, he points out that all the women prisoners were herded together 'cheek by jowl' in one room, and that hardened criminals committed for offences of a brutal character were undergoing the same system of correction as those who had been condemned for the most trifling misdemeanours.

The law itself, as may clearly be seen, recognized no distinction between the thorough-paced criminal, the juvenile offender, and the unfortunate half-wit. In 1813 a poor, crazy, servant girl was hanged at Bodmin for setting fire to a rick.

FROM A M HAMILTON JENKIN, 'CORNWALL AND ITS PEOPLE', DAVID & CHARLES, 1945

Bodmin

THIS MOST forbidding building was built as the County Gaol in the late 18th century. It was rebuilt in the 1850s to include cells, the governor's accommodation, a chapel and an impressive gateway. Public hangings took place here until 1862. It is said that the townspeople relished these executions, crowding the slopes on the opposite side of the valley to watch and cheer. Part of the building became a naval prison from 1888 to 1922. The old Bodmin and Wadebridge Railway can just be glimpsed below the prison.

This bleak institution was closed at the turn of the century, and quickly decayed into a chilling ruin.

Left: BODMIN, CORNWALL, THE PRISON c1955 B129042

Trisha May shared this memory of Bodmin Prison on the Francis Frith website: 'On Halloween night 2007 some friends and myself wanted to do something different for our Halloween night, so where better to do it than at the old Bodmin prison? So off we set at 9 o'clock making tracks to the prison. It was a great evening. We spent some hours in the darkest depths of the prison, and we are convinced we did see a ghost of a man in the Naval Wing, and we did some filming and we got some pictures of what looked like orbs – it was a very interesting evening. We would like to point out that this is not the place to visit if you are easily frightened, as the prison has an odd smell to it and you hear a lot of strange noises and see a number of shadows that are not there when you turn around. It would be worth a visit if you are interested in ghost hunting.'

Haverfordwest

IN MEDIEVAL times Haverfordwest's prison was inside the castle itself. By the 16th century, the castle had slipped into decline, and by 1577 it was described as 'utterlie decayed'; but there was a prison there then – a 'rounde tower, under which is a stronge prison house'. Another prison was built within the castle ward in 1779, along with the Prison Governor's House, but by 1818 this prison was already considered inadequate, and plans were drawn up for a new prison in the outer ward. It was closed in 1878 and subsequently became the headquarters of the Pembrokeshire Police. In 1967 the building was converted to house the Pembrokeshire County Museum and Records Office. One of the doors to these cells pictured here is on display in the museum.

Left: HAVERFORDWEST, DYFED, THE INTERIOR OF THE OLD PRISON c1950 H41004

Maidenhead

ONE OF the most prominent buildings in the streets of almost any town is the public library, and Maidenhead is no exception. A proud modern library (below), built in 1973, has replaced the old Free Library in St Ives Road, shown here when it was newly built – it opened in 1904. It was funded by public subscription and donations; the American philanthropist Andrew Carnegie, who donated to libraries all over the country, was a significant donor, as was Alderman Nicholson. The subscribers were provided with a high quality design by their architects, Arthur McKewan and G H V Cole, who employed a sort of Baroque cum Wren style. It cost £6,000. The cedar tree was a survival from the grounds of Ives Place, a mansion and later a hotel, which stood where the present 1962 Town Hall is located.

Far left: MAIDENHEAD, BERKSHIRE, FREE IBRARY 1904 53148

Left: MAIDENHEAD, BERKSHIRE, THE LIBRARY 2004 M7716K

FOLLOWING the passing of the Technical Act of 1889, Halifax Corporation began this fine building in Hopwood Lane (right); it was completed in 1895. Here, technical education could be carried out away from the pressures of the workplace. Further education remains on this site: the Calderdale College now occupies the building. This photograph shows looms and other equipment installed in a workshop at the technical school; it underlines the importance of the cloth industry to the town.

Straight to the gibbet

The cloth industry was so important to this area that Halifax had been granted permission to make its own laws for dealing with people convicted of stealing cloth. This law was limited to the forest of Hardwick, including the 18 towns and villages within its boundary. Anyone found with stolen cloth 'shall be taken to the gibbet and there have his head cut from his body'. Halifax had had a decapitating machine long before the French Revolution – Dr Guillotine simply improved on the idea.

Halifax

HALIFAX, YORKSHIRE, THE TECHNICAL SCHOOL 1896 38781

BURNLEY, LANCASHIRE, THE MECHANICS' INSTITUTE 1895 35787

BURNLEY TOWN HALL (in the background), with, to its right, the Mechanics' Institute, are perhaps the most impressive buildings on Manchester Road. Opened in 1888, the Town Hall is an elaborate building (perhaps over-elaborate) in the Classical style; it does its job of dominating the Manchester Road very well.

Architecturally the Burnley Mechanics' Institute, which is by the local architect James Green, is a much better building than the Town Hall. It dates from 1855, though in 1887 a new entrance was made to the Concert Hall, and a year later a new wing, once the Burnley School of Art, was added to the Yorke Street elevation. The large entrance with the four Corinthian columns (right) is part of the original building, but the slightly compressed part of the structure, far right, is the 1888 extension. Both the later extensions are by William Waddington.

Mechanics' Institutes provided working men with educational and social opportunities unheard of before. This one served Burnley until 1959. Then, like many similar bodies across the country, a declining membership resulted in its closure. It had been competing with Council facilities, like the library and the college, whose services were often free. Afterwards, the building opened as the Casino Club, and since 1986, it has been Burnley's Arts and Entertainments Centre.

At one time Burnley was described as the town with the most advertising hoardings in the country, probably because of rivalry between local firms. The hoardings here generally inform locals about what is happening at the Mechanics', though there are commercial advertisements too. The three men are clearly more interested in the photographer from Frith.

DESIGNED BY Borough Surveyor Charles Clegg, this amazing 100ft building, affectionately known as Jumbo, was opened amid great civic pomp in 1882. It dominates the landscape for miles around and was built in a monumental Baroque style. (The pond is now replaced by the uncompromisingly modern Mercury Theatre, built in 1972).

Jumbo is the largest surviving Victorian water tower in Britain, and an increasingly rare example of a tower in its original state. Its vast tank and colossal pipes and valves are still there. It is also unusual in that it was built around a central shaft containing a spiral staircase; this leads to a room on the top of the tower, which needless to say affords panoramic views.

Colchester's Jumbo is a monument to the vast improvement in public health that came about in Victorian times thanks to the supply of clean water to all. Previously, deadly diseases like cholera had been spread by water pollution; the Victorian era brought properly engineered sewers, plumbing, reservoirs and water tanks – and an end to the drudgery of fetching water in buckets and to the expense of buying water from water carriers.

COLCHESTER, ESSEX, THE WATER TOWER 1907 57541

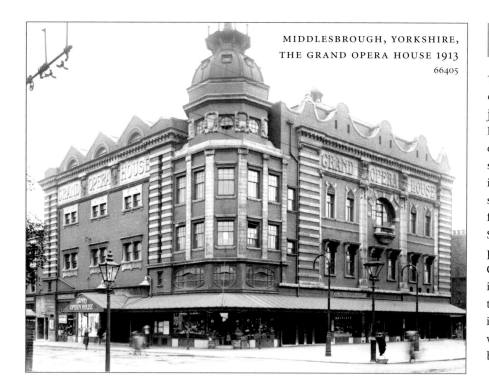

MIDDLESBROUGH, YORKSHIRE,
THE GRAND OPERA HOUSE 1913
66405

Middlesbrough

THIS HIGHLY UNUSUAL, ornate and characterful opera house was built at the junction of Southfield Road and Linthorpe Road in 1903 at a cost of £38,000; it was opened by the local MP, Samuel Sadler. Eight shops and an oyster bar were incorporated into the building. An old farm had once stood here, and then the area was used for fairs and shows; it was known to locals as Swatters Carr. This venue saw many famous people performing on its stage, including Charlie Chaplin and Gracie Fields. It closed in June 1930 and reopened in March 1931 as the Gaumont cinema. The Gaumont closed in 1964, and then the Opera House building was demolished to make way for an office block, sad to say.

Buxton

Above: BUXTON, DERBYSHIRE,
THE OPERA HOUSE 1923   74134

Opposite right: BUXTON, DERBYSHIRE,
THE OPERA HOUSE 1923   74133

THE NEW OPERA HOUSE at Buxton opened in 1903. It was built at the north-eastern corner of the gardens adjacent to the main entrance. The Gardens Company chose the prolific theatre architect Frank Matcham to design the building; despite being built into a rather cramped and irregular area, it was erected in a relatively short time and to very high specifications. A cantilever supporting design for the dress and upper circles obviated the need for supporting pillars, and thus a good view of the stage could be obtained from all parts of the house.

The Opera House was used as a cinema in the 1930s but following a restoration in 1979, it has been used as a theatre ever since. A recent and more thorough restoration, completed in spring 2000 with the aid of Heritage Lottery funding, has restored the building to its original splendour; it is a sight worth seeing for all visitors to the town.

PROMINENT in this mid-50s view of Holywell Street is the Odeon cinema, theatre and ballroom. Holywell Street presents a rather pleasant picture of 20th-century half-timbered revival buildings, some of which would not appear out of place in Chester. The Peter Sellers and Robert Morley film 'Battle of the Sexes' is showing at the Odeon, but also of interest is the Thrift Shop, an early attempt at a discount store. The Odeon is now the Winding Wheel Theatre – named in tribute to the town's coal mining tradition – which has a fine reputation for travelling variety and popular music shows.

Right: CHESTERFIELD,
DERBYSHIRE,
HOLYWELL STREET, THE ODEON
CINEMA c1955 C83041

Chesterfield

Keeping the faith

DOES EVERY town have a Church Street? Certainly, the streetscape in the centre of our towns is almost always dominated by the parish church, whose tower or spire, Gothic details and quiet churchyard give a welcome contrast to the mundane bustle that surround them. We must not forget the nonconformist chapels. The larger Victorian ones, often splendidly extrovert, cheerfully punctuate the busy streets of our industrial towns.

Bradford-on-Avon

THIS SAXON CHURCH had been concealed by sheds and buildings for many centuries. It was rediscovered in the 19th century by Canon W H R Jones, a keen antiquarian; he came across references to it in a text dated 1125. Excavations outside revealed the walls, and repairs revealed the carvings. The simplicity and to some extent the austerity of St Laurence's contrasts with the richness of the churches of later times; we are not used to churches without stained glass, or in fact without windows at all. This church would have been lit by candles. Arthur Mee in his 'King's England' series says about the church: 'It is naked and bare, and all the better for that'. The chancel arch is the narrowest in England at 3ft 6 inches wide. The walls are 2ft 5 inches thick, and the decorations were all cut by Saxon masons. John Chandler and Derek Parker describe the effect of the church on the visitor in 'Wiltshire Churches, an Illustrated History': 'There is an aura of intense mystery, and to submit to its darkness by entering on a sunny day can be a profoundly awesome experience.'

Left: BRADFORD-ON-AVON, WILTSHIRE, ST LAURENCE'S CHURCH 1900   45381

Right: BRADFORD-ON-AVON, WILTSHIRE, ST LAURENCE'S CHURCH INTERIOR 1900   45383

THE MASSIVE tower of St Andrew's Church is mainly Norman work, built of red sandstone with walls 6ft thick. When it was built, Penrith was troubled by border warfare, and the tower was used as a shelter and strongpoint. The rest of the church was rebuilt in the 1720s in the classical style to a design by Hawksmoor. Inside are murals painted by a local artist, Jacob Thompson.

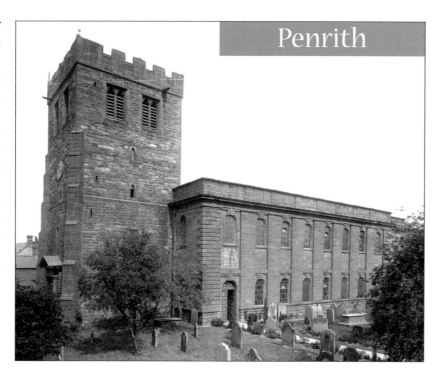

Penrith

The church's rushbearing procession

Originally church floors were made of beaten earth and covered in rushes, and it was commonplace to bury people inside the church as well as in the churchyard. On the church's saint's day, parishioners would bring fresh rushes and herbs to strew on the church floor to purify the air and help keep the worshippers' feet warm and dry. This festivity was known as rushbearing, and continued until as recently as the 1800s – after that, the floors were flagged or tiled. However, the ancient custom is still alive in some Cumbrian parishes, where rushes and flowers are paraded round the village in procession: a band is followed by the clergy and then by the children, who carry a rush or flower cross, which is brought to the church.

Above: PENRITH, CUMBRIA, ST ANDREW'S CHURCH 1893 32924
Right: PENRITH, CUMBRIA, THE GIANT'S GRAVE 1893 32926

The Giant's Grave in St Andrew's churchyard is actually a collection of two badly weathered 10th-century cross shafts and four Norse 'hogback' tombstones. Stories about the grave have been linked not only with the mythical giant Sir Owen Caesarius and the Arthurian legends, but also with Owain, son of Urien, a 6th-century King of Rheged, and Owen, King of Cumbria from AD920 to AD937. The Giant's Thumb stands close to the Giant's Grave and is another badly eroded stone cross dating to about the year AD920. In later years, the Giant's Thumb was used as a public pillory.

Boston

IT IS SAID that the Boston Stump, the tower of the parish church of St Botolph, is 'built on wool'. Some people think this is because sacks of wool were thrown into the foundation pit when the tower was built. This is not so. In fact, it means that the tower was paid for from the profits made by the merchants importing and exporting wool and other goods through the medieval port of Boston.

When we look at St Botolph's Church rising over the riverside wharves or the market place it is hard to believe that it did not get its present appearance until the very end of the medieval period. Boston was no longer as rich as it had been, so it took longer to build the tower than to build the church itself. Begun c1430, it was not completed until about 1520, just a few years before the Reformation. The tower is the tallest on a parish church in England, and because of its height (272 feet), and the imposing scale of the whole building, St Botolph's is often mistaken for a cathedral. It is a remarkable testimony to the skill of medieval masons that the tower still stands despite being so close to a tidal river. The top part of the tower is called a lantern, which refers to its shape, not to a medieval lighthouse with a fire inside its lantern! The name 'Boston Stump' only seems to have been used for the last 200 years or so, and the name was probably intended to tease Boston people, who are justifiably proud of their church tower.

Top: BOSTON, LINCOLNSHIRE, DOUGHTY QUAY 1890 26066T

Above: BOSTON, LINCOLNSHIRE, ST BOTOLPH'S CHURCH, THE NAVE LOOKING EAST 1890 26075

Left: BOSTON, LINCOLNSHIRE, MARKET PLACE AND THE CHURCH 1890 26068

Hitchin

HITCHIN, HERTFORDSHIRE,
ST MARY'S CHURCH 1908   60881T

THE OLDEST of Hitchin's churches is St Mary's, which stands in the centre of the town, to the west of the River Hiz. It was originally dedicated to St Andrew. Development over many years has encroached upon the churchyard, which was originally much larger than it is today; burials have turned up as far away as Brand Street.

The existing church dates from the 12th century, reputedly on the site of an earlier Saxon building. Like most of Britain's churches, additions and alterations have been made to it ever since, sometimes by design, and occasionally by necessity: part of the building collapsed in 'a great wind' in 1115, in 1298 more damage was done by an earthquake, and in 1304 the roof fell in. The 13th-century tower (its buttresses are later) has Roman tiles built into it, and a double sundial dated 1660 supplements the clock. The dial is marked 'Anno Salvus', 'the year of salvation', a reference to the restoration of the monarchy following the Civil War. The tower is topped with a short steeple of a type known as a Hertfordshire spike.

The iron railings were erected around St Mary's churchyard to keep out the resurrection men, or bodysnatchers, who stole corpses for dissection by the medical profession. The railings were erected by public subscription following the theft of the body of Elizabeth Whitehead in 1828; Elizabeth was not the first victim, but the townsfolk were resolved that she should be the last. The railings were removed before the Second World War, and not during it as is sometimes suggested.

Taunton

THIS GLORIOUS TOWER at the end of the street and the Georgian terraces leading to it make a most satisfying composition. The wealth that was created in Taunton in the Middle Ages by both agriculture and the cloth industry was often spent on the construction of fine buildings, especially churches and their soaring towers. A Perpendicular style of church towers developed in Somerset, which is distinctive enough for them to be known as 'Somerset Towers'. The 163ft-high tower of St Mary Magdalene's Church, built of Old Red Quantock sandstone and Ham Hill stone, dominates the skyline of Taunton. It is one of the most beautiful of many exquisite church towers in Somerset, despite being a reconstruction. The rebuild of the tower was completed in 1862 to the lines of the original 15th-century design. During the rebuild of the tower of St Mary Magdalene's, a donkey powered the pulley which took up the stone to the workmen. When the work was completed in 1862, the donkey was taken up to the top of the tower to admire the view!

Left: TAUNTON, SOMERSET, ST MARY MAGDALENE'S CHURCH 1888 20859

Chesterfield

CHESTERFIELD, DERBYSHIRE, THE CHURCH OF ST MARY AND ALL SAINTS 1902   48888P

DESPITE LOOKING as though it is about to topple over, the spire of St Mary and All Saints is stable. The twist is a result of the heat of the sun on the lead plates, which in turn warped the green timber underneath them. A less prosaic story is the tradition that the Devil visited Chesterfield one windy day and sat on the top of the spire so that he could have a good look at the town. To prevent himself from falling, Old Nick twisted his tail round the spire, but he was so shocked when he heard a local speak the truth that he flew off without unwinding his tail, causing the spire to twist. The earliest written record of St Mary's dates from 1100, when the church was given to the Dean and Chapter of Lincoln. The oldest part of the present structure dates from the 13th century, and both the tower and the south transept were added during the 14th century.

A ridgy, spiral spire of puzzling construction

It would be very difficult to convey any idea of it by any description from an unaided pen; and there is nothing extant that would avail as an illustration. The church is very old and large, and stands upon a commanding eminence. The massive tower supports a tall but suddenly tapering spire of the most puzzling construction to the eye. It must have been designed by a monk of the olden time, with a Chinese turn of ingenuity. There is no order known to architecture to furnish a term or likeness for it. A ridgy, spiral spire are the three most descriptive words, but these are not half enough for stating the shape, style and posture of this strange steeple. It is difficult even to assist the imagination to form an idea of it. I will essay a few words in that direction. Suppose, then, a plain spire, 100 feet high, in the form of an attenuated cone, planted upon a heavy church tower. Now, in imagination, plough this cone all around into deep ridges from top to bottom. Then mount to the top, and, with a great iron wrench, give it an even twist clear down to the base, so that each ridge shall wind entirely around the spire between the bottom and the top. Then, in giving it this screw-looking twist, bend over the top, with a gentle incline all the way down, so that it shall be 'out of perpendicular' by about three feet. Then come down and look at your work, and you will be astonished at it, standing far or near. The tall, ridgy, curved, conical screw puzzles you with all sorts of optical illusions. As the eyes in a front-face portrait follow you around the room in which it is hung, so this strange spire seems to lean over upon you at every point, as you walk round the church.

ELIHU BURRITT, 'A WALK FROM LONDON TO JOHN O'GROATS', 1864

Sidmouth

THE FIRST VICAR took up his living here in 1175, around the time the church was first built. It was completely rebuilt in 1450, and restored in 1859. The church is dedicated to St Nicholas, patron saint of sailors, and St Giles, who was much revered by the monks of Mont Saint Michel in Normandy, one-time owners of the manor of Sidmouth.

The Lady Chapel window contains a rare 15th-century fragment of glass known as the Five Wounds Window, depicting the wounds of Christ. The west window was given by Queen Victoria in memory of her father the Duke of Kent, who died in Sidmouth in 1820. The window was designed in 1867 by Hughes and depicts some of St Nicholas's deeds.

Sheep are standing outside the church gate. Could they have been grazing the churchyard grass?

Right: SIDMOUTH, DEVON, ST NICHOLAS'S CHURCH AND CHURCH STREET 1924 76372

BENEATH St Leonard's Church at Hythe is an ambulatory, which contains a collection of human remains. Macabre though this seems, the practice was not uncommon during the Middle Ages, though few such collections exist today. The skulls and bones here pictured make up the remains of some 4,000 people, which are thought to have been disinterred from old graves to make way for new. Most of the remains seem to date from between the 12th and 15th centuries, though some may be up to 300 years older. What is particularly puzzling about the skulls is that they have marked Italian characteristics. It has been suggested that a pocket of Romano-Britons lived in the Hythe area for centuries after the departure of the Romans, who had little to do with their Saxon neighbours. In time, their characteristics died out as the population mingled with newcomers during the Middle Ages.

Left: HYTHE, KENT, ST LEONARD'S CHURCH, THE CHARNEL HOUSE 1903 50381A

Hythe

WIMBORNE MINSTER, DORSET,
ST MARGARET'S CHAPEL AND
THE ALMSHOUSES 1908 60634

Wimborne Minster

A LITTLE outside the centre of Wimborne, on the road to Kingston Lacy, lies this charming group of nine cottages and a chapel. In the 13th century, the chapel was part of a leper hospital. In the 17th century, William Stone, who founded the library at Wimborne Minster, endowed the almshouses. This photograph shows one of the oldest of the houses. Behind the photographer are grouped more of the almshouses around a broad area of pretty cottage gardens. The chapel, built in dark brown stone, has a plain, modest interior with bare walls; the paired windows have trefoil tops. The whole complex, beside a now busy road, looks just the same today as it does in the photograph, and offers visitors an oasis of rest.

Corsham

JUST OUTSIDE Corsham, in Monks Lane, near Gastard, stands the 17th-century Congregational Chapel. The chapel was originally owned by the Society of Friends (the Quakers), and was bought from them in 1690. This fascinating photograph shows the late 17th-century fittings, including box pews and pulpit, and the gallery, which was built in the year the chapel was bought.

Left: CORSHAM, WILTSHIRE, THE CONGREGATIONAL CHAPEL INTERIOR 1907 57808

THIS VERY imposing building stood on the corner of Corporation and Linthorpe Roads. It was affectionately nicknamed 'Big Wesley' by the townspeople. It was built in 1862, at a cost of £4,400. Perhaps the people attired in their Sunday best are on their way into the chapel to listen to the two sermons to be read by the Rev David Wellor as proclaimed on the church board. The chapel was eventually demolished, and British Home Stores took the site.

Right: MIDDLESBROUGH, YORKSHIRE, THE WESLEYAN CHAPEL 1896 47979

Middlesbrough

Defence in troubled times

THE ANCIENT walls and gates that surround the streets of our towns bear witness to more troubled times, when towns needed to be able to defend themselves from marauders and vagrants. A town's gates were also a way of making money – the gatekeeper would impose tolls on people, goods, animals and vehicles. Some towns still have the remnants of very old walls – there are Roman walls at Colchester and St Albans, for example. Most of the walls and gates we see in this chapter are Norman and medieval.

Tenby

Above right: TENBY, DYFED, THE FIVE ARCHES 1890   28078

PROBABLY the best-known and most prominent feature of the medieval walls of Tenby is the Five Arches, built in 1328. This gateway, an innovative design brought back from the Crusades to the Holy Land, had its entrance on the side; this made it battering ram-proof, and brought invaders into the line of fire of defenders along the top of the wall. The original entrance still has a slot for its portcullis. The remaining four arches were knocked through in the 19th century to improve the flow of traffic in and out of the town – originally, opposite the Five Arches were cottages built so closely that only a man walking or a horse being led could pass between them. It is miraculous that the structurally weakened tower survived.

Tenby was never designed for use by the motorcar, of course, and apart from some Victorian road widening, with the demolition of some old terraces and properties, the older part of the town still largely adheres to its medieval street system. Outside the town walls, many streets were laid out in the 19th century principally to provide lodging houses for the many visitors who came to the town once Tenby became part of the wider rail network.

The barrels to the left of the arch in this photograph probably belong to the Bush Inn, whose cellar entrance can be seen between what were probably the naughty boys who cropped up regularly in local newspapers of the day. Although in 1882 the Great Western Electric Company felt themselves in a position to accept an application for the lighting of Tenby with electricity, the lamp on the arches (left) was probably gas.

THE SOUTH GATES at Lynn are always known locally in the plural, no doubt a reference to the gates themselves, rather than the gatehouse. This gate still forms a remarkable entry for visitors into the medieval and mid Victorian town. This handsome tower of brick and stone has a misleading plaque (built into it in the early 1900s) with the date 1520 on it. This relates only to the re-facing of the building in second-hand stone, and work done to the interior arches. Most of the gatehouse was built of brick between 1437 and 1440, on the site of at least one earlier building. There has been a gatehouse here since before 1300. Noble folk in their carriages would use the centre archway, looking down on lesser mortals who had to walk through the small arches.

The gatekeeper was a civic officer in medieval times, and a significant member of the community. He needed to be capable of writing and keeping accounts of the tolls collected. He would be armed with a heavy club; part of his duties was to check on vagrants and strangers, who would not be admitted unless they could give a good account of themselves. Later the job must have become more like that of a council superintendent, for included in its title was 'Keeper of the Muckhills' – the organiser of waste disposal.

Below: KING'S LYNN, NORFOLK, SOUTHGATES 1891 28760P

King's Lynn

THIS WELL-WORN structure of decorative flint work was part of the old medieval town walls, built as a fortification at the end of the 13th century. It was raised in height in the time of the threat of the Spanish Armada. Until the 19th century, building was kept within the old walls. After this date there was an inevitable spreading of streets and tramways, as we can see. The tram is advertising one of Norfolk's most famous products: Colman's Mustard. It is passing the Tower Curing Works, which is to become a museum.

The town walls of Yarmouth, large stretches of which survive, were described by the 17th-century poet Thomas Nash as 'a flinty ring of 15 towers which sent out thunder whenever a Spaniard dared to come near'. The chequer-board pattern still to be seen on this south-east tower was also a feature of the South Gate, pulled down in 1812: it was added in the 16th century. The stretch of wall near Blackfriars Tower had fallen down earlier in the century, and it was repaired using a combination of local flint and limestone from the nearby monastery of the Black Friars, which had burnt down in 1522; the white blocks of freestone can still be seen in the flint wall.

Great Yarmouth

Facing the threat of the Spanish Armada

Great Yarmouth's town walls form one of the half-dozen finest surviving town walls in England – and probably the least well known. The walls were 23 feet high and 2,200 yards long, enclosing an area of 133 acres. There were 15 towers and 8 gates, of which the South Gate and North Gate were by far the largest: both were pulled down in the early 19th century. The walls were last prepared for action at the time of the Spanish Armada in 1588. The walls were neglected for many centuries, and people built houses against them, as we can see in 60653, left. As late as 1901 a stretch of the medieval wall was pulled down to make way for houses along Rampart Road. Twenty years later attitudes had begun to change: in 1919 the Council spent £100 on repairs to a section of the wall which was in danger of falling down.

Left: GREAT YARMOUTH, BLACKFRIARS TOWER 1908 60653

Monmouth

ONE OF the unique attractions in Monmouth has to be the Monnow Bridge with its distinctive fortified gate. Originally a wooden structure (its remains have been found), the bridge is late Norman, built in 1262, and is one of the few Norman bridges still surviving in Britain, and a rare example of a fortified gateway on a bridge. Although impressively built to withstand attack, including the addition of a portcullis, the bridge proved ineffective: the River Monnow which it spanned can easily be forded, and during the Civil War this is exactly what happened, so that the defenders soon found themselves surrounded. Monmouth has retained its medieval street layout, and this helps to give a distinctive feel to the historic town.

The town has a long history. Built on the site of the Roman settlement of Blestium, Monmouth was also occupied by Norman settlers; William FitzOsbern established the first wooden fortress here. This was replaced in the 12th century by a more permanent stone structure. A settlement grew around the castle walls, including a Benedictine priory. Perhaps one of the more famous sons of the town is the 12th-century author Geoffrey of Monmouth.

Above: MONMOUTH, GWENT, BRIDGE OVER THE MONNOW c1891 28780

Left: MONMOUTH, GWENT, BRIDGE ON THE MONNOW c1878 10595

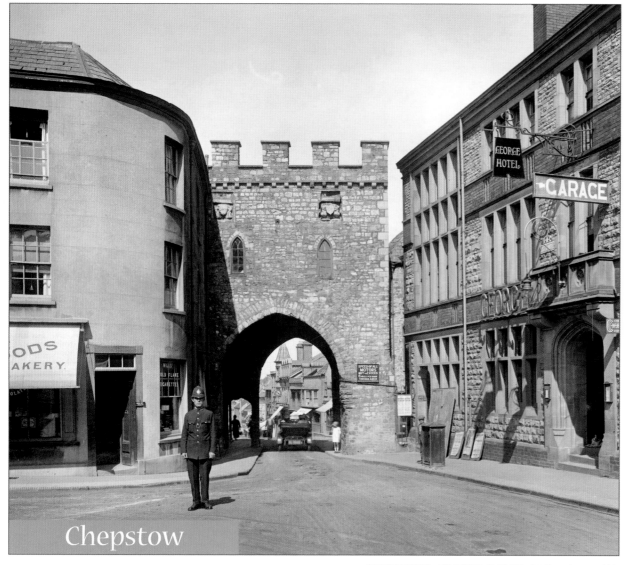

Chepstow

CHEPSTOW, GWENT, WHITE LION SQUARE 2004 C77707K

CHEPSTOW, GWENT, THE GEORGE HOTEL AND TOWN GATE
2004 C77747K

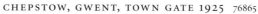

CHEPSTOW, GWENT, TOWN GATE 1925 76865

WE ARE looking at the gate which was originally part of the town wall known locally as the Port Wall, built in the late 13th century during the lordship of Roger Bigod. The wall protected Chepstow on the landward side, while the River Wye protected it to the north and east. It is a surprising fact that this impressive structure was built not for defence, but simply to control access to the town. This kind of wall is known as a customs wall. There was once a toll here, and everything being brought into the town to be sold in the market was liable for market dues.

The Port Wall was over 1,200 yards long, 6 feet thick and 15 feet high. There were probably at least a dozen towers about 27 feet in diameter along its length; outside the wall there was a large ditch about 18 feet wide and 5 feet deep.

The Town Gate, the only landward entrance to the town, was controlled by means of a gate and portcullis. Originally built at the same time as the Port Wall, it was rebuilt later – what we see today dates largely from the early 16th century. The gate was extensively restored in 1986. The room above the arch (note the two narrow lancet windows) has had many and varied uses, including prison, guard room, quarters for the local constable, a tailor's workroom, and museum.

In the 1925 photograph, the notice on the arch restricts the speed of all motors to 6 miles per hour through the arch, while the poster beside it is advertising a fete. Auctions were regularly held in the George Hotel (right), and indeed here there are house auction notices propped up against the wall.

Bridgnorth

BRIDGNORTH, as a fortified hilltop site, dates from Saxon times. Visiting the town at the beginning of the Civil War, Charles I described the view from the castle ramparts as 'the finest in my kingdom'. However, since he was looking for finance from the locals, he may have been laying on the charm.

The North Gate is the only part of the town's medieval defences to survive, apart from the remains of the 12th-century castle. Even in the 1580s, the castle was described by John Leland as being 'totally to ruin', but the Parliamentarians finally destroyed the castle in 1646 with gunpowder. Their activities left a section of the keep leaning over at an angle of 17 degrees, three times that of the leaning tower of Pisa. The North Gate itself was heavily restored during the 18th century.

Left: BRIDGNORTH, SHROPSHIRE, NORTH GATE 1896 38127

The poet Walter Savage Landor had a troubled life. He was expelled both from Rugby and Trinity College, Oxford, and spent a large part of his life abroad. A prolific poet and playwright, he is best remembered today as the author of 'Imaginary Conversations' (1824–29). In 1807 he bought Llanthony Abbey and its land in a beautiful valley in the Welsh Black Mountains. He hoped to create a grand estate for himself, but had so much local opposition that he was compelled to give up the project. He died in Florence in 1864.

THE ONLY REMAINING parts of the walls which once surrounded Warwick are the east and west gatehouses. The fine house on this side of East Gate was modernised in 1692, just two years before the Great Fire of Warwick. Its owner, a Dr Johnson (not *the* Dr Johnson) was so concerned about the approach of the fire that he had a neighbour's house demolished as a firebreak. Unfortunately, the fire went nowhere near his house, and he had to pay £20 in compensation. In 1775 the writer Walter Savage Landor was born in the house – he tended to live up to his middle name. Today the house and East Gate forms part of King's High School for Girls.

WARWICK, THE WEST GATE

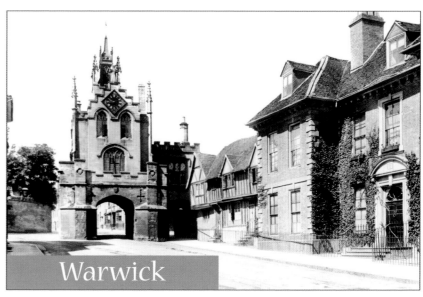

Warwick

WARWICK, WARWICKSHIRE, EAST GATE AND WALTER SAVAGE LANDOR'S HOUSE 1892 31029

'At Warwick the past joins hands so stoutly with the present that you can hardly say where one begins and the other ends … There is a Caesar's tower and a Guy's tower and half a dozen more, but they are so well-conditioned in their ponderous antiquity that you are at a loss whether to consider them parts of an old house revived or of a new house picturesquely superannuated.'
HENRY JAMES, 'ENGLISH HOURS', 1905

Totnes

TOTNES BECAME a walled town in about 1215. Although much of the wall has now disappeared, this eastern gate in Fore Street (21629) still stands. It was rebuilt in the early 1500s, and originally had two gates, one for carts and one for pedestrians. This arch was widened to its present configuration in 1837. On 4 September 1991 an electrical fault caused a disastrous fire. Fifteen fire appliances were needed to get the fire under control - it caused £10 million of damage. The gate was restored and re-opened in 1992.

The steep Fore Street is a delightful mix of ancient buildings. The Butterwalk, beyond Eastgate, was built to provide traders with shelter from the elements as they sold their wares. The pillars are said to be over 500 years old. Nearby was Birdwalk, where poultry was sold, cattle were sold from the square at the top of the street, and meat was sold in the main square down the hill.

'Time was when the town itself was walled, but the wall went with the need of it and two medieval gateways alone remain, the rough arch of the north gate framing one of the prettiest views, and the 16th-century east gate with a panelled room over it in which is a finely coloured frieze and two heads on a chimneypiece, perhaps Henry the Eighth and one of his wives.'

ARTHUR MEE, 'THE KING'S ENGLAND: DEVON', 1938

Above: TOTNES, DEVON, NORTH GATE 1890   25412

Left: TOTNES, DEVON, EASTGATE 1889   21629

Beverley

THE NORTH BAR ranks alongside the Minster, St Mary's and the Market Cross as a feature of Beverley which visitors never forget. It is the only one of the four gates surviving into the age of photography, and it provides a clear point of entry into the town, distinguishing what is outside (North Bar Without and New Walk) from what is inside (North Bar Within).

Built of brick in 1409-10 at a cost of £96 0s 11½ d, it had some defensive role against unwanted intruders, though Beverley was never a walled town but only weakly defended by the surrounding Bar Dyke, which caused it to suffer badly during such conflicts as the Civil War. The Bar may have served as a toll-collecting point for traders attending markets and fairs in Beverley.

Typical Georgian buildings had stood here, but as photograph 17884 shows, while Nos 2 (nearest the Bar), 6 and 8 retained their original appearance, No 4 was given a dramatic Victorian facelift by the Beverley wood carver James E Elwell. He created the black and white timbered facade which is such a recognisable landmark to visitors entering from York – though it gives a misleading impression of the architecture to be found in Beverley.

A breath of fresh air

PARKS AND gardens provide a welcome relief from the streets that surround them. Some towns have long had their open spaces (Harrogate had its Stray, and Southwold its greens, for example), but most parks are a Victorian innovation, provided as an additional draw for tourists or as a philanthropic gesture to promote the health and welfare of the town's workers and their families.

Buxton

Top: BUXTON, DERBYSHIRE, THE PROMENADING CORRIDOR, THE PAVILION c1871 5211

Above: BUXTON, DERBYSHIRE, THE PAVILION INTERIOR 1890 24734

Right: BUXTON, DERBYSHIRE, HALL GARDENS c1865 2795P

BUXTON'S PAVILION in the Winter Gardens was built in 1871 to the designs of Edward Milner. The building was about 400 feet in length with a square central hall for concerts and a wing on either side for promenading in wet weather. In front of the building a terrace walk was built for promenading during dry conditions. The attraction was an instant success, bringing a great many visitors to the town, so much so that by as early as October 1872 pressure was being put on the company to make extensions to the buildings to provide more facilities for visitors.

Its popularity was partly because of the fine performances of the band under the spirited direction of Mr Julian Adams, whose popular concerts were the greatest cause of overcrowding in the central hall of the Pavilion. The concerts were exceptionally well attended and it was quite usual to see some of the audience sitting on the stone sills outside the concert room and standing crowds straining for a glimpse of the orchestra.

The central hall was only 70 feet square, and during concerts in wet weather it was necessary for visitors who wished to move from one end of the Pavilion to the other to force themselves through the audience or else walk outside in the rain. The Improvements Company were constantly being made aware of the problem both by visitors and residents, and it was agreed that urgent action should be taken to remedy the situation.

The new concert hall was octagonal in shape and large enough to accomodate an audience of 2,000. In order to blend in with the existing Pavilion building it was built in a similar style, using iron and glass. Work commenced in 1875, and the building was opened in August 1876.

Concern that the domed roof would distort the acoustic quality of the musical concerts was unfounded; the architect Robert Duke had done his homework. The sound quality of the first concert, held on the opening day, was deemed to be excellent by all who attended. Set into the apex of the domed roof was a gas powered 'Sunlight Burner' to light the hall during evening performances. This burner is still in existence today, but cannot be seen owing to the introduction of a false ceiling at the level of the dome base.

Bournemouth

BOURNEMOUTH, DORSET, INVALID'S WALK 1900   45225

FEW RESORTS have as many green spaces as Bournemouth; these are remnants of the original great chines and wild heathland around which the town was built. Most of these are now formal gardens, where it is possible to stroll, watch the entertainments or just sit and relax. Many of the trees in the various pleasure gardens were planted in Victorian times to 'improve the air quality' on the advice of the influential Dr Granville.

Dr Granville was a connoisseur of favoured watering places and the eventual author of the standard Victorian guide to their health benefits, 'Spas of England and Principal Sea-Bathing Places'. Bournemouth's wily planners gave a dinner in the good doctor's honour, seeking his help in keeping the momentum going. Granville responded magnificently, announcing that the resort was superb for the treatment of consumption, but urging the gathered dignitaries not to allow the burgeoning new town to go downmarket.

On his advice the flowing waters of the Bourne Stream were captured and transformed into the tamer, decorative water feature we see today. The wilder parts of the vale were turned into gardens and walkways. Villas sprang up along the slopes of the hills and the clifftops, each one standing in its own health-giving grounds – just as the doctor ordered. Grateful valetudinarians, but only those who could afford to come, flooded into the area. The results probably were conducive to better health even if, as the frail Robert Louis Stevenson put it some years later, life there 'was as monotonous as a weevil's in a biscuit'.

Bournemouth and its neighbouring towns became a sanctuary for the rich and famous, including writers such as Mary Shelley and Robert Louis Stevenson (left). Royal visitors included the Empress Eugenie, the King of the Belgians, and Edward VII - who discreetly entertained his mistresses Lily Langtry and Mrs Keppel at a hotel on the East Cliff.

AS a spa town, Harrogate relied on its visitors for its prosperity, so it had to keep them happy with every possible amenity. Valley Gardens offered visitors a pleasant walk of nearly a mile from the Pump Room in Low Harrogate to the heights of Harlow Moor; here they could find bright flowerbeds, shady trees, winding paths, lawns to relax on, tennis courts, the rustic Tea House, a boating pond for the children, and above all the bandstand. Concerts were held here to packed audiences every summer afternoon. In this photograph, we see another typical holiday entertainment; the white silk shirts and dunces' caps leave us in no doubt that this is a Pierrot troupe. This type of entertainment owed its popularity to the runaway success of the London production of the mime play 'L'Enfant Prodigue' in 1891 in which the character of Pierrot featured. The Pierrot troupe would perform songs, jokes, mimes and monologues.

Right: HARROGATE, YORKSHIRE, VALLEY GARDENS 1907   58645P

Harrogate

Blackburn

BLACKBURN, LANCASHIRE, CORPORATION PARK 1895   35729

BLACKBURN, LANCASHIRE,
THE PARK FOUNTAIN 1894   34319

CREATING A GREEN SPACE in Blackburn became ever more desirable as the ill effects of industrialisation became apparent. Blackburn as much as anywhere needed somewhere where people could go to escape the rows and rows of terraced housing and the proliferating forest of smoking chimneys.

The land occupied by Corporation Park was bought from Joseph Feilden, lord of the manor, in 1855 at a cost of £50 per acre; fifty acres altogether were acquired. The town's water supply had been there already – there were two small reservoirs fed by Pemberton Clough. Later, in 1847, Blackburn Waterworks Company supplied the town from reservoirs at Guide, Audley, Pickup Bank and Daisyfield.

William Henderson, a landscape gardener from Birkenhead, was engaged to supervise the laying out of the grounds, which he did with the assistance of Mr P McGregor and Mr T Jenkins. The Blackburn contractors Roberts & Walmsley built the entrance gateway and the lodge. The perimeter walls were built by Thomas and John Holden and William Wright, all of Blackburn, using stone from quarries in the park. The promenades, bowling greens and carriage roads were constructed by James Taylor of Burnley.

William Pilkington would have been pleased to see the park so well used 40 years after his inaugural speech. In photograph 35729 there is not a spare bench seat to be had. Something about the smart attire of the people and the full leaf of the trees suggests a summer Sunday afternoon, though the gentleman with their umbrellas are taking no chances.

Blackburn's Corporation Park conservatory is shown in photograph 74069 – what a wonderful place to spend a wet day! The abundance of flowering, exotic plants would cheer up the gloomiest soul. The conservatory was opened on 16 May 1900. A banana plant had produced fruit there by 1903. Plans for heating the conservatory had only recently been approved in 1921, two years before this photograph was taken.

BLACKBURN, LANCASHIRE, CORPORATION PARK, THE CONSERVATORY 1923   74069

Grantham

THERE IS a First World War connection to this paddling pool. After the war, Grantham was allocated a tank for display; it stood in the new park, which is itself a war memorial. The tank was on display exactly where the pool was later dug. The track that enables tanks to crawl over difficult ground was invented in the Grantham works of Richard Hornsby in the early 1900s. Wyndham Park was given to the town as a memorial by the mother of Captain the Hon W R Wyndham, who was killed at Ypres in November 1914. Many years later, it was an ideal and safe place for little ones to enjoy a good splash about and get wet. The roses around the pool added to the happy times.

Left: GRANTHAM, LINCOLNSHIRE, WYNDHAM PARK, THE PADDLING POOL c1955 G43005

Eastbourne

THE FAMOUS Carpet Gardens on Grand Parade were laid out between the pier and the bandstand. Intricate patterns were picked out in bedding plants, and taller plants bloomed along the outer beds. On the left is one of the finest stucco terraces in Eastbourne, the Burlington and Claremont Hotels of 1851: worthy of Brighton.

Eastbourne's Carpet Gardens have been a talking point of the town for many years. Laid out originally in Persian carpet form, they are perhaps less elaborate now than at the beginning of the last century, but other additions have been made, such as small fountains. On average, a total of 39,000 seasonal spring and summer plants and 32,600 carpet bedding plants are used each year. The total cost of maintaining the Carpet Gardens is approximately £18,000 annually.

Right: EASTBOURNE, SUSSEX, THE PROMENADE GARDENS 1912 64974P

Bedford

HERE WE SEE another example of complex planting. The inclined floral bed in the foreground survives, and is planted each year with a different theme. The concrete block walls replaced railings lost during the Second World War. The somewhat utilitarian blocks have now been replaced by low hairpin railings: a considerable improvement. The large inscription attached to the Suspension Bridge, 'Villa Bedfordia', echoed here by the flowers, has been removed: not many Latin-speaking sailors come this far upstream.

BEDFORD, BEDFORDSHIRE, THE SUSPENSION BRIDGE AND EMBANKMENT GARDENS c1960 B51103

Statues and monuments

STATUES AND monuments punctuate and give interest to our streets. They remind us of the history of the town, and they tell us of the people who contributed to the town – and to the nation. Many statues and monuments are great works of art, which turn the street in which they stand into a vast outdoor art gallery.

THE CORONATION STONE was rediscovered only in the early 19th century; it had been being used as a mounting block for horsemen in the Market Square. The stone was recovered in 1730 from the collapsed chapel of St Mary that abutted All Saints' Church. The stone was set into a decorative stone plinth inscribed with the names of seven Saxon kings supposed to have been crowned at Kingston, Edward the Elder, Athelstan, Edmund, Eadred, Eadwig, Edward the Martyr and Ethelred the Unready. Of these the only solid evidence for crowning at Kingston is for Athelstan in AD924 and Ethelred in AD978.

The Coronation Stone and its plinth was set within decorative railings in 1850 right in the heart of Kingston outside the Kingston Municipal Offices, but traffic increased in the 20th century, so it was moved back from the roadway in 1935. The stone now resides alongside the Clattern Bridge over the Hogsmill River outside the Guildhall.

Kingston-upon-Thames

Right: KINGSTON UPON THAMES, GREATER LONDON, THE CORONATION STONE 1893 31767T

Richmond

RICHMOND, YORKSHIRE, MARKET PLACE AND THE OBELISK 1929 82551

THE OBELISK replaced a market cross in 1771; its top finial was removed in 1905, to be replaced by a new one two years later. Around the base were stocks and pillories, and there was a bullring here when bull baiting was an acceptable sport. The fascinating building behind the obelisk was the old Toll Booth, which also contained the town's weights and measures. This was demolished in 1947.

The castle (right of photograph) dominates the centre of this large market town at the entrance to Swaledale. Trinity Church had been given a neat new look in 1923 when a number of shop buildings were removed from around the tower – many still remain lower down. Part of the church is now the Regimental Museum of the Green Howards, and chronicles their 300-year history.

'Richmond stands most romantically: the noble castle, the bridge, the River Swale … Butter sells here for five pence per pound, and a fowl for 10d; and as coals are very cheap, houses very good and at easy rent, walks charming and fly-fishing excellent, Richmond becomes one of the best retiring towns in England.'

JOHN BYNG, 'RIDES ROUND BRITAIN', 1790
ED D ADAMSON, FOLIO SOCIETY

RICHMOND, YORKSHIRE, THE CASTLE KEEP 1908 59493T

THIS WONDERFUL swashbuckling statue (unveiled in 1900) stands at the centre of Bridgwater as a memorial to its distinguished citizen. Robert Blake (1599–1657) was MP for Bridgwater, an important Parliamentarian commander and one of the most famous English admirals in history.

In 1643 he was in Bristol during Prince Rupert's successful siege. Blake then led a surprise attack on Bridgwater, but he was defeated. In 1644 Blake led the garrison at Lyme Regis, where Parliament's navy were shipping in supplies and reinforcements. From Lyme Blake led a daring expedition to Taunton, an important Royalist base; Blake held it for a year and survived three sieges. In 1646 he successfully besieged Dunster Castle in Somerset. Appointed admiral in 1649, he blockaded Lisbon, destroyed Prince Rupert's fleet, and captured the Scillies and Jersey. He defeated the Dutch at the Battle of Portland in 1653. In 1657 came the greatest victory of his career: he destroyed a Spanish treasure fleet of 16 ships at Santa Cruz off Tenerife, only losing one ship himself – Oliver Cromwell rewarded his success with a diamond ring. He died at sea.

Bridgwater

BRIDGWATER, SOMERSET, BLAKE'S STATUE 1901 47868

ONE OF the greatest men in the field of science and mathematics is Sir Isaac Newton; Victorian Grantham remembered him by erecting an imposing and impressive statue of him. To do justice to the great man, the area which is now known as St Peter's Hill was cleared – it had been nicknamed the derogatory 'Wilderness', although its official name was Wood Hill – and trees were set, a number of which are still growing nicely today. The road system laid out then was the same as it still is now. The statue was erected in 1857 and inaugurated the next year. The cost was borne by the public, and Queen Victoria and Prince Albert contributed £100. A generous War Office donated the bronze for the statue, as they had a surplus of metal from a number of Russian cannon captured during the Crimean War. The plinth is of Anglesey marble.

Right: GRANTHAM, LINCOLN-SHIRE, THE ISAAC NEWTON MEMORIAL c1955 G43046

Grantham

St Ives

ST IVES, CAMBRIDGESHIRE, OLIVER CROMWELL'S STATUE, MARKET HILL 1901 48069

Shortly before this photograph was taken, the Town Council approved an expenditure of £850 to be paid to Frederick Pomeroy RA for the design and execution of a statue of the Lord Protector. It had originally been envisaged that it should stand in Huntingdon, Cromwell's birthplace, but that town had always had Royalist inclinations and there was little interest from the people. Cromwell had lived at St Ives from 1631 to 1635, and the townsfolk took the project to heart. The globes in the photograph were made of copper, and were part of the original design. They were removed in the 1970s and never replaced. Today, cast iron replicas adorn the pedestals.

Bedford

BEDFORD, BEDFORDSHIRE, THE HOWARD MONUMENT 1898 40860

THIS STATUE of 1890 is by perhaps England's finest Art Nouveau sculptor, Alfred Gilbert, whose sinuous, slightly disquieting style is seen at its best around the base of the pedestal. He was the sculptor of Eros in Piccadilly Circus in London. John Howard (1726-1790) lived at nearby Cardington, and was twice Mayor of Bedford and in 1773 Lord High Sheriff of the county. He was concerned with prison reform: his name lives on in the Howard League for Penal Reform.

UNDOUBTEDLY BEDFORD'S most famous son – if only because of his imprisonment as the result of religious intolerance – John Bunyan was born into a tinker's family in nearby Elstow and lived something of the high life before becoming a Nonconformist preacher. In 1660 he was arrested for his beliefs and spent the next 12 years in prison. A major outcome of his hardships was the writing and publishing in 1678 of a religious parable – 'The Pilgrim's Progress'. It has become one of the most successful books ever written, being published in over 200 languages. Legend has it that it is possible to trace the pilgrim Christian's journeying through various locations within the county, and the establishment of the John Bunyan Trail attempts to add substance to the possibility.

This statue was created by the noted sculptor Boehm in 1873, and presented to the town by the then Duke of Bedford in June 1874. This is ironic in a way, for Bunyan had been a thorn in the flesh of the establishment in the 17th century, and it was likely that it was the Duke's forebears that had cast him into prison.

At the time of this photograph, the statue and its pier and chain railing is still crisp and fresh-looking, and the replanted limes are young. Around the plinth are bronze panels showing scenes from 'The Pilgrim's Progress'

Left: BEDFORD, BEDFORD-SHIRE, BUNYAN'S STATUE 1898 40857P

Cheltenham

CHELTENHAM, GLOUCESTERSHIRE, THE WILSON MEMORIAL 1923 73482

DR EDWARD WILSON, polar explorer and scientist, was born in Cheltenham in 1872. He first went to the Antarctic with Scott on the 'Discovery' between 1900 and 1904. After his return to England, he performed important scientific research on bird diseases and illustrated natural history books. In 1910 he returned to the Antarctic on the 'Terra Nova' as the chief of Scott's scientific staff. He perished whilst making the homeward journey from the South Pole with Captain Scott in 1912. This fine memorial was erected a few years later.

THE STATUE of Queen Victoria (right) was erected to commemorate her Golden Jubilee in 1887. The sculptor was George Blackall Simonds, born in Reading in 1843, a member of the Simonds brewing family. Instead of joining the family firm, he studied art and sculpture in Dresden and Brussels, developing his skills in stone carving. He lived and worked in Rome for 12 years, where he studied Renaissance bronze sculpture and learnt the lost wax casting technique. According to Benedict Read ('Victorian Sculpture', Yale University Press, 1982): 'It is possible that Simonds could claim primacy amongst English artists in the revival of the lost-wax casting method'. Over the years he exhibited at the Royal Academy over 40 times and created many striking works, including 'The Falconer' (Simonds helped revive the sport of falconry), a version of which stands in New York's Central Park.

As well as Queen Victoria, his sculptures for Reading include a bust of H B Blandy, Mayor of Reading, exhibited at the RA in 1880, the Maiwand Lion (see page 195), and George Palmer in Palmer Park. Simonds stopped making sculptures in 1903 and joined the Simonds brewing firm, becoming chairman in 1910; during his reign the company expanded – by 1929, the year of his death, H & G Simonds was selling 32 million bottles of beer a year.

Right: READING, BERKSHIRE, QUEEN VICTORIA'S STATUE 1904 52011

Reading

Windsor

THIS STATUE was unveiled in 1887 to celebrate the Queen's Golden Jubilee. Queen Victoria stands in her Garter robes, carrying the orb and sceptre, symbols of state and church, and wearing a small coronet. This coronet was made especially for her because the coronation crown was very heavy and she was prone to headaches. The statue was mounted on an Aberdeen granite plinth inside which is a time capsule in a special cavity. This time capsule, which is a hermetically-sealed Doulton jar, contains every coin in circulation at the time.

The position of the statue, both then and now, was significant in that it was the same position on which the old town cross and gallows had once stood and where proclamations had traditionally been made. There is, however, another story which puts a slightly different slant on it. Apparently Mr J E Boehm RA, the sculptor, and the main members of the Jubilee Committee could not decide precisely where they wanted the statue to stand; but with a little creative thought, and with the aid of a railway trolley stacked with champagne cases, which they wheeled round until it looked right, they were able to agree!

The statue of Queen Victoria stands at the junction of Castle Hill, High Street and Peascod Street. This is the oldest part of the town. This area, opposite the King Henry VIII Gate of Windsor Castle, is a compact group of narrow cobbled streets, including Church Street. During medieval times there was a market here – the statue stands near the site of the old market cross. There are some delightful old houses to be found here: some are timber-framed and date back to the 16th and 17th centuries, while others are Georgian.

Above: WINDSOR, BERKSHIRE, CASTLE HILL 1914 66978

Right: WINDSOR, BERKSHIRE, QUEEN VICTORIA STATUE 2004 W111716K

BLACKBURN, LANCASHIRE,
THE GLADSTONE STATUE 1923 74074

Blackburn

TWO DIGNIFIED STATUES stand outside Blackburn's cathedral. This one of the two, the statue of Gladstone, Prime Minister during the Victorian era, was unveiled on 4 November 1899 by the Earl of Aberdeen. It was sculpted by J Adams Acton, and was the first memorial statue in the country erected to Gladstone. It later became an obstruction to bus queues, and in 1955 it was removed to its present site outside the old technical college.

Kendal

IT WAS common practice during the First World War, certainly in the northern towns, to post men from the same town together as 'pals', and Kendal was no exception. By 1915 there were 1,200 Kendal pals who marched, fought and died together. As the war dragged on to the accompaniment of ritual slaughter, the Westmorland Gazette published a growing list of casualties with pages of photographs of the gallant lads who had perished or were missing.

But the Armistice came at last, and the dead were honoured by having their 316 names inscribed on a cenotaph war memorial erected in 1921 on the site of the old library in Market Place facing Stricklandgate. A large company attended the opening; a contingent of children dressed in white sang hymns with the crowd to the accompaniment of a portable organ mounted on a cart. In 1919 Kendal corporation was presented with war trophies for safe care and custody.

Left: KENDAL, CUMBRIA, THE WAR MEMORIAL 1924   75795T

THE TOWN'S war memorial commemorates the men who died as a result of action in the Great War of 1914–18. Out of a total population of around 7,000, over 1,000 men from Hythe served their country during the hostilities.

The memorial, unveiled in 1921, stands in The Grove, Prospect Road: a small winged victory holding a medieval cinque port vessel stands on an orb. The square-section column bears a carving in relief showing twelve servicemen. The lions' heads at the base spout water. The names from both world wars are listed on the wall behind, 154 names for the First World War and 40 for the Second World War. This fine memorial is the work of the distinguished sculptor Gilbert Bayes.

Right: HYTHE, KENT, THE WAR MEMORIAL 1921   71097

Hythe

In 1909 it was decided to form national Voluntary Aid Detachments (VADs) to provide medical assistance in time of war. By the summer of 1914 there were over 2,500 Voluntary Aid Detachments in Britain. Of the 74,000 VADs in 1914, two-thirds were women and girls. A VAD hospital was set up in the Friends School in Kendal's Stramongate. Here nurses cared for the wounded soldiers and a team of women repaired their linen and uniforms. Over at the public baths in All Hallows Lane washerwomen cleaned their clothes, and the soldiers were allowed to use the baths free of charge. Tobacco, mint cake, toffee, chocolate, cake, bootlaces, socks and candles were collected and made up into parcels to send to soldiers on the front.

Harlow

HARLOW, ESSEX, THE STATUE c1965 H22103

THIS IS a striking example of how the new towns strove to give character and distinction to their town centres by acquiring and commissioning fine works of art. In this case, in 1960 the Harlow Art Trust commissioned a cast bronze sculpture by Ralph Brown called 'The Meat Porters' to be placed in the market square. (Ralph Brown's 'Sheep Shearer' also stands in Harlow.)

Ralph Brown has had a long and successful career. He studied at Leeds School of Art, Hammersmith School of Art, and the Royal College of Art from 1948 to 1956, including a period working in Paris with Zadkine. He has had many exhibitions in this country and abroad, and a retrospective of his work was held at the Henry Moore Centre in Leeds in 1988. Today he lives and works in Gloucestershire.

Reading

READING, BERKSHIRE, THE MAIWAND MEMORIAL 1890 27139

IN BUSTLING READING, Forbury Gardens with the old abbey ruins are an area of calm and beauty. This extraordinary monument, with its gigantic lion snarling at the onlooker, was erected here in 1886 to commemorate the 66th Berkshire Regiment's heroism and losses in the Second Afghan War of 1879 to 1880, and records that 11 officers and 318 other ranks died in the mountains of Afghanistan during that terrible campaign, particularly in their rearguard action at Maiwand. In this view the memorial is decked with wreaths and garlands for the anniversary.

This wonderful sculpture was created by the distinguished Reading sculptor George Blackall Simonds (see 52011, page 192); an imposing 31ft long, it took Simonds two years to complete. After the First World War the base of the Maiwand Memorial with its fluted pilasters and stone swags was rebuilt in a harder limestone, for the name panels had eroded badly. The names are now on bronze panels set between pairs of rather more restrained pilasters, and George Simonds' colossal lion looks equally at home on his new plinth.

Sculptor's tragic suicide?

According to an urban legend current in Reading, George Simonds, the sculptor of the lion, made a mistake in his depiction of the lion's stance – a real lion would fall over in this position. Unable to bear the shame of his error, he committed suicide. However, recent research by Reading Museum and H Godwin Arnold and Sidney M Gold has shown that in fact Simonds studied lion anatomy carefully and that the lion's stance is totally true to life – and George Simonds had another 43 years to live!

Street furniture and landmarks

SOME FEATURES of our streets, like clock towers, are prominent, unmissable expressions of civic pride. Some, like stocks or pumps, are ancient reminders of customs now long gone. Some, street furniture like street lamps, railings and water troughs, go almost unnoticed – and yet they add so much character to our streets. And some have gone for ever – do any tram traction standards (the poles that carried the tram wires) still exist?

NEWTON ABBOT, DEVON,
ST LEONARD'S TOWER 1906   56572P

Newton Abbot

Above: BLACKBURN, LANCASHIRE,
SUDELL CROSS 1895   35726T

ST LEONARD'S TOWER is the enduring symbol of Newton Abbot, all that remains of the chapel of ease that saved Newtonians the long walk up to the parish church at Wolborough. The earliest reference to a chapel on this site is in 1350 in a document of Bishop de Grandisson of Exeter, but tradition suggests a foundation of around 1220, the time of William Brewer's foundation of Torre Abbey. The tower remains the place where Newtonians gather on special occasions, such as New Year's Eve, or when kings and queens are proclaimed, or for the announcement of some historic event such as the defeat of the Spanish Armada or the thwarting of the Gunpowder Plot. By 1894 much had been achieved by way of improvement to the town. However, there were still complaints about the width of Wolborough Street and agitation for the demolition of St Leonard's Tower. But the townsfolk retained affection for this monument from Newton Abbot's past and – spurred on by the Society for the Protection of Ancient Buildings – voted to preserve it by 900 votes. It was a wise decision.

RUGBY, WARWICKSHIRE, THE CLOCK TOWER AND ST ANDREW'S CHURCH 1922 72125T

THE VICTORIANS loved to celebrate important occasions, and Queen Victoria's Golden Jubilee in June 1887 was celebrated with especial enthusiasm all over the country. Rugby commemorated the event with the Jubilee Clock Tower in Market Place, on the site of the old market cross. Designed by Mr Goodacre of Leicester, the clock tower was built by Parnell & Son at a cost of £530, which was raised by public subscription. It was formally handed over to the town in January 1889.

The clock tower is 43ft 6in high; it is built of Darley Dale stone, partly filled with Northampton ironstone, on a base of grey Aberdeen granite. Until the early years of the 20th century, there was an underground gentlemen's convenience at its foot. The four-dialled clock, which had to be rewound each week, was made by Evans & Sons at the Soho Clock Factory, Birmingham, and was originally lit by four gas jets on each face. Electricity now both runs the clock and illuminates the faces.

The clock tower's commemorative plaque was for many years obscured by the cabmen's shelter, which was erected about 1893. When the shelter was taken down in 1933, the existence of the plaque came as a surprise to many younger Rugbeians. The inscription reads: 'Erected by the Town and Neighbourhood of Rugby to commemorate the fiftieth Anniversary of Queen Victoria's Accession. 1887'.

Skegness

THE JUBILEE CLOCK TOWER was erected at the junction of Lumley Road with the then seafront's Grand Parade and South Parade. The tower was built to commemorate Queen Victoria's Diamond Jubilee in 1897: this view was taken on 11 August 1899, and shows the clock tower's formal opening by the Countess of Scarborough.

Top: SKEGNESS, LINCOLNSHIRE, THE OFFICIAL OPENING OF THE CLOCK TOWER 1899 44195

Above: SKEGNESS, LINCOLNSHIRE, GRAND PARADE AND THE CLOCK TOWER 1910 62846

MAIDENHEAD, BERKSHIRE,
THE CLOCK TOWER 1911   63802

Maidenhead

ONE OF Maidenhead's best-known landmarks is the clock tower near the station at the south end of King Street. Now on a traffic island on a dual carriageway, and difficult to approach, the splendid clock tower commemorates Queen Victoria's Diamond Jubilee in 1897. Funded by public subscription, the foundation stone was laid on 7 November 1899 by the mayor John Truscott, and the architect was E J Shrewsbury. Behind it, all has gone to be replaced by a four-storey 1990s office block, King's Chase.

Maidenhead suffered greatly in the 1960s when much of its historic fabric was wantonly destroyed. This was in the era when the common belief was that a town could only be hauled from its economic doldrums through rebuilding as much as possible and in the latest style. This was a tragedy, as 1960s commercial architecture was almost universally appalling – indeed, many of those buildings are now being demolished and replaced by better ones, both in design and constructional quality terms.

Bury

BURY, GREATER MANCHESTER, THE WHITEHEAD CLOCK TOWER c1955   B257004

ON THE approach to Bury from the south are the Whitehead Gardens, dominated by this imposing clock tower made of Portland stone. It was the gift of the town's ubiquitous benefactor Henry Whitehead, who had it erected in memory of his brother Walter. Walter was eminent in the field of medicine, becoming a Fellow of the Royal College of Surgeons and later President of the British Medical Association. In contrast, their brother Robert invented the torpedo. The gardens were opened in June 1914, and the opening ceremony was performed by another famous surgeon, Sir Frederick Treves. It is said that Mr Whitehead's grandson started the clock. In front stands the Fusilier memorial of the South African War, which had stood in the Market Place since 1905; it was re-erected in the gardens in 1920.

Another medical link with Whitehead Gardens is the fact that they were built over the grounds of Belle Vue, once the residence of Dr William Goodlad, who owned a private lunatic asylum.

Northleach

NORTHLEACH, GLOUCESTERSHIRE, MARKET SQUARE c1950   N125009

Chapel-en-le-Frith

CHAPEL-EN-LE-FRITH, DERBYSHIRE, THE STOCKS c1960
C400032

THE TIMBER STOCKS at Northleach supply another glimpse of historic ways: miscreants were bundled into the pillory to receive their punishment and supply enjoyment to the locals, who would throw rotten fruit, vegetables and eggs at them. Beside the stocks stands a whipping post.

The half-timbered Kings Head inn in the background recalls the coaching age: Northleach stands on the road from South Wales to London, and so it became an important coaching town where inns such as this provided shelter and accommodation to passengers. The square here is still a place for coaches.

THE ANCIENT STOCKS in Chapel's Market Square (left) have recently been renovated, and probably date from the Cromwellian period. Like the stocks at Northleach (above) they were designed to take two offenders at a time, but these stocks would have been more uncomfortable – the holes for arms as well as legs imply that the unfortunate occupants would have little freedom of movement as they endured the humiliation of becoming the targets for the rotten vegetables thrown by bystanders at the nearby weekly market.

The name of the Peak District town of Chapel-en-le-Frith means literally 'the chapel in the forest', and it was originally the site of a chapel in the medieval Royal Forest of the Peak, where kings and princes hunted deer, wolf and wild boar.

There is an amusing story told of Lord Camden, when a barrister, having been fastened up in the stocks on the top of a hill, in order to gratify an idle curiosity on the subject. Being left there by the absent-minded friend who had locked him in, he found it impossible to procure his liberation for the greater part of a day. On his entreating a chance traveller to release him, the man shook his head, and passed on, remarking that of course he was not put there for nothing.

R CHAMBERS, 'THE BOOK OF DAYS', 1869

Grantham

THE 16TH-CENTURY conduit stands in a corner of the Market Place. In 1314, the Franciscans (the Grey Friars) built a water pipe from springs located to the west of the town to enable fresh water to be available to the people of Grantham, and quite naturally the water was brought to the centre of their world – the Market Place. It was carried in lead pipes, so one does wonder how many inhabitants died of lead poisoning! After the Dissolution of the Monasteries c1538, the water continued to flow; eventually the Borough Council decided that a new building was needed to contain the flowing water, and the conduit was built in 1597. On the front facing the Market Place is the inscription: 'Let thy fountains be dispersed abroad and rivers of water in the streets'. The inscription also tells us that in 1597 Robert Bery was Alderman (Grantham retained the title of alderman for its chief citizen until 1835), and on the north side of the Conduit is a carving of what appears to be a wool staple. Behind is Conduit Lane, leading to where the monastic buildings used to stand.

Left: GRANTHAM, LINCOLNSHIRE, THE OLD CONDUIT 1889 22288

In the days before street lighting (the first gas lamps on posts appeared in about 1810) those who went out at night had to carry a lantern – or if they were rich, they might employ a linkman to walk ahead of them carrying a flaming torch. A few town houses still have a wrought iron extinguisher standing outside them – here the linkman would put out his torch until his employer needed him again.

ANDOVER, HAMPSHIRE, HIGH STREET 1908
70540T (DETAIL)

AT THE bottom end of Arundel's High Street, in the old market place, pride of place goes to the water pump crowned by a gas street light, two vital necessities combined into one decorative piece of street furniture. Arundel had been an important river port and trading centre since medieval times, and the hard-worked horses hauling stage-coaches or trade vehicles up the the busy high street would have welcomed a drink at the trough.

Arundel

ARUNDEL, SUSSEX, HIGH STREET 1902 48792

Chesham

THIS IS a wonderful assemblage of street furniture. The large granite trough could well be one of those put up by the MDF & CTA (the Metropolitan Drinking Fountain & Cattle Trough Association, which was founded in 1859) - at that time cattle and horses were often hard pressed by their owners. The Association set up about a thousand troughs, many of which can still be seen. Notice, too, the cast iron bollard. The first bollards were often made from old cannon (an early example of recycling), and later examples were often made to look like them with a cannon ball protruding from the muzzle. There are two stone bollards here too. Soon after this photograph was taken, a traffic island and the war memorial replaced this street furniture.

On the left is the town cinema, the Chesham Palace, later called the Astoria. It replaced Harding's ironmonger's shop, which accounts for the traditional shop front. It closed in the 1970s. The tall buildings behind the lamp post flanked the entrance to Station Road. This road was cut into the High Street to give access to Chesham's terminus station on the Metropolitan Railway branch, which opened in 1889.

CHESHAM, BUCKINGHAMSHIRE, BROADWAY 1921 70540

Chelmsford

CHELMSFORD, ESSEX, HIGH STREET 1919   69010T

AN OLD conduit used to stand in the market area of Chelmsford. It bore a Latin inscription which might be translated as: 'Bountiful to the bounteous, liberal to the covetous, not diminished by bestowing, thus charity from the heavenly fountain'. The water gushed out of a great spout. Sadly, this conduit-head seems to have been better decorated than it was efficient, and it was replaced in 1791, partly funded by £200 that Sir William Mildmay had willed towards the maintenance of the town's water supply. John Johnson commissioned a new structure; it consisted of a 6ft water nymph grasping a shield and standing on a podium encircled by writhing dolphins. This figure was known as the Naiad.

The flow of water ceased altogether in 1797, and did not radically improve after the wooden pipes were replaced by a brick drain. In 1812, the Naiad was removed, and supplanted by a domed, circular edifice, like a kind of pseudo-classical temple. This time it really was bountiful to the bounteous, as the water flow improved, and the new conduit-head became a long-term feature of the town. Within a few years, the market place was called Conduit Square, and Back Lane was Conduit Street.

ORIGINALLY, PARK GREEN in Macclesfield must have been a big grassy green sloping gently down to the Bollin, which is largely hidden today, and bordering on to the great park or hunting forest that stretched out towards Gawsworth. We can imagine that it was a good place for gatherings and fairs and bucolic games. At the time of Frith's first visits it was still a pleasant wide open space, good for promenading and passing the time of day, with small trees dotted about, fine buildings around it and a splendid cast iron fountain as a focus. This delightful centrepiece was presented by James Kershaw. It was one of the chief landmarks of the town, and gave Park Green an identity which it grievously lacks today. Fountains such as this made a huge contribution to the improvement in public health during the Victorian era. The realisation had gradually dawned that dirty water bred disease, and the provision of a public clean water supply was crucial.

The Congregational Chapel, now the United Reformed Church (left of photograph), was built in 1877 to replace the old Calvinist chapel behind it in Towneley Street, which still stands. The powerful Doric-columned Savings Bank (centre) was built in 1818 – it certainly looks as though your savings would be safe there!

Macclesfield

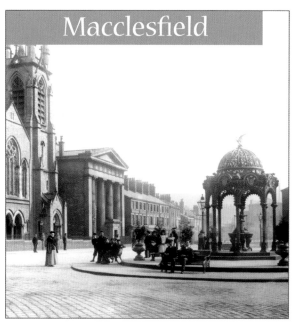

MACCLESFIELD, CHESHIRE,
PARK GREEN 1897   40442

WOODBRIDGE, SUFFOLK, THE OLD
PUMP 1965   W128055

Woodbridge

WHEN THE Seckford Charity received vastly increased revenues from its London estates in the 19th century, this pump with its elaborate Gothic-style shelter was erected for the Woodbridge townspeople at a cost of £250 just outside the Shire Hall on Market Hill. At the base you will see a drinking trough for 'horses, dogs and cattle passing through the town'.

High Wycombe

HIGH WYCOMBE, BUCKINGHAMSHIRE, FROGMOOR LOOKING SOUTH 1921   70607T

FROM 1876 the ancient open space of Frogmoor in High Wycombe was blessed with a fine cast iron fountain and well trimmed trees. The ornate fountain was designed by a lavish hand and with suitably watery imagery: the fountain is supported by pelicans and fierce-looking dolphins.

Highway considerations dominated town planning later in the 20th century. Frogmoor itself was stripped of its trees and paved over in the 1930s, although the fountain survived until it was removed during the Second World War, allegedly for the war effort.

Cheltenham

CHELTENHAM, GLOUCESTERSHIRE, THE NEPTUNE
FOUNTAIN 1912 65100P

CHELTENHAM'S Neptune Fountain has long been a place to linger and relax on sunny days. Neptune was the Roman god of the sea, and here he appears with sea horses and tritons. Before the construction of the fountain, this area was much used for street entertainments.

The Neptune Fountain has adorned the top end of the Promenade since 1893, when it was built as part of a project to improve the ambience of this long avenue. Cheltenham's Borough Surveyor Mr Hall undertook the design of the fountain, supposedly inspired by Rome's Trevi Fountain, and had the new fountain made from Portland stone. It was carved by a local company, Messrs Boulton & Sons; they also made the Boer War Memorial.

THIS IS a wonderful memory of a fascinating part of Teesside which was completely obliterated from the map not long after this photograph was taken. The Five Lamps area was full of character – small shops, old buildings, interesting people. The development of complex new road systems for Teesside removed everything you can see here.

The Five Lamps stood at the junction of Mandale Road, George Street and Westbury Street. They were given to the town by three Justices of the Peace in 1874: Mr Whitwell, Mr Anderson and Mr Richardson. The lamps we see here are relatively modern – this electric lamp standard was put up in the 1950s. The original gas lamps were a typically ornate Victorian design with a solid-looking cast iron standard, with four bollards at each corner; however, it did not have these handy steps where the locals could sit and chat! In 1983 a replica of the original lamps was made and placed near its original location.

Thornaby-on-Tees

THORNABY ON TEES, YORKSHIRE, THE FIVE LAMPS
1957 T122001

THE FIRST gas lamps were erected in 1816 in London's Pall Mall. Thereafter street lighting proliferated hugely; in the Victorian era many street lamps were highly ornamental. In the early days of gas street lamps, a lamplighter had to travel round the town at dusk to light each lamp individually, but later designs had a device that automatically lit the lamp when the gas was turned on from a central point. When electric street lighting came, many gas lamps were adapted for electricity.

The first electric street lighting employed arc lamps, and in the 1870s an experiment was carried out to light Holborn Viaduct and the Thames Embankment in London with arc lamps. The first street in the world to be lit by electric light was Mosley Street, Newcastle-upon-Tyne in 1879. Arc lamps gave out a somewhat harsh light, and the bulbs had to be changed often, so by the end of the 19th century Britain's streets were lit by incandescent bulbs.

Ilkley

Left: ILKLEY, YORKSHIRE, THE STAR HOTEL AND LEEDS ROAD 1906 56474

THIS PHOTOGRAPH looks down from the Town Hall along Hall Quay – along here the electric trams ply their way to Yarmouth. In the foreground, two workmen up a ladder are mingling with the tramline's power cables to repair the street lamp on top. These poles which carried the tram wires were called traction standards.

A ride on a tram was a key memory of many Yarmouth holidaymakers. Horse-drawn trams operated in the last decades of the 19th century. Electric trams began to operate in 1902: the fare was just one penny. In 1922 four million passengers a year were being carried on the trams, at an average fare of just over two pence a ride.

Great Yarmouth

GREAT YARMOUTH, NORFOLK, HALL QUAY 1908
60652

Woodbridge

STEELYARDS WERE used for weighing. The date of this distinctive timber-framed steelyard is uncertain, but most examples can be traced to the early 17th century. It was used to weigh wagons, loaded ones on their way to the river from the market, and empty ones on their way back; steelyards were accurate to within two ounces. In this photograph we can see that the sling chains used to raise the full wagons are still extant, though the steelyard had not been used since the 1880s.

The Bell Inn (now the Bell and Steelyard) stands on New Street, a road first mentioned in the Court Rolls of 1549 and built to allow easier access from the River Deben to Market Hill. The white timber-framed building beyond the inn is the Bridewell. It was used as a poorhouse in the mid 17th century and served as a temporary jail for the Dutch prisoners of Sole Bay.

Above: WOODBRIDGE, SUFFOLK, THE BELL INN
1894 33375

From horses to horsepower

VARIOUS FORMS of transport enliven our streets – or choke them. Before the days of the internal combustion engine much transport was man- or boy-powered; handcarts and trolleys were a common sight, and so were delivery bicycles. Of course, larger loads were moved by horse and cart, and it was the carrier who conveyed poorer people if they needed to go on a long journey. Richer people owned their own carriage, or at least a pony and trap. These photographs also show wonderful examples of early and more recent forms of motor transport, including delivery lorries, and of public transport – trams, trolley buses and even a funicular railway.

Accrington

HERE WE SEE the most basic kind of moving a load: man-powered transport. On the left a labourer is hauling a handcart carrying a barrel of beer to a nearby public house. It must be hot work – he is in his shirtsleeves.

This photograph was taken from outside the Market Hall looking down Blackburn Road towards its junction with Abbey Street. Boots and David Lewis had led the way by being cash-only shops; by 1899, the trend of negotiating over a reduction in the marked price had almost died out. Here we see a Cash Clothing shop on the left, with its 'ready money bargains' piled high in the windows. 'Drink Altham's 2/4d Tea', proclaims the banner further down the street.

Above: ACCRINGTON, LANCASHIRE, BLACKBURN ROAD 1899 43496T

DROITWICH, HEREFORD & WORCESTER,
HIGH STREET 1904 51938

Newark-on-Trent

NEWARK-ON-TRENT, NOTTINGHAMSHIRE, APPLETON GATE 1906 56498

A CARTHORSE pulling a wagon belonging to Dickens & Co, brewers and wine and spirits merchants, waits patiently between trips. Lighter loads were taken around town by handcart or trolley (right).

Droitwich

HERE WE SEE another handcart, this time propelled by boy-power: on the right, outside George Wythes' Wine Store, two delivery boys are pushing a wicker handcart. On the left the Target Clothing Store is displaying a wide stock of straw hats and boaters.

In the Factory Act of 1891, two considerable additions to previous legislation were made. The first was the prohibition on employers to employ women within four weeks after confinement; the second the raising the minimum age at which a child could be set to work from ten to eleven.

Droitwich developed as a spa in the early 19th century thanks to John Corbett, a local businessman, who opened the St Andrews Brine Baths in the town for visitors, and built a magnificent French-style chateau just outside for himself.

Perth

A HORSE-DRAWN brewer's dray loaded down with crates of bottled beer is delivering to James Brown's Wine Store (left), and on the other side of the street a carter bends down as he loads or unloads his cart. Though the busy, cobbled street is thronged with workmen and shoppers, its centre is empty – in the distance is a tram. Everything kept out of its way.

Note the somewhat bizarre and uncomfortable-looking boot trade sign advertising a shoe shop on the extreme left.

Left: PERTH, TAYSIDE, HIGH STREET WEST 1899 43900

Caterham

CATERHAM, SURREY, THE RAILWAY HOTEL 1894 34290

BATCHELAR & SON of Croydon Fire Proof Depository's substantial covered van is parked outside the Railway Hotel. They are probably moving someone into one of the new estates. The coming of the railway in 1856 prompted a rapid expansion of this village: in 1851 it had a population of only 437, which within twenty years had grown to 3,577. These enterprises all sprang up in a new settlement around the station. The Far Famed Cake Company is delivering to the hotel using a much smaller covered cart. Maybe the drivers have stopped for a drink.

Clacton-on-Sea

A HORSE-DRAWN milk cart with a single large churn is delivering to houses. This was how milk was delivered before the coming of the milk bottle and the daily delivery round. The kitchen maid (or the householder) would run out to the van with a jug for the driver to fill from his churn.

CLACTON-ON-SEA, ESSEX, THE CONGREGATIONAL AND CATHOLIC CHURCHES 1904 51539

Cobham

Scunthorpe

ON THE RIGHT of 84920 (left) is a Walls ice cream man, who cycled the streets wearing his uniform with a peaked hat.

FOLLOWING views of man-power and boy-power, here we have woman-power (S78040a, right).
A woman is pulling her electric milk float along. It's bearing an 'L' sign, so she must be new to the job.

COBHAM, SURREY, THE POST OFFICE AND ANYARD'S ROAD 1932 84920

SCUNTHORPE, LINCOLNSHIRE, OSWALD ROAD c1955 S78040A

HORNBY'S of Mansfield are delivering their 'Eclipse' table water from their open lorry (right). Note the poster to the right of the lorry: there was still a drive to recruit soldiers for the army in the fragile post-war peace. The slogan claims that '5 years in the army fits a good man for a better future'.

Mansfield

MANSFIELD, NOTTINGHAMSHIRE, TOOTHILL LANE 1949 M184013

Uttoxeter

Bowdon

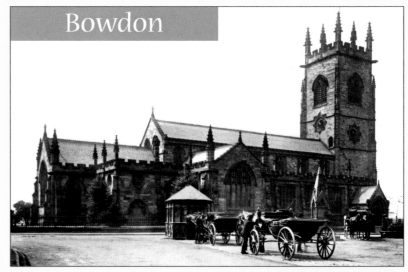

BOWDON, GREATER MANCHESTER, THE CHURCH AND THE CAB RANK 1889 21917

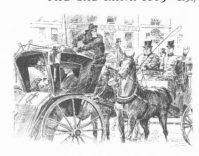

THE WORD 'cab' is derived from 'cabriolet', a horse-drawn two-wheeled two-seater popular for its speed and comfort, introduced about 1825. From the middle of the 19th century two types of cab began to dominate, the two-wheeled elegant hansom cab, and the heavier four-wheeled 'growler' – growlers used to ply their trade at railway stations because they were large enough to carry plenty of luggage. Some horse-drawn cabs survived as late as the 1930s (and London's very last horse cab licence was surrendered on 3 April 1947), but most had gone by the time of the First World War.

This photograph also shows a cabmen's shelter, a typical example constructed from painted timber with a shingled roof. The philanthropic spirit of the Victorian era inspired some wealthier people to concern themselves with the welfare of cab drivers and to subscribe towards shelters where cabbies could rest, keep warm and have something to eat and drink.

THIS IS a nostalgic collection of delivery vehicles. The coal lorry in the foreground belonged to Eckersley Brothers, coal merchants, whose business was run from railway sidings on Bridge Street. Note that the coal is not sacked, but loaded in bulk. The van belongs to W C Hardy.

Left: UTTOXETER, STAFFORDSHIRE, MARKET PLACE 1949 U29015T

PAIGNTON, DEVON, VICTORIA STREET FROM STATION SQUARE 1912 64718T

A MOTORISED bus waits for shoppers in Station Square alongside the horse-drawn cabs. Cabbies' fares at this time were: 'Drawn by 1 horse or 2 ponies or mules – one hour or less 3/- (15p) or extra half hour or less 1/6d, 1/- a mile. To Southfield 6d extra. To Primley Park 6d extra'. Horses were well catered for here with a water trough beneath the ornate lamp standard. Note the smart uniform of the cabbies, complete with top hat.

STEAM TRAMS began running in the streets here in 1881. In 1897 electric trams replaced them, as we see here – note the double-sided traction standards with their wrought iron ornamentation. These trams ran on a 3ft 7in gauge track; the main line went from Norton to North Ormesby, and a secondary route went from Middlesbrough railway station to Linthorpe. About 15 years after this photograph was taken, the trams would be competing with motor buses – their death knell was ringing.

Stockton's iron working industry, which had begun in the 18th century, was booming by the 19th century, alongside ship building and engineering – industry had been greatly boosted when the Stockton and Darlington railway opened in 1825, which made it easier to bring coal to factories in Stockton. By 1851 its population was 10,000, and by 1900 it was 51,000.

The flat oblong building on the left of the street is the Shambles, an indoor market. Behind is the Market Cross, erected in 1768, and the building further back with the clock face is the Town Hall, built in 1735. The hall has had many uses, including a lock-up for law-breakers, a public house and a meeting-place for the town council.

Below: STOCKTON-ON-TEES, COUNTY DURHAM, HIGH STREET 1899   44738P

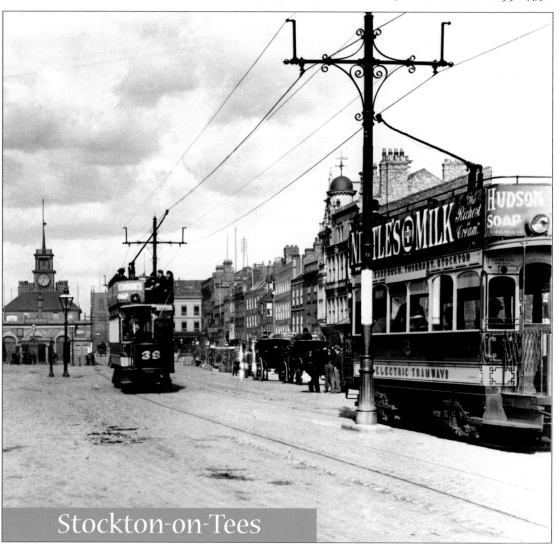

Stockton-on-Tees

NEWPORT, GWENT, COMMERCIAL STREET 1901   47898P

Newport

THE OPEN-TOPPED, horse-drawn tram must be approaching a stop – a man on the top deck is holding tight to the handrail as he prepares to go down the stairs. The tram boasts advertising signs for Lipton's Teas and Milkmaid milk. A beautiful Victorian street lamp dominates the other side of the road, and rising above the rooftops is the spire of St Paul's Church, opened in 1836. From the signs above the shop fronts, we can see that the tram is passing E Cauffman and Scaplehorn, a saddler and harness maker.

CHELTENHAM, GLOUCESTERSHIRE, HIGH STREET 1906 54319T

ALTHOUGH IT lagged behind most towns and cities in the country, Cheltenham did eventually install a tram system. On 22 August 1901 the inaugural service ran from Lansdown Castle to Cleeve Hill carrying VIPs and local notables. From the footplate of the first Union Jack-bedecked car, a bugler sounded the fanfare to announce the clattering convoy's advance. The occasion prompted an enthusiastic response from the Gloucestershire Graphic: 'At last the trams are here! Round the corner comes a huge noise like a small Town Hall on wheels and the quiet respectability of Cheltenham is challenged by the sharp ting-tang on the gong and grinding of the wheels on the rail grooves together with the cars' singing on the wires'.

There had been much opposition to the suggestion that Cheltenham should have trams. The argument of those against the development received a boost when two days before the system was scheduled to open, a tramcar descending Cleeve Hill on a trial run went out of control and overturned at Southam curve, killing two workmen. Once installed, however, trams proved popular and in their first week of operation carried 40,000 fare-paying passengers. Boarding the burgundy with gold coachlined trams of the Cheltenham and District Light Railway Company - the town's coat of arms proudly adorning each side – people discovered red upholstered seats in the downstairs saloon and wooden slatted reversible seats on the open-topped upper deck.

The initial stretch of track from Lansdown Castle to Cleeve Hill was just short of six miles long and took 120 workmen under four months to lay. For some reason Cheltenham's line was 3ft 6in in gauge, rather than the 4ft 8½in in found virtually everywhere else. In 1905 the system was extended to Leckhampton and Charlton Kings. A new loop line also meandered from St James's station via Ambrose Street, into the High Street then up North Street, where a parcel delivery office was opened by the tram company in 1911. This was staffed by young boys who delivered packages to the door by hand, bicycle, or hand-cart. They worked from 8am until 8pm with an hour for lunch and one tea break of 20 minutes for wages of 5/- (25p) a week. By the end of the 1920s trams had been rendered redundant by the quicker, go-anywhere bus. Most tram services ceased in March 1930 and the town's terminal tram ran just after dawn on Wednesday 31 December of that year. The event was of such small public interest that the Echo did not report the demise until five days later. The lines came up, the cables came down and the trams were scrapped.

Llandudno

LLANDUDNO, GWYNEDD, THE GREAT ORME RAILWAY c1960 L71693P

A HIDDEN cable system, the same as is used by the San Francisco tramcars, hauls holidaymakers and enthusiasts up to the Great Orme, the headland that overlooks the Victorian town. The system is a funicular railway, the counterweighted cables hauling the tramcars up and down – as one ascends, the other descends. The railway was installed to exploit the tourist potential of the attractive yet relatively inaccessible Great Orme, and was opened in 1902. This photograph shows the scene as the tramcars pass. From here, as the trams leave the built up area of the town, the views over the bay and out toward the north Wales coast become increasingly impressive as the tram climbs.

Llandudno is the archetypal genteel, middle-class British seaside town with its sweeping promenade, pier, grand hotels and public spaces. The whole town was conceived and planned by Lord Mostyn, the major estate holder in the region. The main streets of Llandudno were linked by a tram system, which at one time connected the town with Colwyn Bay, thus enabling visitors to travel easily between these two popular resort towns. The trams ran down the main streets in Llandudno, beginning at the west shore and travelling down Gloddaeth Avenue into Mostyn Street and then into Mostyn Avenue, continuing its journey via Penrhyn Bay to Rhos on Sea and then to Colwyn Bay. As the bus took over as the predominant form of transport, especially following the First World War, the tram system was streamlined. By the 1950s it was becoming increasingly evident that the tram route would no longer be able to compete and the remaining parts of the tram system were closed on 24 March 1956.

CHRISTCHURCH, DORSET, HIGH STREET,
BOURNEMOUTH CORPORATION TROLLEY BUS
c1955 C99147V

Christchurch

The trolley bus (a Sunbeam MS2) is on its way to the turntable at the Christchurch terminus. The old trolley bus turntable is still in existence in its original location behind Christchurch Jobcentre. It was a popular recreation to watch the mustard yellow with chocolate brown stripe Bournemouth Corporation trolley buses being turned on the turntable – the driver would put his back to the bus and nudge it round. Every now and then the bus driver would allow watchers to help him turn the trolley bus itself; a great bit of fun! The poles had to be lowered prior to turning.

The trolley bus era began in the 1930s, when Bournemouth Corporation had to expand their transport system to cope with increased demand. To double the existing tram routes was prohibitively expensive, but since the corporation already had its own electricity plant supplying the trams, it made sense to use this to power trolley buses rather than lay new lines for more trams. By 1936 Bournemouth Corporation had bought a fleet of 106 trolley buses. They finally ceased to operate in 1969.

Kettering

UNTIL THE 1960s, most people relied on public transport, and the green-liveried buses of United Counties carried workers and shoppers in and out of Kettering on busy timetables. Coach tours became very popular, especially to Skegness ('Skeggy') or Hunstanton ('Hunston') – usually on Sundays. They would leave at 7.30am and often would not return until 10.30pm. This is the view from Northampton Road, with the George Hotel roof visible behind the bus station.

Left: KETTERING, NORTHAMPTONSHIRE, THE BUS STATION C1965 K13079

ALL TRAFFIC has halted for the photographer, including the Great Eastern Railway open-topped bus (centre left). The Southwold narrow gauge railway, opened in 1879, linked the town to Halesworth and the main railway network. Horse-drawn transport is still popular, though, as we can see. The large shop is Thomas Denny, grocer and draper. On the corner is Robert Critten, 'chymist'; further along the High Street are Stead & Simpson and the Crown Hotel.

Right: SOUTHWOLD, SUFFOLK, MARKET PLACE 1906 56845

Southwold

Kidderminster

KIDDERMINSTER, HEREFORD & WORCESTER,
THE TRAFFIC POLICEMAN 1957   K16031

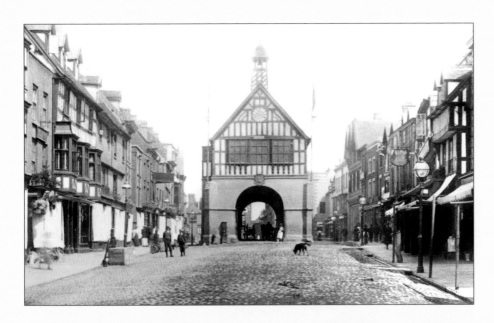

Far left:
BRIDGNORTH,
SHROPSHIRE,
HIGH STREET
1896 38126A

Left:
BRIDGNORTH,
SHROPSHIRE,
HIGH STREET
c1960 B204101

Bridgnorth

THESE TWO photographs give us a vivid illustration of how much the coming of the motor car changed the appearance of our streets. The impression we get from 38126A is of space and ease of movement – and the cobbles add to the picturesque effect. But in B204101, the street seems narrow and choked, and the view from each side of the street is totally blocked by cars.

Francis Moore, whose 'Old Moore's Almanac' is still published every year, was born in Bridgnorth. His first almanac was called 'Vox Stellarum' (voice of the stars) and was published over 300 years ago.

The Town Hall was constructed in 1652 from a redundant tithe barn donated by a Lady Bertie from the town of Much Wenlock. Upstairs are the council chambers. Its position in the centre of the street makes the movement of traffic very difficult along here, and it is a minor miracle that the 1960s town planners allowed it to survive. Fortunately it still stands here, so that traffic is now one-way, going around it on the right-hand side.

THIS IS another photograph that shows the pernicious effects of the car. This wide, spacious street is virtually halved in width by parked cars, and it is busy with moving traffic. It cannot have been a tranquil experience to patronise Annie Martin's greengrocer's stall – a covered wagon with a canopy – or the WI's caravan selling jams, cakes and pies parked next to her (extreme right). However, parking had now become prohibited outside the Coach and Horses (left).

At this time in the 1960s the local council and town planners were becoming more aware of Farnham's architectural heritage, and great care was being taken to retain the Georgian and Georgian-fronted buildings in Castle Street. In the main they succeeded in their aims, so that today Castle Street, whether viewed from the bottom looking towards the castle or from the top looking down the hill, still fulfils its description of being one of the most attractive streets in the south of England.

Hop gardens once covered the western side of Castle Street and extended as far as the back gardens of houses in West Street. The hostelry known as the Hop Blossom is the last remaining link with hop growing in this part of Farnham.

Farnham

Right: FARNHAM, SURREY, CASTLE STREET c1965 F11160

Ripley

THIS BROAD expanse of the old Portsmouth Road is lined with pollarded trees. Twenty-five miles from London, the village was an important staging post in the great days of horse-drawn coach traffic, and both Queen Elizabeth I and Lord Nelson passed through here. The invention of the safety bicycle in 1888 saw the village become a mecca for cycling enthusiasts, who rode here from the metropolis on a day's outing. Up to seven thousand a year came to devour a well-earned tea in one or other of the local hostelries, before returning to the city. In this photograph we can see a car or two and a bus - the motor age has begun.

RIPLEY, SURREY, HIGH STREET 1929   81704

THIS IS a scene that has gone for ever. This kind of small roadside petrol station has been forced out of the market, not only by small margins, but also by health and safety legislation outlawing kerbside pumps. These days, petrol stations are almost all large, hygienic-looking and homogenous.

The first drivers of the 1890s bought their petrol in two-gallon cans from the ironmonger. After the First World War there were more and more vehicles on the road, and the first kerbside petrol stations appeared. They dispensed the petrol from hand-operated bowser pumps, which were not particularly attractive to look at, especially when the garage was selling a variety of brands – and also this meant the additional visual clutter of advertising signs.

In 1928 legislation was passed to control petrol stations, and the larger ones began to look more like the ones we have today with a forecourt, an attendant's kiosk and an island for the petrol pumps. Hand pumps were being replaced by electrical ones which dispensed the fuel more quickly, and the petrol tanks were hidden away. In 1938, petrol cost 1s 5d per gallon for the standard grade, and 1s 7d for premium grade.

With the proliferation of the car in the 1940s and especially in the 1950s and 60s came competition, and the petrol companies realised that logos, company colours and advertising were all-important. Petrol stations had to conform to petrol company guidelines on the exact colours of their paint, uniforms for the staff, and staff training.

The rest of the century saw improvements in the technology of the pumps and bigger, more spacious petrol stations – and a vast increase in the price of petrol.

Epsom

Right: EPSOM, SURREY, HEADLEY PARADE, THE PETROL STATION c1955   E37089

Bridgnorth

THE TOWN of Bridgnorth is divided between High Town on the hilltop and Low Town beside the river. A number of staircases link the two – the Stoneway Steps, shown here, has 178 steps to climb. The iron buttress holding the brick walls apart is known as Pope's Spectacles, named after a man called John Pope who ran the foundry in the town where it was made.

An easier way to get from one part of town to the other would be to take the cliff railway. Rising 111 feet high up the cliff, it is 201 feet long. It was opened in 1892, when a ticket up or down cost 1d (one old penny). Today only return tickets are available, and these now cost 70 pence. The railway was originally worked by a water-balance system, but this was eventually replaced with colliery winding equipment. The poet and railway buff Sir John Betjeman likened a trip upon the cliff railway to a journey to heaven. Bridgnorth is also a centre for another type of railway – the restored Severn Valley Railway with its steam engines.

Left: BRIDGNORTH, SHROPSHIRE, STONEWAY STEPS 1896   38134

Right: BRIDGNORTH, SHROPSHIRE, THE LIFT 1898   42631

Above right: BRIDGNORTH, SHROPSHIRE, THE CLIFF RAILWAY c1955   B204064

Kidderminster

KIDDERMINSTER is famous for its carpet making industry. But without an easy means of transporting coal to the factories and carpets to their customers, Kidderminster would never have been able to develop as it did. The 1700s were to see the building of canals all over the country; but it is interesting that the idea for canals had already been broached locally. In the mid 1600s a local man called Andrew Yarranton first made the River Stour navigable. This was done in order to bring coal to the town; Yarranton had great plans to link the Stour with the River Trent far to the north, but was unable to follow them through for lack of funding.

And so the project had to wait for James Brindley, whose Staffordshire and Worcestershire Canal was finally completed in 1775 at a cost of £103,000. It linked Kidderminster with the great ports of Hull, Liverpool and London as well as Gloucester and Bristol. The canal was 52 miles in length and had 47 locks along it.

This photograph shows the wharf just below St Mary's Church. Notice the narrow boat laden with coal ready for delivery. The canal was built to follow the route of the River Stour very closely, and at this point it is just about to cross over the river by aqueduct before descending through one of its locks. The 'very commodious' warehouses on the left-hand side of the photographs have all gone. The site is instead now used for a supermarket and other large stores.

Left: KIDDERMINSTER, HEREFORD & WORCESTER, THE CHURCH AND THE CANAL 1931   84619

THIS TRANQUIL image makes it hard to believe that the canals were busy, vital transport channels that were created to speed up the Industrial Revolution. The Aylesbury Arm was a branch from the Grand Junction Canal, later the Grand Union Canal, which ran from near Marsworth across the Vale to Aylesbury. It opened in 1815, twenty years after it was first authorised. This view looks along the towpath towards

the Park Street bridge with the Nestlé's factory just out of sight on the right; the boys are fishing from a (surviving) miniature wharf. On the left the meadow is now occupied by Hilda Wharf, 1990s housing.

Aylesbury

AYLESBURY,
BUCKINGHAMSHIRE,
THE CANAL 1897   39642P

ISAMBARD KINGDOM
BRUNEL

THIS DRAMATIC photograph sees a train bravely steaming out of Teignmouth on a day of strong winds and high seas. Brunel's single-track railway of 1846 was set within a cutting at the centre of a 320-yard long tunnel which penetrated Teignmouth's heartland. Unfortunately, the revolutionary atmospheric system introduced on the broad gauge line was a white elephant of monumental proportions that accounted for a £403,000 write-off. An additional investment of £26,000 allowed for the gargantuan task of opening out the tunnels in the 1880s. People on the platform were henceforth warned by the station porter's loud shout of 'Train be a'comin'!

By 1890 the stations of Teignmouth and Dawlish could expect an influx of 400 to 700 visitors a day. In 1892, an enormous workforce spent a day and a quarter heaving the rails closer together to make the line compatible with the rest of the country's rail network. Even today, walkers on the sea wall occasionally see a handful of men suspended precariously from ropes, clearing loose rocks from the cliff face above the line. In the days of steam, the railway employed a 'Cliff Gang' to carry out scarping of the porous cliffs riddled with springs. A local guidebook paints a picture: 'Tis not the samphire gatherer who plies his giddy trade on the cliffs today but the navvy suspended upon an almost invisible rope ladder, picking at the very soil on which he is suspended'.

By 1905, GWR had re-invented itself into a progressive and successful company. Cheap excursion tickets and the advent of paid holidays added to the line's increasing impetus, barely stalled by the Great War. An all-time peak was logged in the 1920s. The holidaymakers failed to arrive in 1939, yet carriage-loads of evacuees and troops did. The line was a vital supply link for Plymouth and, although it was targeted, it never suffered a direct hit. Locals sometimes glimpsed an armoured train passing through as it patrolled between Exeter and Dartmouth on the lookout for E-boats, enemy ships and sea planes.

Increasing car ownership in the 1950s caused a severe decline leading to massive cuts in Devon's railway network. The next decade brought major reductions to services and a huge cultural change. It was the end of the annual summer influx by thousands of visitors travelling the Holiday Line. Scenic splendour aside, the cliff-foot route is still notorious for frequent disruption caused by the sea's determination to undermine the line.

Below: TEIGNMOUTH, DEVON, THE PARADE 1896   37611

Teignmouth

Romford

ROMFORD, GREATER LONDON, THE RAILWAY STATION 1908   59826

A TRAIN arrives at the 'up' platform of Romford Station on its way to London, Liverpool Street. The railway reached Romford in June 1839 when the Eastern Counties Railway proudly brought two trains into Romford running side by side and both with a locomotive at the front and rear. They were met by huge crowds and a civic reception. Within a short time the town's wonderful old inns no longer echoed to the sounds of excitement as the frequent stagecoaches arrived and departed on their way to East Anglia and the coast.

Between the World Wars Romford developed at an astonishing pace. People moving into the new residential estates knew that there was plentiful employment both in the town and close by. Romford had become a commuter town with frequent trains to London from Gidea Park and Romford, and from Upminster, Hornchurch and Elm Park.

Saltaire

SALTAIRE, YORKSHIRE, THE STATION 1909   61871

TITUS SALT was a wealthy manufacturer; his Victorian idealism led him to believe that a happy, healthy and fulfilled workforce was a productive workforce. Saltaire, his model village built in the 1850s, provided all the essential living amenities for his workers and their families, and for recreation he provided a spacious park on the opposite side of the river and canal. Here splendid gardens, with statues of Salt, offered healthy living to the workers at his magnificent Italianate alpaca mill, whose chimney can be seen rising in the background.

Industry needs good communications to be successful, and Saltaire is on the Midland Railway main line from Bradford to Skipton. Metro diesels are now the order of the day, and a steam loco like the one in this photograph is a rarity.

THIS RAILWAY STATION still looks futuristic to 21st-century eyes, but the cars parked outside have an antique look now. Harlow station was opened in 1960 and electrified in 1961. The other station that serves Harlow New Town is near to Old Harlow, and is now called Harlow Mill. The railway first reached Harlow Mill (formerly called Harlow) in 1841. Very soon after, in 1844 the broad (7ft) railway tracks had to be replaced by narrow gauge (56.5 inches) that was becoming standard nation-wide. The company had planned, unsuccessfully, to extend the line to York. The railway brought industry to the area, but it had a bad effect on the canal trade, coach services and innkeepers. The coaching business run by the Gilbey family collapsed, and they changed to dealing in wine (Gilbeys became a major employer in Harlow New Town).

The station is just a few yards from the site of the little gas-lit halt of Burnt Mill. Until 1960 the first New Town settlers used the halt, huddling in a tiny porter's hut on cold mornings, warmed by a small coal stove. It was demolished in 1960.

Right: HARLOW, ESSEX, NEW TOWN STATION c1960 H22066

Harlow

Shrewsbury

THIS BEAUTIFUL railway station – the architect was T M Penson – was opened in 1848. It was built for Shropshire's first railway, the Shrewsbury to Chester line. Some fifty years later it was enlarged with the addition of a new floor inserted below the entire building – the original ground level entry was through what is now a window in this picture, just below the oriel window in the clock tower. The platforms lie over the River Severn. Note the cabs waiting to take the train passengers to their ultimate destination: they are mostly roomy four-wheeled cabs, big enough to carry plenty of luggage.

SHREWSBURY, SHROPSHIRE, THE RAILWAY STATION 1904   51362

Cockles and mussels, alive, alive, oh!

IN EARLIER times, the streets of our towns were thick with street traders of all kinds. Many poor people and beggars (in the 1880s 300,000 Londoners were classified as poor, for instance) made desperate efforts to lift themselves and their families out of their unrelenting poverty by taking on a trade, however small and insignificant. They were reluctant to apply for Outdoor Relief under the Poor Law. The match sellers, shoe blacks and flower girls, very often displaced from the countryside where life was yet more unendurable, were given short shrift by many of the great and wealthy. An 1888 tourist guidebook suggested the following evasive action be taken by travellers: 'To get rid of your beggar, when wearisome, take no notice of him at all. He will only follow you till you meet a more likely person, but no farther'.

Street traders faced suspicion from the public and persecution by the police on a daily basis. Their lives were a constant struggle to win food and shelter; many lived in cheap, crowded lodging houses in poor areas, where they were preyed upon mercilessly by voracious landlords. There was, of course, no social relief, and families were forced back on their own cunning and guile to keep body and soul together.

The Bootblack

SPORTING THEIR red uniforms, the bootblack boys were a familiar sight on the streets of larger towns. The bootblack business grew into a highly organised and philanthropic affair: the Ragged Schools, Saffron Hill, set up the first society, and nine others followed. Their aim was to educate orphan boys and to give them a good start in the world and, by the 1880s, the shoeblack societies had four hundred boys on their books. Members of the Shoeblack Brigade were licensed to trade by the Metropolitan Police and carried on their business unhindered.

THE BOOTBLACK, LONDON 1895 L130114

The Match Seller

THE YOUNG MATCH SELLER, GREENWICH 1884

A YOUNG match seller poses for the photographer. Selling a few lucifers was all too often the pretext for begging. This tiny waif is offering boxes of Bryant & May's fusee 'Alpine Vesuvian' matches, popularly known as Brimstones. His job was hardly a desirable one, but he was considerably better off than those poor girls who were involved in the manufacturing of matches: the yellow phosphorus used in the process caused a debilitating disease of the mouth known as 'Phossy Jaw'. Bryant & May employed 700 girls in their match factories. In 1888 these girls went on strike for better pay and conditions, but such a protest and threat to public order was rare amongst workers in Victorian Britain.

The Hokey Pokey Stall

THE HOKEY-POKEY STALL, GREENWICH 1884 L130110P

SMALL CHILDREN cluster round the hokey-pokey stall licking at the cheap ice cream. They look like ragged street urchins in their rumpled suits and battered boots, and were probably bought their penny treats in return for posing for the photographer. The stallholder, standing in apron and straw hat, is no more than a youth, and is probably one of many hired hands working for a much larger concern.

The Ginger Cake Seller

THE GINGER CAKE SELLER, GREENWICH 1884 L130111

THE OLD ginger cake seller with his laden tray stands in the gutter. His dark-coloured cake of flour, treacle and ground ginger was a favourite snack with Victorians at fairs and street events. The roughly shaped pieces were measured into paper cones and topped with a blanched almond. This old man's ginger cake was probably made by his wife or daughters. His laden tray has seen better days and the strap has been given makeshift repairs on more than one occasion. The old man's foot rests on what is probably the tray cover, which is gathering dust in the road.

The Chair Mender

A CHAIR MENDER squats in the passage outside the kitchen of a London house. There were once 2,500 cabinet-making shops in London, many employing children. When powered sawmills and mechanical production methods brought ready-made furniture onto the market, many thousands of craftsmen lost their jobs. Here, an old man re-canes a child's chair. The housekeeper maintains a wary eye.

Left: THE CHAIR MENDER, LONDON 1877
L130112

THE CHIMNEY SWEEP, LONDON 1884 L130115

The Potato Seller

THE POTATO SELLER, LONDON c1890 L1302001

THIS STREET TRADING woman is offering potatoes from her basket. Baked potatoes were even more popular, and handcarts fitted with ovens and chimneys plied the streets offering inexpensive hot snacks. This potato seller looks relaxed enough, but the weight of the potatoes must be excruciating to her.

The Chimney Sweep

THE VICTORIAN social critic Henry Mayhew reported that the chimney sweeps were a tight-knit community, and that master sweepers often let rooms to families in the same trade. The climbing boys, often from the workhouse, earned 2d or 3d a day, but were sometimes given an extra 6d by grateful householders. They climbed easily up through wide flues using their elbows, but often found themselves stuck and near-suffocated in narrow nine-inch chimneys. For young children it must have been the most terrifying experience. George Smart's invention of the familiar set of hollow rods topped with a broad bristle brush encouraged an end to

the cruelty, and an Act of Parliament finally made child sweeps illegal in 1875.

THE ORGAN GRINDER, LONDON 1895 L130109

The Organ Grinder

THE BARREL ORGAN always drew a huge crowd with its wheezy renderings of popular tunes. When a trio of frightened monkeys was introduced the attraction for children was irresistible. Here they crowd closely round while the monkeys, dressed in waistcoats, are goaded into reluctantly performing their tricks.

Can you help us with information about any of the Frith photographs in this book?
We are gradually compiling an historical record for each of the photographs in the Frith archive. It is always fascinating to find out the names of the people shown in the pictures, as well as insights into the shops, buildings and other features depicted.

If you recognise anyone in the photographs in this book, or if you have information not already included in the author's caption, do let us know. We would love to hear from you, and will try to publish it in future books or articles.

Share Your Memories
We have a website dedicated to memories from the public that relate to our photographs. Seeing a place from your past can rekindle forgotten or long held memories. We would love to hear from you!
www.francisfrith.com/memories

Our production team
Frith books are produced by a small dedicated team at offices in the converted Grade II listed 18th-century barn at Teffont near Salisbury, illustrated above. Most have worked with The Francis Frith Collection for many years. All have in common one quality: they have a passion for The Francis Frith Collection.

For further information, trade, or author enquiries please contact us at the address below:
The Francis Frith Collection, Frith's Barn, Teffont, Salisbury, Wiltshire, England SP3 5QP.
Tel: +44 (0)1722 716 376 Fax: +44 (0)1722 716 881   Email: sales@francisfrith.co.uk

www.francisfrith.com